University of

Media &
Politics

Media & Politics

An Introduction

Wayne Errington
Narelle Miragliotta

OXFORD
UNIVERSITY PRESS

OXFORD
UNIVERSITY PRESS

253 Normanby Road, South Melbourne, Victoria 3205, Australia

Oxford University Press is a department of the University of Oxford.
It furthers the University's objective of excellence in research,
scholarship, and education by publishing worldwide in
Oxford New York
Auckland Cape Town Dar es Salaam Hong Kong Karachi
Kuala Lumpur Madrid Melbourne Mexico City Nairobi
New Delhi Shanghai Taipei Toronto
With offices in
Argentina Austria Brazil Chile Czech Republic France Greece
Guatemala Hungary Italy Japan Poland Portugal Singapore
South Korea Switzerland Thailand Turkey Ukraine Vietnam
OXFORD is a trademark of Oxford University Press
in the UK and in certain other countries

National Library of Australia Cataloguing-in-Publication data

Errington, Wayne.
Media and politics : an introduction.

Bibliography.
Includes index.
Textbook for 2nd and 3rd year Politics and Media and
Communications students studying subjects on Media and
Politics.

ISBN 9780195558340 (pbk.).

1. Mass media - Political aspects - Textbooks. 2. Mass
media policy - Textbooks. 3. Press and politics -
Textbooks. 4. Government and the press - Textbooks. I.
Miragliotta, Narelle. II. Title.

070.44932

Edited by Pete Cruttenden
Cover and text design by Mason Design
Typeset by Mason Design
Proofread by Roy Garner
Indexed by Neale Towart
Printed in Hong Kong by Sheck Wah Tong Printing Press Ltd

Contents

Preface

This book critically examines the dominant assumptions about the role of the media in a liberal democracy like Australia. These assumptions about the relationship between the government and the media underpin the behaviour of journalists and the expectations of media audiences, and are crucial to the process of holding governments accountable. We consider the government and the media as institutions that both compete for power and cooperate when necessary to achieve their goals. The book takes account of the dynamic technological and regulatory environment in which the media operates, and the consequences for these changes for journalists, politicians and ordinary citizens.

Chapter 1 traces the historical development of liberal concepts such as freedom of the press and accountability, and the way these ideals have been translated from Europe to Australia. It also sets out the problems with the liberal model in the Australian setting, such as the unrealistic assumptions about the role of the market, the power concentrated in the hands of media owners, and the conditions under which government intervention in media markets may be required.

Chapter 2 sets out the structure of the Australian media and the tension between the various government and private actors. It shows the importance of media audiences in sustaining old and new media formats, provides an overview of media ownership in the private sector, and underlines the concentration of ownership in some media platforms. It also introduces the government bodies that regulate the media and the types of laws they enforce.

Chapter 3 takes a critical look at our understanding of the relationship between the media and its consumers. It considers that relationship in light of the liberal concepts introduced in Chapter 1, and provides an overview of the various theories of media effects. These theories are used to shed light on the practical concerns of the community with issues such as violence, consumerism and the representation of women.

Chapter 4 introduces the values of the journalism profession. Those values are compared with the more abstract ideals about the relationship between the government and the media, and the constraints provided by the journalist's need to deal with powerful media companies and politicians. This chapter also considers the causes of the declining level of public trust in journalists.

Chapter 5 compares the liberal ideal of an independent media with the reality of government efforts to influence the output of journalists and news organisations. It considers the efforts of politicians in projecting a favourable image, describes the growing number of media units within government agencies and the growing difficulties for journalists attempting to maintain the standards of their profession in this environment. Efforts to use government advertising campaigns to bypass media scrutiny and promote the interests of political parties are also critically examined.

Chapter 6 explores the various strategies used by political parties to harness the media in their election campaigns. In particular, the chapter considers the advantages of the various public resources set out in Chapter 5 to the election campaigns of the parties in government. We also question the media's role in concentrating power in the hands of political leaders and the utility of election campaigns in holding governments accountable.

Chapter 7 examines the highly contested area of media content and censorship. We show the various rationales used to challenge the principle of media freedom and the history of their application in Australia. The chapter sets out the laws under which content is restricted or prescribed and the way that regulations change in line with social mores, as well as the development of ideas about nation-building and culture.

Chapter 8 extends the analysis of media ownership developed in Chapter 2. It shows the way in which ownership rules for traditional media platforms have been influenced not only by liberal principles of diversity but also by lobbying from incumbent media owners. The challenges to regulators provided by new media technologies and the Howard Government's arguments in favour of the deregulation of media ownership are also analysed.

Chapter 9 sets out the principles of public broadcasting. It explains the historical circumstances surrounding the creation of Australia's public broadcasters, and questions whether the ABC and SBS have fulfilled their charters. We also discuss the political pressures that public broadcasters are forced to endure and whether these pressures affect their output.

Chapter 10 considers the ways in which the new media technologies introduced earlier in the book are changing the relationship between journalists, media companies, governments and consumers. We discuss the sources and quality of information on the internet, and how ever-present digital media will affect the economics of news gathering, copyright law and the way in which we as citizens engage with powerful institutions.

Chapter 11 shows the way in which foreign policy priorities put unique pressures on the liberal conception of a free media. We introduce the CNN effect: the idea that rapid mass communication can influence foreign policy decision-making. This chapter also outlines the way that governments have historically insisted on stringent management of information during times of conflict, and questions whether such controls are viable in the current global environment.

THE LIBERAL DEMOCRATIC TRADITION AND AUSTRALIA'S MEDIA:

An Introduction

This chapter will:

- explain the dominant assumptions that underpin liberalism, and their implications for the organisation and structure of the Australian media system
- discuss the key roles liberals ascribe to the media
- consider some of the criticisms levelled against the liberal model of the media.

The media are an intrinsic feature of Australian society. They play an important role in all facets of social, political, economic and cultural life. It is for this reason that the form and development of the Australian media has not been entirely left to chance. Australia's media institutions and practices have been informed by certain political principles and values. Of these, the liberal doctrine has been especially powerful, not only in shaping our expectations of the media's role in society, but also in influencing the structure of the industry.

Liberalism is a political doctrine that takes as its starting position a belief that individuals are rational, self-interested and competitive, and who are capable of living freely and with minimum external interference (Ball

& Dagger 2004, pp. 44–5). Its origins lie in European medieval society, and developed largely as a reaction to religious intolerance and hereditary privilege. Liberalism's stress on the virtues of freedom, liberty and autonomy directly and irrevocably challenged the repressive political, economic, religious and social order on which medieval society was based. The ideals that inspired liberalism, along with the democratic tradition, were later to strongly influence the organisation of the state throughout the Western world. The modern Western liberal state is defined by a commitment to rule by the people, limited government, representative political institutions and a belief in the rights of the individual (Ball & Dagger 2004, pp. 50–60).

For their part, the media are conceived as an institution to shield and to protect the individual from the excesses of the state and to facilitate the rights and liberty of the citizenry. The media are regarded as a servant of the people and one of the key guardians of the independence of the political system. In order to facilitate this function, liberals typically believe that the media sector must be open and pluralistic in terms of its ownership. Media outlets should be privately owned and permitted to operate unhindered by excessive governmental regulation. This chapter introduces the principles underlying regulation of the media in Australia, its development and evolution, and its critics.

What is media?

Before we proceed any further, it is instructive to take the time to consider what we mean by 'media'. Many of the scholars who write on the media rarely bother to define the term, assuming that the reader understands all that the term encompasses, an assumption that is not wholly unreasonable. On those occasions when an effort has been made to clarify the term, there is remarkable uniformity in the definitions proffered. Consider the following descriptions:

- 'messages that are distributed through the technologies, principally text in books, study guides and computer networks; sound in audio-tapes and broadcast; pictures in video-tapes and broadcast; text, sound and/or pictures in a teleconference' (The World Bank 2007)

- 'organising technologies which make mass communication possible' (McQuail 1994, p. 10)
- 'methods of communication that can reach a large and potentially unlimited number of people simultaneously' (Hague & Harrop 2004, p. 10)
- 'the technological vehicles through which mass communication takes place' (Turow 2003, p. 15)
- 'the main means of mass communication, *esp.* newspapers, radio, and television, regarded collectively; the reporters, journalists, etc., working for organizations engaged in such communication' (Oxford English Dictionary Online 2007).

What becomes quickly apparent is that across these different definitions there is agreement that the 'media' refers to an instrumentality that is capable of communicating information, facts, opinions and ideas via a number of different platforms such as, but not limited to, newspapers, books, DVDs, radio, television, videocassettes, telephones, magazines, cinemas, the internet and MP3 players.

Quite apart from the seemingly endless definitions of this term, there are also different ways of categorising media. Classifying media is useful because it allows us to make sense of what is a fairly complex and diverse array of media that have different capacities and impacts. How one groups different media tells us quite a bit about an individual's particular interest in the subject matter. While there are potentially many ways of classifying media, some of the more popular approaches include:

- *Technology*—Different media rely on different technology to operate (i.e., print versus broadcasting, and electronic versus computer systems). This, historically, has had implications for the type of rules developed to regulate different media silos. The nature of the technology that supports a medium not only has important consequences for what the medium can do and who it can reach, but it also often places different regulatory demands on the government.
- *'New' versus 'old' media*—Distinctions are drawn between media that have a long-standing presence and those that are new to consumers (i.e., internet versus print). This distinction is useful in allowing scholars to consider the possible applications of new media and their consequences in political, social and economical terms.

- *Mainstream versus alternative*—Some media have popular appeal and are enjoyed by a broad cross-section of the population, such as television. In contrast, other media are utilised by a specific demographic, such as computer games. Such a distinction allows scholars to contemplate which particular media individuals and groups are using, and for what purpose.

- *'Hot' versus 'cold'*—This is associated with the ideas of Marshall McLuhan (1964), who argued that media could be divided into 'hot' and 'cold'. Cold media (for example, cartoons) are those that require active participation from the user because they are typically low in information and content, and thus force the subject to fill in what is missing. In contrast, hot media (for example, television) are jam-packed with visual and verbal content and, as a result, require low participation from the user. By categorising media in this manner, it draws attention to the demands that different media place on our senses.

Liberal democracy and the development of the media

While the liberal tradition strongly supports the notion of a free press unhindered by state intervention, it has only been practised in the last 200 years and, even then, only in Western nations. Historically, there was no natural consensus between the state and the public about the necessity of a free press. It is a freedom that was hard fought and won in Europe and North America, and one for which many around the world continue to struggle.

Advocacy of press freedom within the Western tradition began in the late 1600s and early 1700s. The invention of the printing press in the 1400s is significant to the claim to such a right. It was not long before the printing press infiltrated Europe, with presses being constructed in Germany, Italy, France, Spain, England and the Netherlands. Despite the fact the new technology was embryonic, the application and output of the early presses was formidable. By the end of the fifteenth century, it is estimated that there were around 15 to 20 million pamphlets and publications in circulation. This was an astounding achievement given that the population in these countries was fewer than 100 million and literacy rates combined were incredibly low (Thompson 1995, p. 55).

While the printing press made possible the proliferation of political and religious pamphlets, it was not a technology lauded by Europe's ruling elites. The new invention was to have a major impact on the political authority of both the church and the absolutist monarchies. For as long as printed matter was reproduced manually by scribes, production times were slow and output low. This decelerated the transmission and dissemination of new ideas within society. However, the creation of the printing press resulted in the proliferation of printing firms and outlets capable of mass production, and, in the process, made it increasingly difficult for both the church and the political rulers to control the free flow of ideas and information within their respective societies. For the church, it meant that the people could now read the Bible for themselves and were no longer dependent on priests to interpret the scriptures. In the case of the monarchs, publications overtly or implicitly critical of their rule became increasingly commonplace. Up until this time, the power of monarchs was challenged only by brute force, not by new ideas (Thompson 1995, pp. 55–6).

The response of the monarchs to the new technology was predictable. In England, particularly, from the 1400s to the late 1600s, the state operated a highly repressive licensing system. There were explicit restrictions on the number of printing presses that could function. Those fortunate enough to hold a licence were subject to pre-publication censors. This effectively meant that the state inspected all printed matter prior to distribution. Moreover, the British monarchy sought to consolidate its control over the production of printed material by dispensing favours and privileges to those who published state propaganda. Those willing to serve the state were often rewarded with lucrative monopoly printing rights (Wheeler 1997, pp 32–3).

The attempt on the part of the British monarchy to control the press was not popular, particularly among the emergent capitalist class—the **bourgeoisie**. This new class had benefited from the breakdown of feudalism and the growth of capitalism. They were affluent and well educated, and resentful of the power and privilege of the monarchy and the aristocracy. They were highly intolerant of the state's attempts to censor news and information, particularly when the sole purpose of the monarchy's strict system of regulation was intended to preserve and protect traditional power structures. The bourgeoisie agitated for change, demanding more freedom, fewer restrictions and greater participation in political life. Freedom of the press became one of their key demands (Keane 1991).

▶ **bourgeoisie** a term often used in reference to the middle class; in Marxist terminology it is specifically applied to the ruling capitalist class that owns the means of production

According to John Keane (1991), the earliest claims for press freedom relied on at least four different species of argument. These are the *God defence*, the *natural rights claim*, *instrumentalism* and the *truth argument*.

The God defence, or the theological approach, criticised state censorship in the name of the God-given faculty of the individual to reason. The argument is associated closely with an essay written by John Milton entitled *Areopagitica* in 1644. In his thesis, Milton put forward two arguments. First, he criticised the repressive licensing restrictions imposed by the state on practical grounds. He believed that the system of press controls administered by the state was simply unworkable and unenforceable, requiring the state to employ additional censors and giving rise to the likelihood of arbitrary decisions. Second, and perhaps more importantly, Milton's claims rested on spiritual considerations. He argued that a free press was needed to enable the love of God and the human spirit to flourish. Without it, he said, the exercise of the individual's freedom to think, to exercise discretion and to choose a Christian way of life was stifled. Moreover, Milton claimed that the censors were not infallible. It was his contention that God had blessed humankind with the gift of rationality, and hence the capacity to choose between right and wrong. He believed that individuals could only develop their true capacities by engaging contrary opinions and experiences (Keane 1991, p. 12). This, Milton claimed, was an essential part of the individual's spiritual development and growth, for 'God uses not to captivate under a perpetual childhood of prescription, but trusts us [sic] with the gift of reason' (Milton quoted in Keane 1991).

Beginning in the mid 1600s, a new type of argument was advanced in favour of press freedoms based on the notion of the rights of the individual. This argument was heavily influenced by the ideas of John Locke (1689), but was applied specifically to the campaign to secure a free press by the likes of John Asgill (1712) and Mathew Tindal (1704) (Keane 1991, p. 13).

The natural rights argument rested on the assertion that all men are essentially rational beings capable of making decisions and choices in their own best interests. Unlike Milton's God defence, the proponents of the natural rights argument rejected any suggestion that press freedom should be advocated on religious grounds. Instead, they declared that the rights of man—the right to life, liberty and property—were inalienable, belonging to all persons and not just monarchs. A free press was essential to allow the individual to achieve enlightenment and knowledge, a condition that could only be achieved if ideas were able to flow freely within society (Keane 1991, pp. 14–15).

In the 1800s, the argument in support of press freedom shifted to new ground. During this time, a more practical or instrumental defence of press freedoms became the raison d'être rather than an argument predicated on either spiritual or moral considerations. This strand of thinking was propounded by the Utilitarians, a new generation of liberals who believed that the claim to freedom and liberty owed less to natural rights than it did to the promotion of general happiness within society (Ball & Dagger 2004, pp. 65–6).

The instrumental thesis is associated with the works of James Mill (*Liberty of the Press*) and Jeremy Bentham (*On the Liberty of the Press and Public Discussion*). Both men argued the role of the state is to produce the greatest happiness for the greatest number. The likelihood of such an outcome depends on the state, and more specifically the government, being subject to constant and vigorous oversight. Mill and Bentham believed that it was impossible to guarantee and sustain the development of a just and fair political system without the existence of a free press. The reason, they argued, is that government is always ruled by self-interest. While periodic elections go part of the way to checking governmental conduct, it is insufficient in itself to guarantee prudent policy decisions by elected officials. A free press could mediate the worst excesses of governmental self-interest by publicising instances of governmental misconduct. Unless restrained by the fear of what the public might think and do, there would always be a propensity for Members of Parliament to misbehave. Thus, the instrumentalists argued that the press was a critical part of the checks and balances of government by 'helping to control the habitual self-preference of those who govern, expose their secretiveness and make them more inclined to serve and respect the governed' (Keane 1991, p. 16).

The fourth species of argument in support of a free press was devised by John Stuart Mill, the protégé of Bentham and Mill. JS Mill agreed with the idea that a free press could help to constrain government. However, he also believed that a free press was important for the advancement of truth. Keane (1991) refers to this as the truth argument.

Mill advanced three reasons for a free press based on the claim of 'truth'. The first is that one cannot be certain that any opinion that the government seeks to silence is indeed false—the government is not infallible, and by suppressing an alleged falsehood there is a risk that the truth itself would be denied. Incorrect ideas and opinions could be best contradicted by exposing them publicly. It is only through a robust and vigorous debate that truth can emerge. Basically, government censorship can result in the suppression of important truths. Second, even if it later transpires that an opinion is false, it does not preclude the possibility that it contains a small ounce of truth. Sometimes, Mill claimed, we have to be exposed to a number of competing arguments before we are able to properly ascertain the 'truth' of a situation. In public affairs, truth necessitates 'combining and reconciling opposites'. Even dissentients have something worth hearing, and we should not resile from divergent opinions just because one is opposed to different points of view. Freedom from censorship, therefore, helps to engender a clearer understanding of the truth and to reach better decisions. Third, without free discussion, even truth will degenerate into dead dogma. Unless ideas are subject to constant questioning, they turn into prejudice, assumed to hold true for all time and applicable to every circumstance (Keane 1991, p. 19). The problem with this scenario, according to Mill, is that the 'deep slumber of decided opinions' overpowers the moral courage and dignity of the human mind. Thus, censorship encourages ideas to stagnate and, by extension, humankind and the society in which they live.

CONTEMPORARY JUSTIFICATIONS FOR AN INDEPENDENT MEDIA

It is true to say that the God defence, the natural rights claim, the instrumentalist thesis and truth argument continue to resonate among liberals. Today, however, the liberal claim to a free media is commonly expressed in terms of three interrelated sets of arguments: a watchdog role; the provision of information; and the facilitation of the public sphere.

The watchdog role is arguably the most critical in democratic societies. In a representative democracy, it is important that governments, as well as other powerful figures, are scrutinised. The media are essential to this task, evaluating and questioning the government on behalf of a public which, owing to time and other constraints, is frequently unable to perform this task in its own right. By maintaining a continuous presence in Parliament, active attendance at government press conferences and the pursuit of potential stories, the media are able to bring instances of official impropriety to the public's attention.

The second role ascribed to the media is that of information provider. The media are able to draw together news and information about events occurring within both the domestic and international arena. In doing so, the media are able to hold a mirror to the world, allowing the public to glimpse events outside their immediate personal experiences. In the context of societies that value representative democracy, the role of the media as information source is especially critical because citizens are required to make informed decisions when they vote. For most of us, our only exposure to politics and politicians is through the media. While we may have direct experience of issues like unemployment and the health system, it is the media that give us the information we need about the policies of political parties.

The third function of the media in modern society is that of facilitator of the public sphere. The idea of the public sphere was introduced by Jurgen Habermas (1989) to describe the emergence of laws, places and media that facilitate public debate. Hitherto, such conversations could only take place in a private sphere. The public sphere enables us to have unhindered conversations about ideas and governments of which the media are a vital component. The media act as a conveyor belt that disseminates ideas and information and, in the process, enables the public, notwithstanding their geographical location, to engage in a dialogue with their elected officials, fellow citizens and, increasingly, governments and people living on the other side of the globe.

REGULATING FOR A FREE MEDIA: THE AUSTRALIAN EXPERIENCE

Liberals are cognisant that the media's capacity to perform its roles of government watchdog, information provider and defender of the public sphere is contingent on the existence of a particular set of political conditions. Liberal theory recognises that the ability of the media to serve the public interest is inhibited by forces that militate against such an occurrence. Because of this, liberals typically argue that the regulation and organisation of the media should be informed by two essential rules. First, a critical distance between the media and the government must be secured through private media ownership (Curran 2000, p. 123). That is, the government should not be in the 'business' of owning media outlets. The sector should ideally be exclusively, if not predominantly, privately owned. Second, the media should be 'lightly regulated, subject only to libel and decency laws and the tenets of good taste and decency' (Wheeler 1997, p.6). The level of official regulation should be minimal and only to prevent unscrupulous business practices (that is, the formation of media monopolies) and maintain general standards.

The belief in the importance of a free media was imported into Australia, along with a host of other political and social institutions, largely from the UK at the time of white settlement in 1788. One of the important rights secured by the press in the UK at the time of Australia's colonisation was freedom from prior restraint—the right to publish news and information without first having to obtain the government's permission to do so (Schultz 2002 p. 103). Despite the recognition of this principle in the UK, it did not result in its ready acceptance in Australia. For many years, there were clashes between the **governors** of the Australian colonies and early media proprietors. The governors put in charge of the country's various administrative regions exercised absolute power in the areas under their control, and refused to allow newspapers to publish without their approval. However, thanks in large part to the introduction of a new charter of justice in the Sydney colony, the press was eventually able to free itself from the strict pre-publication censorship regime imposed by the colonial governors (Lloyd 1999, pp. 10–14). By the 1820s, the doctrine of the absence of prior restraint was fully accepted, even if resented, by the governmental authorities. Today, the commitment to this principle remains salient, although it has not been codified in any of the Australian constitutions.

> **governors** officials of the UK government who were appointed to manage the affairs of the various Australian colonies

The other important expression of the liberal ethos in Australia is the dominance of the private sector in the provision of media services. Despite the desire on the part of the governors of the colonies to strictly control the publication of printed matter, they had no interest in establishing their own newspapers. As in the UK, the governmental authorities opted to refrain from ownership of newspapers, preferring instead to rely on the supply of such services from private citizens. However, the emergence of the broadcasting media (initially radio and later television) did prompt the Australian government to reconsider this position. As a result, beginning in the 1930s, public broadcasting services were established alongside the private broadcasting sector.

PROBLEMS AND CONTRADICTIONS OF THE LIBERAL MODEL AND ITS IMPLICATIONS FOR THE AUSTRALIAN MEDIA

While the organisation and control of the Australian media is strongly influenced by liberal ideals, the model is contested. Criticisms include, but are not limited to:

- the practical difficulties of operationalising liberal principles into practice
- the idealisation of the media's capacity to perform its roles as watchdog, information provider and facilitator of the public sphere
- misplaced trust in the virtues of the market in regulating the sector
- problematic assumptions about the nature and capacity of private media power.

One problem associated with liberal theory, and theory more generally, is in applying what are, essentially, fairly abstract political principles and values to real-life contexts. While the notion of a free press unhindered and unrestrained by excessive government interference is intuitively appealing, there are hurdles to translating that ideal into an internally coherent set of policy outcomes. The liberal model struggles to identify clearly when government has a legitimate role in regulating the media in the public interest, and knowing how far the government should be allowed to go in this regard. Liberals recognise that a regulatory presence by government is vital to ensure that society remains orderly and productive. In the case of the media, there is a belief that, at a minimum, the government should play a role in ensuring that the channels of communication remain open and clear.

There are normally three situations in which government intervention in the activities of the media is considered both necessary and beneficial. First, liberals typically contend that restrictions should exist on what can be said and shown in the interests of protecting an individual's reputation, physical safety and assets. That is, speech or material that is violent or pornographic or that incites violence does not necessarily serve the community and should be prohibited. Second, restrictions on the media should be imposed in the interests of national security. Liberals believe that the state has a responsibility to protect the individual from foreign aggressors. It is for this reason that it is considered legitimate to ban the press from attending important meetings of the state, such as cabinet meetings. Finally, liberals recognise the importance of some form of restriction on private media ownership. Government, they contend, should act to prevent the formation of media monopolies, which can arise if the market is left entirely to its own devices.

At first glance, the circumstances under which it is not reasonable for the state to intervene in media's activities seem fairly straightforward. In practice, achieving the right balance is very difficult. The government is constantly forced to make compromises between its obligations to protect the rights of the individual and its obligation to regulate interaction between its citizens. This means liberal democratic governments must find a way of balancing individual rights with those of the broader community, which can result in unsatisfactory trade-offs. Take, for example, the issue of media reporting during times of war. It is generally accepted that the media should not report on matters that might imperil the security of the nation. Information that threatens the safety of the state must not be permitted to enter the public domain. However, it is not always clear when the national interest should take precedence over the right of the individual to be apprised of certain activities and events. In 2004, photographs were published of prisoners held in Abu Ghraib in Iraq. The photos revealed the abuse and torture of prisoners at the hands of US military police. It was argued that the release of the photos was in the public interest because they exposed the maltreatment of the Iraqi prisoners at the hands of US prison guards. Conversely, others put forward the case that the publication of the pictures compromised the US administration's standing in the international community, particularly among the Arab and Muslim states. The resulting political furore damaged the credibility of the USA (and its allies) in its military operations in the Iraq War at a time when it could least afford to become embroiled in further scandal. In doing so, it not only increased the vulnerability of US troops stationed overseas, but also weakened the resolve of the American public to a war to which its government is irrevocably committed. As this case study so clearly demonstrates, liberalism only provides governments with a loose guide as to when it is appropriate to intervene for the public good, and little help in reconciling competing policy objectives.

A second criticism of the liberal model is its confidence in private ownership arrangements to guarantee the supply of objective, quality media content. That is, liberals have essentially ascribed mythical powers and virtues to the media that fail to match its actual capacities or which reflect the political and economic realities in which it operates.

Liberals mostly justify the call for press freedom on the grounds that an uninhibited flow of information is necessary to keep government accountable between elections. In the literature, both historical and contemporary, the media are sometimes referred to as the fourth estate. The notion of the fourth estate refers to the idea that the media (and particularly the press), along with the church, Parliament and courts, exist as a watch on the activities of government. Implicit in the notion of the media as 'the fourth estate' is the idea that they are unbiased, objective, capable of reflecting a diversity of views and opinions within society, and willing and able to check officialdom. Essentially, the media are seen as a 'virtuous' institution, which serves the public interest by seeking out truth and exposing mendacity.

However, a number of scholars have expressed the view that liberals underestimate the impact commercial imperatives have on the media's capacity to perform its fourth estate functions. Liberals have been accused of paying limited attention to the relationship between private ownership and its likely effects on the selection, quality and choice of media content. With the small exception of print, the media allocates very little of its time to news and current affairs, despite being mostly privately owned. As Curran explains, 'the liberal orthodoxy defines the main democratic purpose and organisational principle of the media in terms of what they do not do most of the time' (2000, p. 122). Many commentators claim that much of the media content that is produced by the commercial sector is geared to infotainment, and not the disclosure of news and information. Ironically, many Australians in seeking quality current affairs rely on the government-owned media enterprises, such as the ABC, rather than the privately owned commercial broadcasters. This begs an important question: if the commercial media are not adequately performing the task envisaged by liberals, do the media have a legitimate claim to the extensive freedom that liberals propose?

A third criticism is that liberal theorists overestimate the power of the marketplace to restrain the natural proclivities of the media industry. As explained previously, liberals tend to conceive the media as a check on the activities of government. The state, they advance, should be the main target of media scrutiny because it alone has a monopoly on the legitimate use of force. Because of this, the media should be insulated from overt governmental interference, with its fate largely left to market forces.

While there is merit to the claim that the media plays an important role in monitoring the actions of the state, it is also true that society's reliance on the media to perform this function has been diminished over time. It is important to remember that the media's claim to being a critical watch on the government was forged at a time when other institutions to check government power were either non-existent or ill-defined. Today, however, with the extension of suffrage, the independence of parliament from the sovereign, constitutional protections to the judiciary, and codified constitutions, our reliance on the media to check the government is far less crucial (Tiffen 2004, p. 204). Because liberals have generally focused on the perils of government, they have largely ignored the potential evils that can arise from a market-driven media sector. As a result, it is claimed, liberals have not developed sufficient mechanisms to counter the influence of commercial imperatives of the private media, particularly in relation to dampening the natural propensity to media monopoly. Tiffen contends that this problem is largely a function of the circumstances that gave rise to the liberal claims for press freedom. He suggests that much of the 'rhetoric about freedom of the press was fashioned in the heat of the fight against tyranny' and as a result 'the tradition is much stronger at criticising those forces which restrict press freedoms than prescribing those which enhance it' (2004, p. 201). Because of this, liberals tend to appeal to 'civic responsibility' and other voluntary mechanisms as the best means of curtailing the activities and behaviours of the media, rather than building and developing strong institutions. In modern Western societies like Australia, this has real implications for the provision and maintenance of a 'multiplicity of media voices' in the public sphere.

A further, and related, concern advanced by some scholars is that liberals do not adequately address the political, cultural and economic implications that arise from the growing commercialisation of the media (Curran 2000, p. 122). This argument has been made in light of the growing recognition that the modern media is big business. Historically, media organisations were mostly small-scale local and family-run concerns with limited media holdings. Today, however, a growing section of the world's media has been taken over by major industrial and commercial concerns such as General Electric, Toshiba and the like. Others have grown into huge leisure conglomerates that are among the largest corporations in the world. The American Federal Communications Commission estimates that worldwide revenues of media exceeded $1 trillion per year beginning in the 1990s (Hague & Harrop 2004, p. 99). This development has prompted some commentators to suggest that the media's close ties with the commercial world make it part of the established order and hence less vigilant in its willingness to scrutinise its activities. The enmeshing of the media with corporate interests means there are 'no go areas where journalists are reluctant to tread for fear of stepping on the corporate toes of a parent or sister company' (Curran 2000, p. 123). This trend is regarded as highly problematic. While the activities of modern governments are subject to stringent accountability, this is not always so for the actions of private economic interests. The media's resolve to check the corporate sector is weakened because they, too, are members of it. How likely is it that a media corporation will pursue stories on businesses in which it also has a pecuniary interest? Would the *Bulletin* magazine, which is owned by PBL, necessarily commence an investigation on one of the various casinos owned by that company? As the business interests of the commercial media extend beyond media enterprises, there are fewer incentives for the media to scrutinise the activities of the various non-media companies to which they are connected.

SUMMARY

It would seem that many of the lofty values and ideals that inform the Australian media industry are difficult to apply in a real world setting. It seems likely that the realisation of a truly free and open media, as envisaged by liberal theory, is unattainable in a world where politics rules. Maybe the true virtue of liberal theory is that it creates a standard by which we evaluate and judge the efficacy of our media system. However, this should not be taken to mean that the Australian media can be seen as a completely failed institution just because there are faults with the orthodoxy that has influenced many of their institutions and practices. Despite liberalism's flaws and miscalculations, it has made and continues to make an important contribution to the form and style of the Australian media.

Questions

1 What has been the impact of the influence of the liberal doctrine on the form and structure of the Australian media? Do you think liberal values have had a beneficial impact on the structure of the media in Australia?

2 How important is the media in Australia society and what is its most significant function? Do you believe the media has managed to meet the expectations set for it by liberals?

3 Is it right to assume that government poses the greatest threat to the freedom and plurality of the media?

FURTHER READING

Hallin, D. & Mancini, P. 2004, *Comparing Media Systems*. Cambridge University Press: UK.

Keane, J. 1991, *The Media and Democracy*. Polity Press: UK.

AN OVERVIEW OF THE AUSTRALIAN MEDIA:

The Actors, Institutions and Processes

This chapter will:

- examine how Australian audiences use and interact with media
- provide an overview of those who own Australia's media industries
- explore the role of government in the management and regulation of the media sector.

The media are of little use if there is no one to watch them, no one to supply them, and no one to monitor and regulate their use. It is for this reason that three groups are especially important to operation of the Australian media: audiences, media proprietors and government. These groups are not only critical to the media's existence and viability, but are also highly inter-dependent. Audiences consume media products and services, the proprietors supply the content that audiences demand, while the government determines and shapes the environment in which the key stakeholders operate.

While each of the groups takes an active interest in media, they do so with a different end goal in mind. Consumers look to the media to provide escapism, information and entertainment. It is important therefore, that the industry can deliver choice, reliability, and quality at a reasonable price. In contrast, the media owners have a mostly pecuniary interest in the media. Their financial success is contingent on a combination of strong consumer demand for their product, a stable economy and some protection from the vicissitudes of the marketplace. For its part, the government umpires the relationship between consumers and proprietors, and ensures, as far as possible, that neither group is in a position to exert an unfair advantage over the other. Coincidentally, the government has an interest in cultivating the media for its own sake. The government relies on the media to communicate with the public and, ultimately, to advance its electoral position.

It is clear that each of these groups plays a unique role in sustaining the media. The next section of this chapter explores the nature and contribution each group makes.

The audience

Consumers are critical to the viability of the media industry. Without audiences, private media corporations would have little incentive to invest in the industry.

The Australian audience consists of approximately 20 million people who either have or will have use for the media at some time in their lives. The Australian market is small compared with other countries (for example, the US market consists of 260 million people) but sophisticated nonetheless. Australians are enthusiastic consumers of media products, with significant financial capacity to procure media goods and services. It is estimated that 81 per cent of the population are moderate or heavy users of some form of media, with only 19 per cent claiming to have a low involvement with all media forms (Productivity Commission 2000).

Although the public has access to a variety and diversity of media products, the most popular of these, at the present time, are newspapers, the broadcast media (radio and television) and the internet. There is a good reason for this: these media are among the most accessible in terms of availability and reach.

One of the characteristics of the Australian newspaper sector, and one that is not uncommon to most liberal democracies, is that it is privately owned and lightly regulated. Private ownership has been a feature of the industry since the publication of the *Sydney Gazette and New South Wales Advertiser* by George Howe in 1803. Although Howe, and the many newspaper men who followed him, initially operated under fairly restrictive conditions imposed by the colonial authorities, the precedent was nonetheless established that Australian newspapers, much like their British counterparts, would be provided by private rather than public interests.

The Australian newspaper industry has undergone significant change since its inception. Newspapers have come, gone and changed hands; improvements in technology have revolutionised production; formats have been altered; and content expanded. Today, the Australian newspaper industry consists of a mix of daily state-based metropolitan dailies (for example, *Sydney Morning Herald*); national daily metropolitan newspapers (the *Australian* and the *Australian Financial Review*), regional daily papers, non-daily papers and free papers. It is estimated that around 39.5 per cent of Australians read newspapers daily (Denemark 2005, p. 2) and those who do spend an average five hours a week doing so (Roy Morgan Research 2003).

While significant numbers of Australians regularly read newspapers, there is mounting evidence the industry is in decline. Although the imminent demise of the newspaper industry have long been posited, more recent evidence appears to add weight to these claims. This is reflected across two trends. First, only a small percentage of Australians (16.8 per cent) cite newspapers as the medium they most rely upon for their news and information (Denemark 2005, p. 4). Second, circulation is waning. Over the last 20 years, newspaper circulation has decreased significantly: between 1980 and 1995, the sales volumes of metropolitan newspapers fell from 26.2 million copies to 18.2 million, representing a drop of 31 per cent (Kirkpatrick 2000, p. 76). This trend has not abated: since 1998, the average circulation of Australian metropolitan newspapers has declined a further 4.8 per cent. Similar trends have been identified in comparable countries, such as the US. Since the late 1980s, US newspaper circulation has fallen by 13 per cent (Wood 2005). Despite this, the received wisdom is that newspapers still play an important role in setting the news agenda for Australian politics.

Along with the print medium, Australians are heavy users of radio and television. These media are collectively referred to as 'broadcasting', a name coined by early radio engineers in the US. The expression is thought to have been inspired by the farming practice of 'broad casting' whereby seeds are spread using a wide toss of the hand (Turow 2003, p. 351). The creation of radio and television broadcasting services marked a fundamental break with the print media on a variety of fronts. Not only was the new broadcasting technology unparalleled in the ease with which it was able to reach a mass audience, but its audio and visual qualities also allow communication in a 'seemingly close and personal fashion' (Alger 1989, pp. 59, 65). Few would challenge the assertion that the broadcast media have had a major impact on society and politics, more specifically.

Radio was introduced to Australia in 1923. Although its popularity and prestige suffered following the commencement of television, commentators note that 'Australians spend more time listening to the radio than any other medium' (Miller & Turner 2002, p. 133). It is estimated that 95 per cent of the population listen to radio at least once a week, and that those who do listen to an average of 22 hours per week (ABC 2003, p. 22). This finding should hardly come as a surprise, given the estimated 37 million radio sets in the country, which equates to an average of 5.1 sets per household (Commercial Radio Australia 2000).

Radio's capacity to connect with a mass audience is matched only by television at the present time. Television was introduced to Australia in 1956, a number of years behind the US and the UK. Despite the delay in its launch, the take-up rate for the new medium was phenomenal. Within 10 years of its introduction to Australia, 80 per cent of homes in established markets possessed one television set: a remarkable feat, given the comparatively high costs of purchasing the new technology at that time (Given 2003, p. 175).

Television is the most ubiquitous of the media forms in terms of reach and accessibility. It is estimated the 99 per cent of Australians own at least one television set, with 60 per cent of households owning two or more (ABS 2004–05). Australians spend an average of 20 hours per week watching television; that is, one third of their leisure time is expended by this activity. Most Australians claim that it is the main source of their household entertainment. Moreover, research shows that Australians rely more on the television for their news and information than any other media. According to Denemark, 65.2 per cent of Australian have indicated a preference for television as their primary information source (2005, p. 2).

While commercial free-to-air television has proven extremely popular, the take-up rate for pay television has been slow. Launched in 1995, pay television is a fairly recent addition to the Australian stable of media. As of June 2005, there were 1.694 million pay-television subscribers, or 22 per cent of all households (DCITA 2006). While this is a major improvement on previous years' levels, it is significantly lower than take-up rates in New

Zealand (45 per cent), the UK (50 per cent) and the US (80 per cent). The Australian public's reluctance to embrace this technology is matched only by their apathy towards **digital** television. Although digital television commenced in 2001 (effectively replacing the old **analogue** technology, which has traditionally underwritten the broadcasting sector), only 15.5 per cent of households have access to digital free-to-air television, and a further 12 per cent if digital pay television is added (Coonan 2006, p. 4).

digital information-processing techniques that convert the actual data into binary (or machine language) code for more efficient transmission and storage; it is regarded as being more secure than its sibling, analogue, and also relatively impervious to static or fading signals

analogue a form of transmitting information characterised by continuously variable quantities, as opposed to digital transmission, which is characterised by discrete bits of information in numerical steps

Arguably, the newest of the most popular media forms is the internet. The internet was created in 1992, and is distinguished from other media on the basis of its hyper-interactivity. The internet is unique in terms of its ability to not only allow the user to interact with content, but also to create their own content and to transmit their ideas to a mass audience. As Barr explains, the internet is a new kind of communications 'beast': a 'communications hybrid: partly an information system where people can go searching for information' but 'also a medium where people can create their own content and distribute it widely using the platform of the World Wide Web' (2002, pp. 22–45).

Internet usage in Australia is one of the highest in the world. Approximately 57 per cent of Australia's 7.8 million households are connected to the web. As would be expected, the households that are most likely to have access to the internet are those that have children under the age of 15 years, are located in the metropolitan areas, and are generally among the highest income earners. Moreover, the evidence suggests that Australians are spending an increasing amount of time surfing the net. In 2001, the average amount of time spent online per month was nine hours. In 2003, this figure climbed to thirteen hours per month (ABC 2003). The most popular use of the internet is emailing or visiting and participating in chat sites (91.5 per cent), although other uses, such as finding information (58 per cent) and paying bills (46.9 per cent), are becoming increasingly popular (DCITA 2006). The internet is also beginning to compete directly with more traditional media as an information source, albeit on a fairly modest scale. The research shows that a little over 10 per cent of the population use the web on a daily basis for accessing information, and that around 3 per cent claim to rely on it as their main source of news and information (Denemark 2005, p. 3).

The media proprietors

Whereas audiences drive demand for media products, it is the media proprietors who attempt to satiate the public's appetite for financial gain and, some say, to acquire power, influence and prestige.

Table 2.1 The big hitters of Australian media by sector

Princes of print	Queens of screen	Regents of radio	Lords of the net
Newspapers	*Commercial television*		
APN News and Media • 21% of regional circulation	Network 10 (CanWest) • Audience reach of 65.77% (five licences)	Austereo • Audience reach of 58.50% (10 licences)	Bigpond (Telstra) • More than 1.5 million subscribers
Fairfax (Investors) • 22% of capital city circulation	Nine Network (Packer) • Audience reach of 52.45% (four licences)	Australian Radio Network • Audience reach of 50.89% (eight licences)	iinet (Malone) • More than 400 000 subscribers
News Ltd (Murdoch) • 66% of capital city circulation	Prime (Ramsey) • Audience reach is 24.99% (nine licences)	Broadcasting Operations P/L • Audience reach of 27% (28 licences)	Optus Net (Singapore Telecommunications) • More than 600 000 subscribers
Rural Press Group • 27% of regional circulation	Seven Network (Stokes) • Audience reach of 73.26% (six licences)	DMG • Audience reach of 56.27% (eight licences)	iPrimus • More than 400 000 subscribers

	Southern Cross Broadcasting (Investors) • Audience reach of 41.86% (15 licences)	Macquarie Regional Networks • Audience reach of 22% (90 licences)
	WIN Corp (Gordon) • Audience reach of 25.71% (26 licences)	Southern Cross Broadcasting • Audience reach of 52.59% (seven licences)
Magazines	*Pay television*	
Pacific Publications (Stokes) • 14 titles, seven of which are in the top 30 titles	Austar (Austar United com. Ltd.) • Approximately 571 000 subscribers	
PBL (Packer) • 63 titles, 14 of which are in the top 30 of titles.	Foxtel (PBL, Telstra and News Ltd) • Approximately 1.29 million subscribers	
	Optus TV (Singapore Tele-communications) • Approximately 142 000 subscribers	

Source: Australian Film Commission (2006); Gardiner-Gardens & Chowns (2006).

The proprietors are critical to the operation and success of the Australian media sector. It is their capital and resources that are invested into the Australian market, and which give rise to the services that are eagerly devoured by local audiences. Moreover, they provide employment to a significant number of Australians. By way of example, the Fairfax Group employs a workforce of just under 5000 people (Fairfax Holdings 2005, p. 83), News Ltd maintains a staff of 8000 (News Corporation 2007) and PBL has over 10 000 employees on its books (Publishing and Broadcasting Ltd 2006).

Media owners can generate revenue in a number of ways. Some proprietors make money by selling content to audiences. An example of this is pay television, which earns the bulk of its revenue from the sale of television channels to the public. Others generate revenue from the sale of advertising space to interested parties. In this case, the media proprietor attracts income through the creation of an audience base, which they then sell to advertising companies in the form of air-time. The audience, in theory, does not pay to use the service. Free-to-air commercial radio in Australia generates approximately 95 per cent of its revenue through this means. Most, however, generate income through a combination of advertising revenue and sale of content. A classic example of this is the newspaper industry. Newspapers earn revenue not only by selling a tangible product to consumers for a fee, but they also allow interested parties an opportunity to buy advertising 'space' in order to promote their products and services.

One significant characteristic of the Australia media, and one that will be discussed further in Chapter 8, is the extent to which the most popular and profitable media are controlled by a small number of owners. As shown in Table 2.1, within each sector a handful of players dominate, some of whom also have vested interests in other media. PBL, for example, possess four free-to-air television licences, a 25 per cent stake in Foxtel, 63 magazine titles, and interests in cinema and internet services (not to mention its substantial non-media holdings). It is also true that profits tend to be concentrated among the largest firms in any given medium. In the case of the electronic media, the 15 largest businesses attract 70 per cent of all revenues of the market (Ruthven 2005).

There are powerful economic incentives that motivate media owners to capture as big a share of the media market as the law will permit. The industry is highly lucrative, thanks to the spending habits of Australian audiences and companies. Australian households disburse substantial sums of money on media products. Total household expenditure on newspapers in 1998–99 totalled $943.3 million, while $1533.8 million was spent on broadcasting, electronic media and film. It is estimated that the average household spends around 3.8 per cent of its total expenditure on media-related goods and services. Moreover, the trend reveals, if anything, a propensity to spend more rather than less over time. In the 10 years between 1989 and 1999, expenditure on broadcasting, electronic media and film alone increased by over 60 per cent (ABS 2004, pp. 25–6). This, along with the $10.3 billion annual advertising market in Australia, has the effect of rendering the media industry highly profitable (Westerman 2006).

Nonetheless, some sectors of the media are stronger economic performers than others. The print media are regarded as modest revenue earners, despite the fact their share of the Australian advertising market, while declining, still remains the highest across all media at 38 per cent (Catalano 2006). Notwithstanding some financial volatility, Australian newspapers continue to record profits; for example, Fairfax Holdings, which has substantial press holdings, registered a $126.1 million net profit for the first half of the financial year 2004–05 (Tiffen 2006, p. 110).

The free-to-air broadcasting sector is the most profitable of the mainstream media. While there is some variability across the sector (depending on location, competition and demographic reach), it is generally true that both radio and television are solid financial performers. Revenue from the commercial radio sector in the 2003–04 period was $825.5 million, up 11.4 per cent from the previous year. In terms of profitability, the industry recorded a profit before interest and tax of $149 million. Television is the more lucrative of the two media. In the 2003–04 period, television revenue was $3724 million, up 9.23 per cent from the previous year (ACMA 2005).

The internet is regarded as having enormous, but as yet untapped, commercial potential. This is evidenced by the amount of money some media companies, such as News Ltd, are prepared to outlay in order to buy online businesses. In 2005, News Ltd invested heavily in interactive businesses, paying $776 million to procure the online business Intermix, owner of the site MySpace.com, which offers blogs, email, instant messaging, and video and music-clip downloads. The internet is fast proving to be a financial goldmine. The audited figures for the 2004–05 financial year show continued exponential growth. Locally, internet advertising is worth $488 million, up 63 per cent, with search engine and classified advertising the main drivers. By 2007, it should reach $800 million and begin closing rapidly on the printed product, which generates more than $3 billion annually (Sinclair 2005).

The only mainstream media sector that is struggling at present is the pay-television industry. As of June 1998, Optus TV (satellite service) had accumulated losses of $1000 million, and Foxtel (the largest pay-television provider) losses of $512 million (Productivity Commission 2000, p. 102). These losses result from the fact that the pay-television sector is a maturing industry. The high costs of rolling out the infrastructure and connecting customers, combined with the reluctance of Australians to embrace this service, has resulted in a fairly dismal economic performance. It is only more recently that some of the pay-television providers have come close to breaking even or even begun to register a profit.

Box 2.1   Industry bodies of select media

In order to promote the interests of their particular sector, media proprietors have created industry groups. Industry bodies are typically funded out of financial contributions made by its members, and serve the objective of protecting and advancing the interests of their sector. Industry groups perform a range of roles, including lobbying government, preparing discussion papers relevant to their constituents, undertaking research, and providing general assistance and advice to the industry leaders they represent. While there are many different media industry bodies, among the most influential of these are:

- *Magazine Publishers of Australia*—Represents Australia's 'leading' consumer magazine publishers in order to promote a 'dynamic and vibrant medium' and further the interests of the industry (http://www.magazines.org.au).
- *Australian Subscription Television and Radio Association*—Formed in 1997 following the amalgamation of the Australian Narrowcasting Subscription Services (FANSS) and the Confederation of Australian Subscription TV (CAST), it represents the interest of the pay-television sector by providing a 'single unified voice on issues affected by subscription television'. Its membership consists of the three subscription television platforms, the program channel providers and communications companies and other associate members (http://www.astra.org.au/home.asp).
- *Free TV Australia*—The industry body that has represented all commercial free-to-air television licensees for over 40 years. It provides a forum for discussion of industry matters as well as a public voice of the industry. It is governed by a board of directors, which in turn is supported by a number of committees that offer advice across a range of issue of importance to the industry (http://www.freetvaust.com.au/).
- *Commercial Radio Australia*—The national body representing Australia's commercial free-to-air radio was established in 1930, under the name Federation of Australian Radio Broadcasters. It has 252 members, representing 98 per cent of commercial stations on-air (http://www.commercialradio.com.au/).
- *Community Broadcasting Association of Australia*—The peak body for community radio and television stations, it provides 'leadership, advocacy and support' for its members (http://www.cbaa.org.au).

- *Internet Industry Association*—Australia's national internet industry organisation, it provides policy input to government and advocacy on a range of issues relevant to the industry in the interests of promoting laws and initiatives that enhance the medium. Members include telecommunications carriers, content creators and internet publishers, web developers, e-commerce traders and solutions providers, among others (http://www.iia.net.au/).
- *Press Council*—Established in 1976 with the twin objectives of preserving the press freedoms within Australia and ensuring that the press acts in a responsible manner: It consists of 22 members representing industry, journalists and public interests and is funded by the newspaper and magazine industries. At the present time, there is no comparable industry body for the print media—as exists for the broadcasting and other media—although there has been in the past (http://www. presscouncil.org.au/).

To what extent would you regard the existence of industry bodies legitimate, particularly if it allows the media proprietors to use their collective influence to gain concessions from the government?

The regulators: the government

The government is the third major player in the Australian media, responsible for establishing and enforcing the regulatory setting. The government is required to manage the various and often competing interests connected to the media, and to oversee and monitor the allocation and distribution of scarce media resources. The government acts to ensure that consumers are not subject to offensive material and content, are protected against unscrupulous business practices, and that there is both choice and a continuous supply of services at a reasonable price (for example, **anti-siphoning legislation**). The government sees to the interests of the media proprietors by seeking to create a stable and prosperous economic environment.

anti-siphoning legislation a scheme that ensures that certain events are available on commercial free-to-air channels by preventing pay-television licensees from acquiring exclusive rights to certain listed events

The sheer volume of laws that have been enacted to regulate the sector reflects the perceived importance of the industry in economical, political and cultural terms. Many of the regulations, such as rules regarding the allocation of broadcast spectrum, attract very little attention. Other matters, however, such as censorship and media ownership, generate heated public debate.

More particularly, the government performs a number of important functions in relation to the organisation and management of the media. These include:

- *Who can own media*—The government makes rules about which kind of people or organisations are permitted to own media. The objective is to ensure that only 'suitable' candidates will be allowed to enter the market. Historically, this has meant fairly tight restrictions on foreign ownership. While such considerations are becoming less important over time, it remains the case that government continues to take an interest in the nationality of potential media owners.

- *How much of any particular media an individual or company can own*— The government determines how much media one person or company can acquire. This is achieved in a variety of ways. First, the government imposes limits on ownership that restrict the amount of any one particular medium a person or company is entitled to purchase. Second, cross-media rules have been devised that limit the number of different types of media that can be acquired. Finally, the government can prevent mergers between media companies and thwart hostile takeovers if it believes that such action would have an adverse effect on the diversity, plurality and cost structure of the industry.

- *The conditions under which both individuals and companies use media*— The government also imposes terms and conditions on both the users and providers of media. In the case of broadcasters, the government attaches conditions on their right to broadcast. They must observe programming and content standards in order to retain possession of a broadcasting licence. In the case of audiences, the government outlaws access to content that it believes is unsavoury, and makes it illegal for consumers to act in ways that may injure the legitimate pecuniary interests of media owners (for example, imposition of fines for accessing pay-television services that have not been subscribed to).

- *A provider of media*—In addition to regulating media, the government is also a direct provider of media services. As will be explained in greater detail in Chapter 9, the government is a media owner, with interests in broadcasting and, until recently, telecommunications.

It is also important to note that while the government is active across all media, it applies different rules to different media. For example, the print media are subject to a much weaker legislative regime than the electronic media, being exempt from a licensing process, specific content regulations or subject to the oversight of a government agency. This, according to Butler and Rodrick, is a vestige 'of the constitutional history of England, where removal of newspaper licensing and regulation in the late 1600s was regarded as an advance in civil liberties' (2004, p. 566). The convention persists and, today, is given further legitimacy on economic grounds; namely the lower barriers of entry to the industry in comparison to other media.

In contrast, the government's approach to the regulation of the broadcasting sector has been both prescriptive and interventionist, tightly controlling both ownership and use. This is a response to a mixture of concerns. The sheer ubiquity of the broadcasting media in terms of their immediacy and mass coverage forced the government to concede that it would be unwise to leave the new sectors to their own devices, lest the technology be used 'against', rather than 'in' the interests of the greater good (Albon & Papandrea 1998, pp. 3–4). It was also justified on the basis of technological considerations. Traditionally, broadcasting programs were delivered exclusively via **radio frequency spectrum**, regarded as a national, public resource. While in theory radio frequency spectrum is finite, in practice the number of frequencies that can support broadcasting channels is not. Because of this, the government assumed responsibility for the allocation of spectrum in the interests of 'fairness' and 'efficiency' (Butler & Rodrick 2004, p. 486). As a result, the government determines the number of broadcasting stations per market and the conditions under which licensees operate.

> **radio frequency spectrum** alternating current having characteristics such that if the current is input to an antenna, an electromagnetic field is generated suitable for wireless broadcasting and/or communications

The machinery of regulation

The formulation of media policy is largely the responsibility of the national government (Commonwealth) located in Canberra. The Commonwealth derives its authority to legislate on virtually all forms of media on the basis of powers afforded to it under the federal **Constitution**. However, as we will see a little later in this chapter, there is still some scope for state governments to play a role in shaping some aspects of media policy.

▶ **Constitution** enacted in 1900, the Australian Commonwealth Constitution is a legal compact that sets out the fundamental political principles of government, describing important political institutions, actors and processes

In relation to the electronic media (that is, broadcast and internet), the Commonwealth's authority to devise policy is outlined in s. 51, part 5 of the Constitution. This section, known colloquially as the 'telecommunications power', specifies that the Commonwealth has the power to make laws in respect to 'postal, telegraphic, telephonic and other like services'. Despite opportunities for the state governments to legislate in this area, since 1935 particularly, broadcasting has been a matter for the Commonwealth (Harding 1985, p. 234).

Responsibility for the regulation and administration of the electronic media falls to the Minister for Communications. The role of the **minister** is to set the overall policy direction for the portfolio and ensure any resultant initiatives are properly reflected in law. The minister is assisted in such duties by the Department of Communications, Information Technology and the Arts (DCITA). DCITA, a **government department**, is required to offer 'strategic advice and professional support' to the minister, as well as contribute to legislation relevant to the portfolio.

▶ **minister** a person appointed to head an executive or administrative department of government; in the Australian context, a minister is in charge of one or more portfolio areas and is answerable to Parliament for both his/her actions and those of the department under his/her jurisdiction

> **government department** a department established by the government in order to advise and assist in the formulation and delivery of policy in a specific area, such as health or defence; individual departments are directly answerable to the relevant minister

Whereas DCITA provides the minister with assistance in the formulation and administration of policy, other government agencies also play an important role in administering the various laws that regulate the media. The Australian Communications and Media Authority (ACMA) is a key government body. ACMA's tasks consist of the regulation of aspects of the electronic media, including broadcasting, radio-communications, telecommunications and online content. It plans the channels that commercial and community broadcasting services use; issues and renews **licences**; regulates content; and administers the ownership and control rules for broadcasting services. In recognition of the politically sensitive role performed by ACMA, it enjoys the status of a **statutory body**. This designation affords the agency a modicum of independence from the minister and, ultimately, the government.

> **licence** a contractual arrangement between the government and individual/organisation, which affords to the later the right to operate broadcasting services; since 1992, the process of assigning broadcasting licences is based on a price-based system whereby they are auctioned to the highest bidder

> **statutory body** a form of government department that has a largely corporate function and is, for the most part, autonomous in its operations as compared with government departments

While the Commonwealth is clearly pre-eminent in the regulation of the broadcast media, it does not have exclusive responsibility for the internet. Regulation of the internet is shared between the Commonwealth and state governments. Most aspects of the internet, and more particularly the activities of **Internet Content Hosts** (ICH) and **Internet Service Providers** (ISP), fall to the Commonwealth and the portfolio of the Minister for Communications. With the help of ACMA, the Commonwealth classifies material, determines the broad framework for the **industry code of practice** and investigates public complaints about internet content. The state governments have authority for content providers/creators and ordinary internet users. The state governments are essentially responsible for prosecuting internet users who create and post 'unsuitable' material online and/or those who download such material.

> **Internet Content Host (ICH)** persons, groups or organisations that host internet content

> **Internet Service Provider (ISP)** a company that provides access to the internet to individuals or companies; they provide local dial-up or broadband access from your personal computer to their computer network, and their network connects you to the internet

> **industry code of practice** a document that outlines how to achieve the standard required by the relevant government Act and regulation; codes of practice are generally developed through consultation with representatives from industry and the relevant government agency or agencies

Both the Commonwealth and state governments share responsibility for the regulation of the print media. There is 'no single piece of legislation' that regulates the print media (Butler & Rodrick 2004, p. 566). Most, but not all, state and territory governments have some form of legislation that deals with the print media. The Acts passed by the state governments are relatively innocuous, and typically take the form of a requirement for the proprietor to formally register the newspaper, and that the proprietor's/company name and contact details are displayed somewhere in the paper (Butler & Rodrick 2004, p. 567). According to Brown, such provisions are not intended to impose a barrier against entry into the industry, but rather to 'facilitate legal action in the event of proceedings for defamation and obscene publication' (1986, p. 30).

Although the Commonwealth lacks an explicit right to legislate for the print media, it is still able to exert considerable influence and control over the medium. The Commonwealth is able to leverage a role for itself in the print sector, as well as the electronic media, through s. 51(10) of the Constitution, which permits the Commonwealth to legislate in relation to 'Foreign Corporations, and trading or financial corporations formed within the limits of the Commonwealth'. This section of the Constitution is known as the 'Corporations power'.

The Corporation's power gives rise to two important Acts, which have important implications for ownership of all forms of media in this country. The first of these is the *Foreign Acquisitions and Takeover Act 1975* (FATA), which allows the government to make laws with respect to foreign ownership of all media. The second is the *Trade Practices Act 1974* (TPA). The TPA covers barriers to entry and mergers legislation designed to constrain and limit uncompetitive and unfair behaviour on the part of firms. The TPA can be used to prohibit mergers that are likely to substantially lessen market competition and to prevent the misuse of media power. In combination, both Acts enable the Commonwealth to determine the terms and conditions under which newspapers, and other media businesses, can buy and sell, and to intervene where the government believes a company is engaging in unfair and uncompetitive behaviour.

Both FATA and the TPA are administered by the federal Treasurer. The Treasurer, who is largely responsible for economic, business and taxation matters, is assisted in managing both Acts by the Foreign Investment Review Board (FIRB) and the Australian Competition and Consumer Commission (ACCC). Both the FIRB and the ACCC oversee the day-to-day administration of FATA and the TPA, respectively.

The Commonwealth Attorney-General (AG) also plays a role in regulating the print media. The AG's responsibilities are chiefly confined to the regulation of media content, except electronic media content (such as television, radio, telephony and the internet). The AG's authority arises from s. 51(1) of the Constitution: 'the trade and commerce power'. This provision gives rise to the *Customs Act 1901*, which controls and regulates all goods imported into the country. The *Customs Act* provides the AG with the legal authority to rate and classify all imported films, DVDs and computer games. While the AG, in conjunction with his/her **cabinet** colleagues and the **Parliament**, is responsible for determining the broad criteria on which the material is assessed, the task in practice is delegated to the Classification Board. The Classification Board, a 20-member panel selected by the AG, views, reads or plays relevant material and determines its classification status. The state governments do retain the power to classify locally produced printed material, films, video games and internet content. Since the 1980s, there has been a concerted effort to operate a uniform classificatory regime. Nonetheless, there remains some variation in permissible content between the different states and territories.

▶ **cabinet** the supreme decision-making institution of government, consisting of the prime minister/premier and his/her most senior ministers

▶ **Parliament** an assembly of those men and women who have been democratically elected to make laws for the country

Table 2.2 Overview of Australian media law

Constitutional authority	'Telecommunications Power': Section 51(v)	'Corporations Power': Section 51(10)	'Trade and Commerce Power': Section 51(1)
Federal minister	Minister for Communications (http://www.minister.dcita.gov.au/)	Treasurer (http://www.treasurer.gov.au/)	Attorney-General (http://www.ag.gov.au/agd/www/Minister Ruddock home.nsf)
Public service department	Department of Communications, Information Technology and the Arts (DCITA) (http://www.dcita.gov.au/)	Treasury (http://www.treasury.gov.au)	Office of the Attorney-General (http://www.ag.gov.au/)
Relevant legislation	*Broadcasting Services Act 1992* (http://www.austlii.edu.au/au/legis/cth/consol_act/bsa1992214/) *Radiocommunications Act 1992* (http://www.austlii.edu.au/au/legis/cth/consol_act/ra1992218/) *Special Broadcasting Services Act 1991 (SBS)* (http://www.austlii.edu.au/au/legis/cth/consol_act/sbsa1991254/) *Australian Broadcasting Corporation Act 1983 (ABC)* (http://www.austlii.edu.au/au/legis/cth/consol_act/abca1983361/)	*Foreign Acquisition and Takeovers Act 1975* (http://www.austlii.edu.au/au/legis/cth/consol_act/faata1975355/) *Trade Practices Act 1974* (http://www.austlii.edu.au/au/legis/cth/consol_act/tpa1974149/)	*Customs Act 1901* (http://www.austlii.edu.au/au/legis/cth/consol_act/ca1901124/)

Relevant legislation (continued)	*Radio Licence Fees Act 1964* (http://www.comlaw. gov.au/comlaw/ management.nsf/ lookupindexpages byid/IP200403899? OpenDocument)		
	Television Licence Fees Act 1964 (http://www.comlaw. gov.au/comlaw/ management.nsf/ lookupindex pagesbyid/ IP20040133 2? OpenDocument)		
Regulators	Australian Communications and Media Authority (ACMA) (http://www.acma.gov. au/)	Australian Competition and Consumer Commission (TPA 1974) (http://www. accc.gov.au/) Foreign Investment Review Board (FATA 1975) (http://www.firb. gov.au/)	Office of Film and Literature Classification (http://www.oflc. gov.au/) The Classification Board
Responsi-bilities	Management of electronic media (internet, radio and television)	Regulates aspects of ownership and control of the media sector, including the print media	Classification of imported films, DVDs, computer games and publications.

Debates and controversies: the future of regulation—convergence and deregulation

Over the last 15 years, new media technology has presented a challenge for government and prompted calls for reform of the regulatory setting. Driving much of the debate has been a phenomenon known as convergence. Convergence refers to a process whereby television, telecommunications and computer services are becoming increasingly integrated owing to digitisation. Convergence is dissolving the old boundaries that formerly existed between different media in terms of services and platforms, putting pressure on the government to re-write the regulatory rule book to address these changes. At the core of much of the policy rhetoric that shrouds this debate is the claim that special rules should not apply to the media sector and that it should be treated like any other area of the economy. Essentially, media specific legislation should be repealed and the sector regulated under generic competition laws.

The Howard Government, along with previous governments, acknowledges that 'the media landscape is changing rapidly, and a flexible system is needed to allow media companies to adapt and prosper in the new digital environment' (Coonan 2006, p. 1). The Howard Government's reforms are outlined in a document entitled *New Media Framework for Australia*. Among other things, the new laws, introduced in April 2007, relax the cross media regime, remove foreign ownership restrictions for TV and newspapers, and dilute Australia's antisiphoning scheme. The aim of the new laws is to deregulate the media sector so as to facilitate a greater role for free market forces in shaping the configuration and structure of an industry currently undergoing transformation and change.

> **deregulation** the removal (either in part or in whole) of government controls over an industry; this is done ostensibly in the interests of improving the economic and productive efficiency of the industry in question

There is little agreement about the impact deregulation will have on either the industry or consumers. Some scholars contend that it is unwise for the government to pursue liberalisation because it will only benefit large media owners and result in poor market outcomes for audiences and small media firms. They believe in the retention of stringent government controls, particularly in relation to cross-media and foreign ownership. Others, however, argue that the government's agenda is timid and does not go far enough to inject real competition into the sector, which should be the key objective of deregulation. Chris Berg (2006a) claims that the reforms 'merely add more rope'. He argues that some initiatives, such as the decision to water down the cross-media rules, are only a 'minor adjustment', which disappoints 'advocates of genuine deregulation'. Berg, a Research Fellow for the Institute of Public Affairs, maintains that the retention of cross-media rules will, if anything, lead to a loss of significant efficiencies in the media market, and effectively prevent the existing players from further investing and developing the industry (2006b, pp. 5–6).

The lack of consensus that surrounds the Howard Government's reforms are indicative of the difficulty in formulating policy that meets the interests of all the key stakeholders. Government is forced to balance a range of competing interests simultaneously—those of the public, who elect them to office; the media industry, which has the power to use its outlets against the government should they so choose; and, at the end of the day, their own interests and those of the **Parliament** to whom they are accountable. The problem is compounded because the industry is oftentimes internally divided about the kind of policy outcomes they expect. Contrary to popular belief, the media industry is not an amorphous block. While the media owners have much in common (the desire to be successful and profitable), they are also rivals with different needs. The Howard Government's latest offer to relax cross-media ownership is welcomed by James Packer's PBL, but not by News Ltd owner Rupert Murdoch. News Ltd has complained that the reform proposal is 'highly discriminatory' because of the government's refusal to issue a fourth commercial television licence, and unwillingness to disband the anti-siphoning list. It claims that the reform plan 'shore[s] up protection for the dominant and highly profitable free-to-air television industry' and 'pose[s] a significant threat to the viability of Australia's emerging subscription television industry' (Murray 2006b). Adding to the Howard Government's problems is the high degree of uncertainty about the likely impact that convergence and digitisation of the media will produce. Because the full impacts of the new technology are yet to be fully felt, governments have little choice but to proceed with caution. This can result in the temptation to approach reform in a piecemeal manner, which many regard as undesirable and compromised.

SUMMARY

The chapter has provided a brief snapshot of the Australian media. It has shown that three groups are particularly crucial to the operation and success of the industry. Australian audiences drive market demand for media, which creates powerful economic incentives for media proprietors to invest in media technologies, and supply media products and services. The government is also an integral player, regulating the media market ostensibly in the public interest. While each of these groups is interdependent, their interests are not always compatible; nor are they easy to reconcile. It is the tension that exists between the key stakeholders—their conflicting hopes, expectations and objectives— that drives the logic and dynamic of the Australian media.

Questions

1 Which medium would you consider the most powerful and why? What, in your opinion, does the future hold for radio, television, newspapers and the internet in terms of popular usage?
2 Do you think that ownership of the media industry is too concentrated?
3 Is it legitimate for the government to impose fewer restrictions on the print sector compared with the broadcasting industry?

WEBSITES

Australian Communications and Media Authority (ACMA)—Responsible for the regulation of broadcasting, radio communications, telecommunications and online content (http://www.acma.gov.au).

Department of Communications, Information Technology and the Arts (DCITA)— Provides strategic advice and professional support to the Australian Government on a wide range of significant and rapidly changing policy areas including: arts and culture; broadcasting and online regulation; Indigenous programs; information and communications technology; information economy; intellectual property; post; sport; and telecommunications (http://www.dcita. gov.au/).

FURTHER READING

Cunningham, S. 2006, 'Policy', in S. Cunningham & G. Turner (eds), *The Media and Communications in Australia*, 2nd edn. Allen & Unwin: St Leonards.

Gardiner-Garden, J. & Chowns, J. 2006, 'Media Ownership Regulation in Australia'. *E-Brief*, Australian Parliamentary Library, Canberra.

THE PUBLIC AND MEDIA:

Couch Potatoes or Rational Consumers?

This chapter will:

- explain the dominant assumptions about the relationship between the media and the individual in liberal democratic societies

- provide an overview of the literature and research on media effects.

It is widely accepted that the media possess the power to shape ideas, beliefs and behaviour. It is for this reason that governments prohibit and restrict certain content. However, it is also recognised that it is not easy to ascertain the extent of the media's influence. In liberal democratic societies, there is an implicit understanding that the media's power is held in check by three key factors. First, there is a belief that adults are self-selecting and rational with different needs and wants. Society is not an amorphous, undifferentiated mass, but consists of individuals with diverse abilities and tastes. As a result, individuals are thought to have different needs and uses for media, and will be attracted to different media forms and content. The underlying assumption is that the individual will be affected by the media in different ways and at different times. It is for this reason that much of public concern about the effects of the media is directed at children and young people, rather than adults.

Second, the media's power to influence the individual is thought to be diluted by powerful economic considerations. The accepted wisdom is that for as long as the media are predominately privately owned, there is scope for the individual to influence the type of media content that is produced. The industry's financial success is contingent on the creation of a media product that is popular among the buying public. In order to turn a profit, proprietors must cater to the public need (Wheeler 1997, p. 6). What individuals watch, listen and read reflects their needs, desires and demands. If this were not the case, why would broadcasters waste their time with audience ratings, or newspaper owners concern themselves with circulation figures? Implicit in such thinking is the belief that if audiences are capable of exerting some influence over media content, then surely they are able to control their reaction to that material.

Third, any concern about media owners using their outlets to manipulate the public is tempered by the belief that power in society is relatively diffused. In liberal democratic societies, such as Australia, it is thought that there is no permanent power elite capable of exerting its influence over society. Power in society is assumed to be fragmented, and constantly shifting between many groups. Whatever power the media owners do have is likely to be counteracted by other sources of power in society; namely, other non-media business interests and groups. More importantly, any use of the media for ill, self-serving purposes can be negated by governments enacting laws that proscribe content that might prove offensive or injurious to the public.

Such assumptions, when taken in combination, imply that the power of the media can be both contained and controlled. For the most part, liberals believe that some individuals will be more affected than others by the media, that its effects are likely to be transitory, and that these evils can be managed through legislative oversight. Yet, while much of government policy appears to be predicated on such assumptions, this does not prevent concerns being voiced episodically about the media's ill effects. While there are a number of issues that have sparked public disquiet, the more high profile of these includes:

- unease about the effect of the media on the mental and physical development of children
- anxiety about the impact of the media on violent and antisocial behaviours
- outrage at the representation of women and minority groups in the media
- fears that the media are promoting rampant consumerism.

At the core of these concerns is the sneaking suspicion that the rationality of the human mind is inherently fragile, and that individuals have the potential to absorb messages and ideas uncritically, and can be easily swayed by media content. The uncertainty that shrouds the nexus between media content and audiences has prompted a great deal of scholarly activity aimed at helping us to better understand the nature of this relationship.

The who and why of media effects

As a field of academic endeavour, the attempt to understand media effects is relatively new. While academics took more than just a passing interest in the political, social and cultural impact of the print media, it was not until the emergence of the broadcast media that the level of academic interest was substantially piqued, or that research techniques to measure such phenomena were fully developed. Since this time, countless studies have been conducted on the effects of the media. Durkin estimates that more than 1000 empirical studies have been undertaken on the subject of television violence alone (Durkin 1995a, p. 1).

There are two broad research traditions associated with the study of media impacts: the dominant paradigm and the alternative paradigm (McQuail 1994, pp. 41–6). The *dominant paradigm* is strongly associated with the **media effects** tradition. It has a strong scientific basis, drawing heavily on both **quantitative research** and **qualitative research** techniques, but the former more particularly. Most researchers working within this tradition have a decided preference for 'precise measurement and quantification, usually based on observations of individual behaviour' (McQuail 1994, p. 44). This tradition assumes that there is a linear transmission model of effects (which visualises communication as a sequential process) and takes as its starting position a conception of 'the good society' predicated on Western liberal values. The *alternative paradigm*, in contrast, rejects the assumptions that underpin the dominant paradigm and more particularly its preoccupation with the effects of the media on the individual, which they contend ignores the broader political and cultural impacts of the media. Essentially, the alternative paradigm seeks to 'engage critically with the political and economic activities of the media; to better understand the language of the media and the ways of media culture; to discover how meaning is constructed … and to explore the diverse meanings of the practices of using the mass media'. The alternative paradigm tends to favour qualitative research methodologies (McQuail 1994, p. 48).

media effects attempts to account for how the media affects audiences; it is associated with an empirical, qualitative research approach that attempts to scientifically measure the relationship between the media and audience behaviour

quantitative research attempts to measure quantitatively the impact that exposure to media has on our actions and attitudes by 'converting observed behaviours into numbers that can be systematically analysed using mathematical tools generally known as statistics' (Traudt 2005, p. 16)

qualitative research attempts to 'study the lived experience' by 'observing how individuals act' and by 'describ[ing] their actions in society' (Traudt 2005, p. 30); Turow describes this approach as one that endeavours to 'make sense of an aspects of reality by showing how different parts of it fit together in particular ways' (2003, p. 131)

Box 3.1   Selected examples of Australian research into media effects

Much of the literature that currently exists on media effects is American. This preponderance of American effects studies, versus those from Australia, is the result of the high costs associated with undertaking such research. However, there is a growing body of Australian scholarship on the subject, which spans a number of academic disciplines:

- Bean, C. 2005, 'How the political audience of Australian public and commercial television channels differ'. *Australian Journal of Communication*, vol. 32, no. 2, pp. 41–55.
- Brown, M. 1996, 'The portrayal of violence in the media: impacts and implications for policy'. *Trends & Issues in Crime and Criminal Justice*, no. 55, pp. 1–7.
- Denemark, D. 2002, 'Television Effects and Voter Decision Making in Australia: A Re-examination of the Converse Model', *British Journal of Political Science*, vol. 32, no. 4, pp. 663–90.

Morris, M. & Frow, J. 1993, *Australian Cultural Studies: A Reader*. Allen & Unwin: St Leonards.

Sheehan P. W. 1986, 'Television viewing and its relation to aggression among children in Australia'. In L. R. Huesmann & L. D. Eron (eds), *Television and the Aggressive Child: A Cross-National Comparison*. Erlbaum: Hillsdale, pp. 161–200.

Skouteris, H., & Kelly, L. 2006, 'Repeated-Viewing and Co-Viewing of an Animated Video: An Examination of Factors that Impact on Young Children's Comprehension of Video Content', *Australian Journal of Early Childhood*, vol. 31, no. 3, pp. 22–30.

A number of academic disciplines within the social sciences, humanities and health sciences take a keen interest in the study of the media, even though they have slightly different foci. What unifies the various approaches, however, are two broad areas of agreement about the nature of media effects. First, almost all scholars and researchers agree that the media exerts an influence over individuals. That is, there is a general consensus that the interaction between the media and the individual is 'complex' but not without effect. Second, most agree that television, at the present time, is the most powerful and persuasive of all media, even if it is not the most important in political terms. This view results from the particular conjunction of properties possessed by the television medium. Television's ubiquity (virtually every Australian household owns a set); the limited obstacles to access and usage (that is, literacy is not relevant to one's comprehension or enjoyment of the medium); the high level of intimacy with the viewer; and its large-scale reach (that is, it's capable of transmitting a single message to a large audience effortlessly and simultaneously) renders it not only one of the most researched media, but also one of the most powerful.

While scholars broadly agree that the media exerts an influence and that television is the most influential medium, there is disagreement about the size of the media's influence. Within the literature, there is a difference of opinion between those who contend that media effects are 'big' and 'powerful' and those who argue that that its effects, while apparent, are limited and diffused. The next section of this chapter explores this debate in further detail.

Box 3.2   Is television making you antisocial?

In 1950, David Putnam set out to explain declining levels of social capital in US society, particularly evident in the postwar generation. Putnam defined social capital as 'features of social networks—networks, trust and norms—that allow people to participate more effectively to achieve shared objectives'. He noted that declining membership in social groups, less time devoted to socialising and the decrease in political participation were evidence of declining social capital. He posited various explanations for this trend, such as general busyness of modern society, the emergence of the welfare state and the advent of the working woman. However, of the 11 variables he outlined, he argued that only one stood out as a plausible explanation for declining levels of social trust: television. Since the late 1950s, television has penetrated more than 90 per cent of US homes. Concomitant with this phenomenon has been a marked increase in the amount of time spent watching television (the civic generation precedes the onset of television). Putnam argues that television watching is the only leisure activity that inhibits participation outside of the home, resulting in 'time displacement'. Moreover, he notes that television 'induces pessimism about human nature (1995, p. 679). In essence, Putnam argued that 'each hour spent watching TV is associated with less social trust and less group membership' (1995, p. 678).

Putnam's thesis was challenged by Pippa Norris, who argued that while the tendency to lay the blame at the altar of television is intuitively appealing and likely to 'strike a popular chord', 'many of the attacks on the media are drawn in black and white terms, as though there is one television experience ... and one audience ...' (Norris 1996, p. 475). On the strength of her research findings, Norris argued that those who watched a lot of television news and public affairs programs were more likely to be involved in all types of political activity, compared with those who preferred other types of programs. She argued that current affairs programs did not damage the 'democratic health of society' but appeared to improve it (1996, p. 479). As far as Norris is concerned, the problem lies not with television but with the content people are watching.

Do you think that declining levels of social capital are the net result of television, as proposed by Putnam, or do you think it has the potential to be of benefit, as suggested by Norris?

The size of media effects: powerful or mediated?

The earliest academic contributions to the media effects debate subscribed to the view that the media were a powerful agent of change. The 'powerful effect' thesis was commonly associated with the hypodermic model, although the tradition sometimes goes under other names, such as the 'transmission model' or the 'magic bullets' approach. The hypodermic model suggests that media messages are like a needle that, once injected into the audience member, renders the recipient helpless to reject its message. Predicated on a simplistic stimulus–response model, it assumes that the individual, once exposed to the message, will react according to the sentiment the message is intended to engender (Ward 1995, pp. 23–5).

The hypodermic model supposed that any given audience would interpret the same message in much the same manner. Regardless of one's level of educational attainment, age, social and economic circumstances, we are all destined to respond to the same media stimuli in exactly the same way. Essentially, audiences were viewed as passive processors and receivers of information, lacking the innate capacity to think critically about the information to which they were exposed (McCullagh 2002, p. 152).

While various theories were offered to explain this phenomenon, the dominant thesis was the theory of mass society. According to this theory, the process of industrialisation had disrupted established modes of living. Individuals were forced to abandon small-scale, intimate communities and live in anonymous large-scale cities. In this faceless urban setting, people found themselves without stable ties to community, family and the church. Mass society was an anchorless existence that made people vulnerable to the media due to their lack of strong group or individual identity. In the absence of strong community structures to offer direction, individuals turned to other institutions such as the media to provide them with their cues (McCullagh 2002, p. 153; McQuail 1994, p. 34; Ward 1995, pp. 29–31).

There appeared to be strong, albeit superficial evidence to support such conclusions. The public was flocking to the media in droves. The high attendance at films and movies tended to suggest that the public was innately attracted to the media: captive to its charms and 'hanging out' for their next media fix. Both government and businesses also seemed intrigued by the potential of the new media, and eager to exploit it for their own purposes.

Scholars surmised that neither group would willingly invest heavily in pro-motional campaigns if they did not believe the media served their interests in some way. Moreover, scholars were able to point to instances where the media had incited public hysteria. Orson Welles's radio dramatisation of *War of the Worlds* became a much referred-to case study among academics. The radio play, based on H.G. Wells's novel about an alien invasion, created havoc in the streets of New York, with people fleeing their homes because they thought spaceships had landed. What was surprising about the reaction was that at various points during the program the radio announcer had indicated that it was a work of fiction. Moreover, on the basis of the sequence of events being described, any thinking, rational person should have realised that it would be impossible for aliens to have blasted off from Mars, conduct a major military battle in New Jersey and destroy New York all in the course of an hour (Ward 1995).

While there seemed to be plenty of anecdotal or observational evidence to support the argument that a direct and unmediated relationship existed between the individual and the media, there was little hard scientific evi-dence. Beginning in the 1940s, new research techniques were developed to assess the veracity of these assertions; techniques that were able to test for a range of different variables, and lay claim to the principles of neutrality and objectivity (Taylor & Willis 1999, p. 158; Ward 1995, p. 32). As this research began to bear fruit, the findings appeared to contradict the view that the media exerted a powerful effect on audiences. This resulted in the repudiation of the hypodermic model and belief in an all-powerful media.

In the 1960s, a new wave of scholars began to revisit the 'powerful effects' contention. These scholars, loosely defined for our purposes as exponents of the critical tradition (also see the earlier discussion of the alternative para-digm), argued that the media exerts a powerful effect over society. However, unlike their 'powerful effects' antecedents, the critical tradition diverged on two essential points: how best to study the impact of the media, and the underlying theoretical assumptions that inform the nature of media power.

In terms of differences to their approach to the study of media, the critical tradition maintains that 'neither large-scale surveys nor detailed experiments replicate or reflect the actual experience of viewing' (Street 2001, p. 93). It tends to be sceptical of claims that the impacts of the media can be measured in a neutral, scientific and objective way. More particularly, its advocates argue that the scientific approach fails to properly explore the nexus between broader power structures in society and the production of media texts (Taylor & Willis 1999, pp. 160–1). Instead, the critical tradition maintains that 'media power is best conceived not in the form of separate and discontinuous effects but in terms of ideological influence and requires recognition of the wider context of those interpretations' (Curran 2002, p. 139). In keeping with this sentiment, the critical tradition tends to be much more interested in a macro-level (society) analysis of media effects rather than micro-level (individual) responses. Essentially, much of critical theory is interested in how the media engenders broader social change rather than how it impacts on the individual's attitudes, opinions and short-term behaviour (for example, imitation).

The other distinguishing feature of the critical tradition is that it proposes a slightly different set of reasons to support a powerful media thesis. In the first place, critical theorists do not believe that the effects of the media are immediate or direct, but that they are cumulative. They argue that the media does not just change one's behaviour, but that it encourages or reinforces certain behaviours over an extended period of time. The effects of the media are long term—actively cultivating certain attitudes and behaviours—and do not merely produce short-term changes in behaviour. Second, the critical tradition rejects the idea that the media's ability to exert a powerful influence results from the inherent passivity of individuals, believing instead that it is a function of how elites within society use and exploit the media to their own ends.

The critical tradition is strongly influenced by Marxist scholarship and its variants. In very simplistic terms, the Marxist position takes the view that the media are instruments of the dominant class (ruling elite within society), which is used to maintain and produce inequalities in society. Basically, the media ensure that the rich and powerful remain rich and powerful, and that the masses remain oppressed and unaware of their true situation. This is essentially achieved through a dominant **ideology** that produces **false consciousness** so that the hegemony of the ruling elite is maintained.

▶ **ideology** a comprehensive set of beliefs, ideas or values that inform how people order and make sense of the world around them

▶ **false consciousness** the failure of the oppressed to recognise that their situation results from their acceptance of the views of their oppressors

There are, essentially, two dominant approaches within the critical tradition: political economy and cultural theory.

POLITICAL ECONOMY APPROACH

This approach is strongly associated with such writers as Edward Herman, Noam Chomsky, Graham Murdock and Ben Bagdikian. This perspective focuses on the importance of economic processes and how patterns of ownership affect media output. It is primarily concerned with how economic forces and the need to produce a profit lead inevitably to concentrated patterns of media ownership, whereby there is a reduction in independent sources, less diversity and plurality of voices in the marketplace, and a concentration on the largest lucrative niche markets at the expense of poorer and smaller segments of the marketplace (McQuail 1994, p. 82). It is suggested that, as a result of these forces (namely the particular configuration of political and economic structures in society), and the structure of ownership and control over the media, the ruling elite are able to maintain the status quo or, to quote Herman and Chomsky, 'manufacture consent'(1988).

CULTURAL THEORISTS

Associated with the work of the Frankfurt school and writers such as Theodor Adorno, Louis Althusser, C. Wright Mills, Antonio Gramsci and Herbert Marcuse, the cultural theorists explore the interrelationship between the media and its cultural effects (Macnamara 2003, p. 4). They contend that the media exert influence through cultural hegemony, and its means of doing so are largely imperceptible to society at large. They concentrate more on ideas and the process of **socialisation**, and how these are used and exploited by the dominant elite to cultivate acquiescence among the public. As McQuail explains, 'cultural products (images, ideas and symbols) are produced and sold in media markets as commodities ... These can be exchanged by consumers for psychic satisfactions, amusement and illusory notions of our place in the world'. This is a process that results from our dependence on the mass media. This occurs not through the exertion of economic or political power, but by way of a dominant discourse that gives preferential status to the values of the ruling elite (1994, p. 99).

▶ **socialisation** the process whereby individuals learn to behave in a manner consistent with societal expectations as regards the norms, values and culture of their society

Box 3.3   Is television making you fat?

The Australian population is one of the fattest in the developed world, with the number of overweight and obese people doubling over the last century. Sixty-seven per cent of men between the ages of 25 and 64 are either obese or overweight, while the figure for women in the same age group is 52 per cent. Research shows that there is a strong relationship between obesity and television viewing habits, with one Australian study showing that 'the odds of being obese were highly dependent on TV viewing time' (Cameron et al. 2003, p. 431).

Of most concern is the high rate of obesity in children between the ages of 5 and 17. Research shows that 20–25 per cent of Australian children are obese or overweight and that the numbers are growing. Concerns about a looming child obesity epidemic have prompted demands for television advertising of junk food during children's television to be banned. Australian children spend an average of 23 hours per week watching television and are exposed to four hours of advertisements per week, or 208 hours per year. The problem is compounded, some argue, by the high number of food advertisements shown during children's programming. In fact, Australian television shows have the highest number of food advertisements for children in the world, with an average of 12 per hour compared with 11 per hour in the US, seven per hour in Greece and one per hour in Austria. Moreover, 75 per cent of the advertisements are for unhealthy foods (Centre for Health Promotion 2006).

The combination of high caloric intake, heavy television viewing and junk food advertising is believed to have resulted in weight gain in children. A recent study undertaken in the US—which examined the television viewing, eating habits and physical activity of more than 500 children aged 11 and 12, over a 20-month period— found that watching television for an hour can increase a child's dietary intake by 167 calories and add about 6.5kg to their weight over a year. Researchers also discovered that children were eating significantly larger quantities of the snacks, sweets and fast foods that they had seen advertised most frequently on television (Nikkhah 2006).

The weight gain, in turn, is producing health complications in children, as Kaye Mehta, lecturer in the Department of Nutrition and Dietetics at Flinders University, explains: 'We are also seeing children with high blood pressure and raised blood cholesterol, which are both risk factors for cardiovascular disease ... [it is also] associated with arthritis, sleep apnoea, gout, and a whole lot of sociological factors associated with low self-esteem, bullying and so on'. More concerning is that this might be the first generation in modern history that has lower life expectancy than their parents.

So far, the Australian federal government has resisted a ban on junk food advertising during children's peak television viewing hours. This is despite calls from health experts (Australian Media Association), parents' groups (Parents Jury) and other bodies (Youth Media Australia). The government maintains that it is a problem best left to parents to manage. Instead, the government has agreed to invest heavily in public education campaigns and schools in order to encourage children to get physically active, including a $6 million campaign to encourage children to exercise one hour a day.

Do you believe that government should ban junk food advertising during children's television viewing hours?

Mediating conditions model

A second school of thought recognises that the media have the capacity to affect behaviour, but rejects the view that they are all-powerful. This tradition is mostly, although not exclusively, associated with a **liberal/pluralist** perspective. According to Curran, the liberal tradition views the media as 'reflecting rather than shaping society' (2002, p. 127). It adopts the position that audiences are not passive users of media but actively respond to content and even select content based on their own needs. It is associated with a range of media-effects traditions including the **limited effects** school, the **uses and gratifications** model, the **reinforcement thesis**, **agenda setting** and **agenda priming**, and the **encoding/decoding** model.

> **liberal/pluralist perspective** a view that holds that power in society is diffused and rented among a number of competing groups
>
> **reinforcement thesis** linked to the limited effects school, it suggests that the media tends to reinforce existing attitudes rather than change or create new attitudes

▶ **limited effects** sometimes referred to as minimal effects theory, this school
of thought has its genesis in the work of Paul Lazarsfeld and his colleagues, and
champions the view that media effects are largely of a minimal and indirect nature

▶ **uses and gratifications** a theory that focuses on how audiences use media and
why; it assumes an active audience that selects different media based on fulfilling their
particular needs

▶ **agenda priming** coined by Iyengar and Kinder, it draws on and expands upon
the agenda-setting thesis; Iyengar and Kinder argued that media helps to 'prime' or
influence how people think about particular issues—the media sets the context (on
the basis of the stories it presents) in which audiences make political judgments, not
only about the 'issue' but also perceptions about how well political candidates and
organisations are doing their job in relation to that issue

▶ **agenda setting** associated with the work of Shaw and McComb, it posits that the
media does not tell us what to think, but rather tells us what to think about

▶ **encoding/decoding** derives largely from the critical tradition; however, it does
use tools of quantitative analysis; media messages are believed to be open and have
multiple meanings, and are interpreted according to the context and culture of the
receiver—it assumes that audiences can in fact resist ideological influence by applying
oppositional readings according to their own experiences and outlook

The 'mediating conditions' tradition coincides with the development of new research techniques that attempted to scientifically measure the impact of the media, beginning in the 1940s. One of the earliest influential works was by a group of academics led by Paul Lazarsfeld. Lazarsfeld and his team had initially set out to prove the hypodermic theory of the media, hoping to draw a link between election advertising and the voting choices of electors (Ward 1995). However, their research findings proved counter-intuitive. Much to their surprise, their findings suggested that the media only exerted a relatively limited impact. Their research revealed that people did not necessarily change their voting choices as a result of their exposure to the media. Instead, they found that the opinions of one's primary group—that is, their friends, family and opinion leaders—were much more influential in shaping voting choices than election campaigns. In fact, family members and opinion leaders were extremely important in mediating media messages, acting as an invisible barrier between the message and the individual (Taylor & Willis 1999, pp. 158–9).

A number of studies followed, based on different research methods. Studies were conducted on a diverse range of topics, including, but not limited to, political campaigns, violence in the media, pornography, the representation of women and ethnic groups, propaganda effects and advertising campaigns. It facilitated the identification of an expanded range of variables that are likely to mediate the effects of the media: not just the influence of social relationships.

Those who argue the case for mediating conditions assert that the effect of the media is filtered by a host of variables that affect the individual's receptivity and use of different media. Some of the variables that have been identified include:

- *Socio-economic and demographic factors*, such as a person's age, gender, employment status and social location, which appear to influence not only what type of media we consume but also the type of media content to which we are attracted (Graber 1989, p. 158).
- *Situational factors*, such as what we are doing and who we are with at the time of utilising media, which also appear to have an impact on our ability to process information. If we are not actively engaged with the medium, then there is a reduced chance we will take in messages. For example, chatting with friends or thumbing through a magazine while simultaneously watching television is likely to distract the viewer and act as a barrier to the absorption of information (Graber 1989, p. 159).
- *Individual factors*, such as age, level of intelligence, one's innate level of political interest and personality predisposition which are also critical not only to the selection of media but also to how the individual processes the information to which they are exposed. The research tends to indicate, for example, that certain types of individuals have a decided preference for certain media and certain content. Moreover, children (as distinct from adults) are less equipped to separate fact from fantasy.
- *The medium, the nature of the appeal and the means by which the message is delivered*, which is also a crucial variable that is likely to mediate the effect of the media on the individual. It is acknowledged that not only do different media enjoy a different credibility rating among the public, but also that perceptions of the impartiality of the source is an important determinant

of whether we accept or reject the information it provides (Street 2001, p. 84). Similarly, how information is presented is also important. Graber points out that factors such as the length of the story, the degree of repetition, whether the information is presented in an interesting manner or even if there have been prior presentations of that information are likely to substantially impact on whether the individual is attentive to the story (1989, pp. 165–6). Moreover, who is presenting the information also appears to have a bearing on the degree to which the individual is willing to trust the authenticity of what they are being told or have read.

More importantly, perhaps, the various studies have shown that the effects of media are tempered by the machinations and cognitions of the human mind. Three important discoveries about the workings of the brain point to evidence of a high degree of discretionary selectivity on the part of the individual.

First, individuals make deliberate choices about the media they utilise. Known as selective exposure, it holds that certain individuals are drawn to certain programs. We often are attracted to those programs that contain information or material in which we have an innate, prior interest (Vivian 1999, p. 391; Graber 1989, p. 161). It is this phenomenon, for example, which helps to explain why different radio listeners might prefer different talkback hosts over others. It is safe to assume that those who listen to the right-wing views of Alan Jones are unlikely to tune in to the left-wing musings of Phillip Adams.

Second, as a result of cognitive dissonance models developed by psychologists, it has been discovered that individuals perceive content selectively, an occurrence known as selective perception. This is essentially the idea that the human mind screens out messages and ideas with which it disagrees, and gravitates towards those ideas and messages that it approves. Unlike selective exposure, this is a subconscious phenomenon. Sometimes the human mind will distort or ignore information that does not square with pre-existing beliefs (Vivian 1999, p. 392).

Third, research has shown that not only are individuals capable of both selective exposure and selective perception, but that they also suffer from poor retention. That is, we tend to not absorb all that we are exposed to, and, even then, we are really only likely to absorb messages or information that is of personal interest. Moreover, it has been established that our recall is deficient. American research shows that rates of miscomprehension are often very high, ranging between 16 per cent and 93 per cent (Vivian 1999, p. 392).

For the most part, the 'mediating conditions' model takes the view that media effects are greatest when an individual has no existing views on a topic. The media are likely to change our views when we do not have an established view on the topic or we are actively looking to the media to help us to reach an opinion on a matter. The media only reinforce existing beliefs, and individuals respond best to communications that are consistent with their predispositions, primarily because we tend to see and hear those messages that conform to our pre-existing beliefs (McQuail 1994)

Just as the 'powerful effects' school has its critics, so too does the 'mediating effects' tradition (for a full list, see Boyd-Barrett 2002). Macnamara (2003) suggests there are a number of flaws inherent in the mediating conditions model. First, it downplays the capacity of the media to reinforce particular messages or ideas. Critics suggest that reinforcement is itself powerful, particularly when it is reinforcing a selective discourse. They argue that growing concentration of media ownership, combined with the globalisation of the industry, has seen the media industry fall under the control of 'fewer and fewer' media corporations. The decline in the number of media owners, they claim, has caused a reduction in the diversity of media content. More particularly, it is beginning to result in the production and distribution of 'homogenised media content worldwide' (Macnamara 2003, p. 7). As a result, the capacity of the individual to make oppositional readings or interpretations of mass media content, which depends on having access to contrary viewpoints, is made increasingly difficult.

Similarly, the 'mediating condition' tradition is contested on the grounds that it does not properly consider the vicious cycle of media influences. This means that, even if an individual is more influenced by friends and family than by the media, it remains the case that the people who they rely on for information are likely to be media consumers, and may, as a result, have been influenced in their opinions and views by something they saw in the media. Under these conditions, the media's impacts, while of an indirect nature, are nonetheless real. Related to this point, the 'mediating conditions' model tends to downplay the fact that, even if an individual claims to not depend on the media for information, it is highly plausible that some 'seepage' does and can occur due to the ubiquity of the mass media in modern society. Even those individuals who are smart enough to interpret their own meanings and media texts will find themselves exposed to some of the messages intended by the producers of the media.

Finally, there is the concern that this research is limited in its capacity to measure the long-term or cumulative effects of media influence; that is, the long-term impacts of mass media representation. Critics contend that so-called 'scientific' approaches to research studies are unable to detect the presence of repeated and consistent messages in their studies, and, in most cases, are not designed to do so. In their haste to prove the influence of the media on one's attitudes and behaviour, more insidious effects—such as how the media might influence one's world view or the operation of our key political, social and cultural institutions—are simply not explored (Macnamara 2003, p. 8).

Box 3.4   Does the media encourage violence?

The issue of violence of the media is perhaps the most discussed and researched aspect of media effects (see Van Evra 1990). Understandably, much of the concern has centred on the relationship between media violence and child development and behaviour. Studies confirm that children, like adults, spend considerable time watching television and that much of what they view contains considerable violent content. In fact, US studies show that the prevalence of violence is higher in children's television (69 per cent) than other types of programming (57 per cent) and that children witness 10 000 violent incidents each year (Kaiser Family Foundation 2003). Moreover, violence is frequently 'glamorised, sanitised and trivialised' (Strasburger & Wilson 2002, pp. 77–8). Up until the age of seven, most children lack the capacity to differentiate fact from fiction or fantasy from fact. Research has also shown that children lack the ability to conceptualise or think in abstract terms. Young children are more inclined to pay attention to what the leading characters look like and their explicit behaviours, and lack the capacity to follow a plot or to integrate information. This means, for example, if a violent act and a scene featuring remorse for that act are separated by a commercial, young children are typically unable to link the two events (Strasburger & Wilson 2002).

There are three major explanations posited to explain why media violence might facilitate aggression within children (Strasburger & Wilson 2002, pp 90–4):

- *Cognitive priming*—Berkowitz (1989), among others, argued that violent images activate or elicit aggressive thoughts, which can then 'prime' or encourage other closely related thoughts stored in the memory. Following exposure, a person is in a state of activation whereby the violent thoughts are at the forefront of the mind and trigger pre-learned aggressive behaviours. Cognitive priming is thought to explain short-term violence only.
- *Social learning*—This perspective was devised by Bandura (1965, 1977) and suggests that children learn new behaviours either by direct experience (trial and error) or by imitating the behaviour of others. If violent and aggressive actions are modelled and, in some way, sanctioned, it can lead to positive reinforcement of those behaviours. It is assumed that children selectively pay attention to different aspects of modelled behaviour, and in evaluating and interpreting that behaviour are influenced by their own experiences.
- *Social informational processing*—Formulated by Huesmann (1998), this theory attempts to explain the long-term impact of exposure to media violence. It suggests that as a result of what we watch, we develop a mental script (mental routines stored in memory) of how we should respond in particular conditions. A child who is exposed to violence (either in the media or through personal experience) is likely to develop scripts that encourage aggression when dealing with problems.

Many scholars believe that the evidence is inconclusive and that it is not possible to state with any certainty that television induces violent or negative behaviours in children (in Australia, see Durkin 1995a; Turnbull 2001). Nonetheless, the Australian Government recognises that children, due to their developmental levels, require special consideration in areas such as advertising and the presentation of material that may be harmful to them. As a result, Children's Television Standards (Standards) have been established, to which free-to-air television stations are obliged to adhere. Among other things, the standards dictate that children's programming must be suitable. Suitability is defined as content that is not demeaning (physically, sexually, regarding religion or race, etc), does not 'unduly' frighten children; depicts 'unsafe' use of products or situations; and does not advertise products considered to be unsafe by the government.

In light of the research on the effects of media violence on children, do you think the government should do more to limit violent content on television? What kind of restrictions should be put in place and why?

SUMMARY

This chapter has shown that there is no agreement about the nature of the media's effect on the individual—only that media does have an effect and that television is regarded as the most powerful medium at the present time. In part, this is because the research can and does yield contradictory findings. It is not unknown for studies that attempt to replicate a particular research experiment to produce a very different set of results. There can be no doubting the fact that research into the media is complicated because of the human element. Not only is there the possibility that human beings will in some way err in some aspect of their research design or application, but that the very test matter—human beings—are inherently unpredictable. This is not to suggest that the research endeavour is fruitless, only that it is difficult to conclusively determine the nature of the relationship between exposure to media and its effects on both the individual and society more generally.

Questions

1   Do you think that liberals are correct in thinking that individuals are rational and self-selecting, and thus capable of controlling their reaction to the media content?

2   What influence do you think the media has on society? Do you believe its impact is minimal or powerful?

3   What factors complicate the ability of policy makers draw definitive conclusions about the nature of media effects?

WEBSITES

CCMS Infobase—Infobase of resources for communication studies, cultural studies and media studies students at school or early university (http://www.cultsock. ndirect.co.uk/MUHome/cshtml/index.html).

Media and Communications Studies Site—The MCS (pronounced 'mix') site is an award-winning portal to internet-based resources useful in the academic study of media and communication. It is hosted by the University of Wales, Aberystwyth, and is intended to give priority to issues of interest to both British scholars in the field and to others who are interested in media in the UK (http://www.aber.ac.uk/media/index.php).

Young Media Australia (YMA)—A national, non-profit, community-based organisation providing information, advocacy and research on the impact of the media on children and young people (http://www.youngmedia.org.au).

FURTHER READING

Boyd-Barrett, O. 2002, 'Theory in Media Research'. In C. Newbold, O. Boyd-Barrett & H. Van den Bluck (eds), *The Media Book*. Arnold Publishers: London.

McQuail, D. 2005, *McQuail's Mass Communication Theory*, 5th edn. Sage Publications: London.

THE NEWS MEDIA IN ACTION:

Pawn, Villain or Saint?

This chapter will:

- explain the liberal conception of the role of journalists in political and social life
- outline the transformation of journalism from a trade to a profession
- discuss the mechanisms used to regulate journalists
- consider the factors that constrain journalists in the performance of their responsibilities
- examine the phenomenon of declining levels of public trust in journalists and consider its political implications.

Journalists have been described as the 'heart and brains of the media' (Von Dohnanyi 2003, p. 15). They are crucial to the operation of a liberal democratic media, and key to the health and vitality of democratic life. Journalists collect news stories, investigate and follow up on leads, and organise and present the information on which we depend. They serve as the chief conduit through which the public accesses news and information about the world around it. The information that journalists gather and supply does, in theory, enable the public to make informed choices and decisions, and, in the process, facilitate popular participation in democratic society. In this sense, journalists make an important contribution to the preservation of free speech by helping to ensure the channels of communication remain free, open and clear.

Journalists also perform a 'watchdog' function, protecting the public interest in much the same way a guard dog defends the family home. Journalists expose official wrongdoing and other abuses by reporting on the activities of elected officials in order to keep them accountable to the public between elections. This role is sometimes referred to in the literature as the **fourth estate** function. Journalists also keep tabs on the media owners, standing as a bulwark between the pecuniary ambitions of the proprietors and the public's right to receive information that is reliable and of a high quality (Wheeler 1997, p. 7). In doing so, journalists keep a close eye on those who have the greatest capacity to thwart liberty and freedom.

> **fourth estate** thought to date from the first half of the nineteenth century, this term in its modern form refers to the role of the media (press) as a check and counterbalance on the power of the executive, **Parliament** and courts—the three arms of government

Liberals believe that journalists are predisposed to bear the burden of these important public functions. The nature of the journalistic endeavour—investigation and reporting—requires journalists to 'verify information by drawing on alternative sources and representing rival interpretations' (Wheeler 1997, p. 7). These proclivities are reinforced by the procedures, routines and values that inform journalistic work practices. The culture of the profession is marked by a commitment to public service and the norms of journalistic responsibility, and built on the values of objectivity, truthfulness and accuracy.

In order to ensure that the journalist's natural inclinations are encouraged, liberals maintain that a particular set of basic conditions must exist. First, the training of journalists must be heavily focused on the public service element of their craft. This norm, along with its associated values, must be reinforced in a **code of ethics**, which outlines the principles of good journalistic practice and acts as the standard against which journalists should be judged (Wheeler 1997, p. 7). Second, journalists must be permitted a certain degree of independence from both the government and media proprietors.

Independence from the government requires recognition of the principle of freedom from restraint; that is, government must acknowledge and support the right of journalists to operate free from the prying eyes of official censors. Independence from the media proprietors can only be properly secured through the existence of alternative employment opportunities within the industry. This allows journalists to seek out other employment in the event of a professional or ethical disagreement with their employer.

▶ **code of ethics** a statement of principles that outlines the expected behaviour of members of a professional group, and that reflects the values that it members are required to observe

It is true to say that the Western liberal view of journalists is heavily contested. There exists a disjuncture between the theory of how journalists 'should' operate and the manner in which they 'do' in practice. As we will see a little later in this chapter, the conditions that are thought to enable journalists to undertake their core functions are not easy to secure, even in countries that support the principles of press freedom.

Box 4.1 **Balancing the right to know with journalistic responsibility: the case of the Muhammad cartoon controversy**

In 2005, a (right-wing conservative) newspaper in Denmark published a series of twelve editorial cartoons, most of which depicted the Islamic prophet Muhammad. Danish Muslim organisations staged protests in response to the cartoons, which were viewed as blasphemous and culturally insensitive to Muslims. The Danish Prime Minister defended the publication of the images on the grounds that 'the government does not control the media or a newspaper outlet; that would be in violation of the freedom of speech'. The problem was compounded when some of the images were subsequently reprinted in newspapers in 40 other countries. This led to unrest around the world, particularly in Islamic countries, resulting in death threats against Danish citizens, the setting alight and forced closure of Danish embassies in some Arab countries, and protests and riots in those countries where newspaper editors made the decision to reproduce the images.

The incident highlighted the fine balance that exists between press freedom and journalistic responsibility. While it is generally understood that press freedom is a core value in Western societies, this right is ultimately tempered by the belief that journalists should not abuse their power by broadcasting or publishing material that has the potential to cause more good than harm. The difficulty, however, is striking the right balance.

Do you believe that the images should have been reproduced in newspapers in other countries, given the chaos that followed their publication in Denmark? Is it responsible for editors to knowingly publish images and stories that they know will inflame and offend certain sections of the community and compromise physical safety?

Australian journalism: from trade to profession

Although most of us would consider journalism to be a white-collar professional occupation, this was not always the case. In the early years, the average journalist was lowly paid and the working conditions poor. Mayer (1964, p. 193) notes that in the 1890s a reporter often worked 15-hour days for very little money. Despite the 'occasional strike or principled stand', journalists exercised very little discretion to decide what they wrote about and how they approached the task (Schultz 2002, p. 113). The prestige of the vocation was further weakened due to the absence of a tradition of tertiary education, as in law and medicine. Journalism was regarded as a trade—a label which suggested that reporters acted with limited independence and autonomy (Hamilton 1999, p. 99). As a result, it lagged behind white-collar professions in both status and pay.

Over time, however, the status of journalists improved. The formation of the **Australian Journalists Association** (AJA) in 1911 was a critical first step. The AJA campaigned successfully to improve wages and conditions of employment. Further gains were achieved in the 1940s with the creation of professional standards in the form of a Code of Ethics (Code). While designed in part to improve the public's perception of journalists, the Code also represented an 'important assertion of journalists' professional responsibility' (Schultz 2004, p. 113; Hirst & Patching 2005, p. 87). The 1970s and 1980s witnessed an increase in the number of people entering the profession with tertiary qualifications, and a growth in journalism degree courses offered at universities (Schultz 1994a, pp. 209–15). In this period, journalists became increasingly vocal in their demand for independence, showing a willingness to use industrial tools such as strikes and walkouts in order to further their professional objectives (Shultz 1999, pp 270–1). Such events unfolded against a backdrop of changing management and ownership structures within media organisations. Media organisations began to evolve from small owner–operator concerns to large-scale media corporations with diversified interests run by a new class of professional managers. As Schultz explains, this prompted growing operational separation between editorial content and management, which enabled journalists the professional 'space' to demand greater control over their output. By the 1980s, this manifested in the demand for charters of editorial independence from the proprietors, as well as facilitating an unprecedented era of investigative journalism; a period many journalists and scholars believe was the 'high-water mark' of journalism (McKnight 1999, pp. 155, 166–7).

> **Australian Journalists Association (AJA)** formed in 1910 and registered federally in 1911, this union served its members until 1991 when it amalgamated with the Australian Commercial & Industrial Artists Association; in 1993, the AJA (along with the Australian Theatrical and Amusement Employees Association and the Actors Equity of Australia) amalgamated to form the Media, Entertainment and Arts Alliance (MEAA)

Journalists have achieved many of the trappings of a profession, with better pay, resources and greater autonomy than their predecessors enjoyed. Despite this, journalism does not assume an equal place alongside other professions. Unlike other white-collar vocations, journalists do not face any significant 'qualification' hurdles in order to practice their craft. As the Senate Committee on Constitutional and Legal Matters (1994, p. x) explained: 'No formal tertiary qualifications, professional recognition, registration or licensing is required before a person can create a piece of writing, film, or video, or audiotape and have it published.' It has been suggested that until some form of professional registration is established, journalists cannot expect to attain the same status and respectability as other white-collar professions.

Regulation of Australian journalists: self-regulation or bust

The regulation of Australia's journalists, much like their contemporaries in other liberal democratic states, is informal and built on a culture of peer review. As has been noted elsewhere in this chapter, Australia's journalists quickly acquired the right to publish free from overt interference from government censors. This early grant of freedom from restraint has had an important impact on how the profession is regulated. More particularly, it resulted in the removal of direct statutory controls on journalists, with voluntary mechanisms becoming the chief means by which Australian journalists are regulated. Over the years, various informal instruments have evolved to monitor the activities of journalists, such as the ABC's **Media Watch** program and the **Australian Press Council**. However, the most important instrument for regulating journalists is the Code of Ethics (the Code).

> **Media Watch** an ABC television program dedicated to exposing deceitful and duplicitous behaviour in the Australian media

> **Australian Press Council** the self-regulatory body of the print media, established in 1976 with two main aims: to help preserve the traditional freedom of the press within Australia and to ensure that the free press acts responsibly and ethically

The Code was devised in 1944 by the AJA, now known as the **Media, Entertainment and Arts Alliance (MEAA)**. It is an attempt to square away the concerns of those who reject the idea of government regulation, but who believe that journalists should not be permitted to act with impunity. As shown in Box 4.2, the Code consists of 12 points or clauses that set out and prescribe how journalists should conduct themselves.

> **Media, Entertainment and Arts Alliance (MEAA)** The Alliance is the union and professional organisation that covers everyone in the media, entertainment, sports and arts industries; it was created in 1992 and consists of 36 000 members, including people working in TV, radio, theatre and film, entertainment venues and recreation grounds; journalists, actors, dancers, sportspeople, cartoonists, photographers, and orchestral and opera performers, as well as people working in public relations, advertising, book publishing and website production

Despite the perceived benefits of the Code, a number of shortcomings have been identified. First, the Code only applies to journalists who are members of the MEAA. Non-unionised journalists cannot be sanctioned for breaching the Code's provisions, nor can editors and media proprietors: those who have the most power in determining editorial content (Chadwick 1994, pp. 170–1). Second, the Code is inherently constrained by its form. Such an instrument cannot 'deal with all situations in all contexts', and is limited in its capacity to provide answers and guidance to all ethical dilemmas. In part, this is because ideas about what constitutes good or bad conduct are relative 'within varying religious, cultural, political and ideological frames of reference' (Apps, cited in Hirst & Patching 2005, p. 90). On a more practical level, the language of the Code is vague. This invites journalists to interpret the Code according to their own beliefs, and, in doing so, courts the possibility that its intent will be subverted, even if unintentionally (Hirst 1997, p. 65). Third, because the Code is policed by a private (rather than government) body, this constrains the range of penalties that can be applied. Sanctions for wrongdoing are limited and include rebuking (that is, a nasty letter from the MEAA), monetary fines of up to $1000 or expelling the journalist from the union (Alliance Online 2006).

In recent years, critics have raised new concerns about the legitimacy of the Code. Turner (1994), for example, has argued that self-regulation is proving ineffective in coping with the threat to press freedom posed by the growing trend to concentration of media ownership. Turner has proposed the formation of an independent tribunal with 'legislated maximum discretion' to regulate journalists, to be supervised by a quasi-government body or group; in this case, an all-parties parliamentary committee (Turner 1994, p. 1). This model essentially calls for the use of statutory controls, albeit modest.

Despite Turner's enthusiasm for reform, not everyone supports a retreat from self-regulation. Others have countered that self-regulation is the only reliable means of imposing standards and accountability on journalists. Hirst and Patching (2005, p. 118) have argued that it is fundamentally dangerous to open the door to the possibility of a return to government control, however innocuous. Hirst and Patching are not alone in their views. The Senate Standing Committee on Legal and Constitutional Affairs (1994, p. xxiii) expressed similar concerns when it reported: 'The dangers of political interference and the development of fetters on freedom of speech are seen by the committee to be real enough to prefer the continuing encouragement of self-regulation.'

Box 4.2   MEAA Code of Ethics

MEAA members engaged in journalism commit themselves to:

- honesty
- fairness
- independence
- respect for the rights of others

1 Report and interpret honestly, striving for accuracy, fairness and disclosure of all essential facts. Do not suppress relevant available facts, or give distorting emphasis. Do your utmost to give a fair opportunity for reply.

2 Do not place unnecessary emphasis on personal characteristics, including race, ethnicity, nationality, gender, age, sexual orientation, family relationships, religious belief, or physical or intellectual disability.

3 Aim to attribute information to its source. Where a source seeks anonymity, do not agree without first considering the source's motives and any alternative attributable source. Where confidences are accepted, respect them in all circumstances.

4 Do not allow personal interest, or any belief, commitment, payment, gift or benefit, to undermine your accuracy, fairness or independence.

5 Disclose conflicts of interest that affect, or could be seen to affect, the accuracy, fairness or independence of your journalism. Do not improperly use a journalistic position for personal gain.

6 Do not allow advertising or other commercial considerations to undermine accuracy, fairness or independence.

7 Do your utmost to ensure disclosure of any direct or indirect payment made for interviews, pictures, information or stories.

8 Use fair, responsible and honest means to obtain material. Identify yourself and your employer before obtaining any interview for publication or broadcast. Never exploit a person's vulnerability or ignorance of media practice.

9 Present pictures and sound that are true and accurate. Any manipulation likely to mislead should be disclosed.

10 Do not plagiarise.

11 Respect private grief and personal privacy. Journalists have the right to resist compulsion to intrude.

12 Do your utmost to achieve fair correction of errors.

Do you think the Code goes far enough? Are there any omissions in the Code? Do you think the current sanctions for breach of the Code are sufficient? If not, what could be done to improve this state of affairs?

Constraints on journalists

While a career in journalism is associated with excitement and adventure, it can also be fraught with danger. According to the **Committee to Protect Journalists**, approximately 400 journalists have been killed in the line of duty in the last decade. A small proportion died while reporting either in a combat zone or a non-combat conflict situation, such as violent demonstrations. However, the overwhelming majority (76 per cent) were murdered in reprisal for their reporting (Committee to Protect Journalists 2006).

▶ **Committee to Protect Journalists** an independent, non-profit organisation dedicated to the global defence of press freedom

Fortunately, there have been no reported cases of journalists being deliberately killed on Australian soil as a result of an investigation. This should not be taken to mean that the professional life of Australian journalists is without hazard. While Australian journalists are not at high risk of political assassination, there is a range of factors that impede their ability to fulfil their journalistic responsibilities. Key among these are the legal setting, government manipulation, declining levels of media ownership and workplace constraints.

LEGAL CONSTRAINTS

A common complaint is that aspects of Australia's legal system have a 'chilling' effect on the free expression of the media. Although the legal system exists to provide protection to the public, it does not automatically follow that laws that are designed to serve genuine and legitimate purposes are not used for illiberal ends.

Defamation law is a good example of how laws enacted for legitimate ends can undermine the activities of journalists. Defamation law is designed to offer redress to individuals where their reputation has been tarnished unjustly by published information. While Australia's defamation laws underwent a major overhaul in 2005 (that is, the introduction of a uniform code), a number of problems remain. In particular, the laws are criticised because they place a relatively heavy burden on the defendant (that is the onus of proof resides with the person accused of defamation). There are also high costs associated with defending an action, and significant outlays if the action ultimately succeeds. Moreover, the Australian Constitution offers journalists 'limited' protection against defamation action, brought by public persons, those who generally have the means and motivation to pursue grievances via legal channels.

The absence of strong constitutional protections against defamation actions, combined with the complexity of the law can result in journalists becoming embroiled in costly and drawn-out defamation suits. This, many commentators fear, discourages investigative journalism, fostering tentativeness and passivity, and even a willingness to withhold information in order to avoid expensive legal proceedings. In the USA, because defamation law generally requires the plaintiff to prove actual malice, and the Constitutional protections for journalists are more robust, more defamatory articles are printed than in Australia. Whereas 15 per cent of Australian articles included defamatory allegations against either individuals or corporate entities, in the USA this figure was 43 per cent (Dent & Kenyon 2004, p. 115).

Another problem identified in Australian law is the dearth of legal protections for journalists' confidential sources. This situation puts Australian journalists at great risk of being charged with the tort of disobedience contempt. Disobedience contempt involves defiance of an order of the court to disclose certain information. Journalists are especially vulnerable to disobedience contempt because they have an ethical (rather than legal) obligation to preserve the confidentiality of their sources when they have given an undertaking to do so. The journalists' approach to the issue of 'confidentiality' is unique in that, unlike other professional codes, they do not have an 'escape clause' that allows them to reveal confidential information when called upon by the courts. As a result, once a journalist has agreed to accept information in confidence, he or she is bound to respect that confidence (Pearson 2004, pp. 235–8).

For many years, the issue of confidentiality was of little consequence, primarily because the courts displayed a reluctance to compel journalists to reveal the names of their informants, and because proprietors often chose not to defend those defamation cases where a journalist might be compelled to reveal a confidential source (Pearson 2005, p. 240). However, since the late 1980s a number of Australian journalists have fallen foul of disobedience contempt laws; three have been imprisoned, one sentenced to community service and countless others fined.

According to Magnusson (1999, p. 37), the ethic of protecting confidentiality under all circumstances is ingrained deeply in the culture of journalism; something he regards as ironic because, while 'journalists have a phobic aversion to breaching their own undertakings of confidentiality', they are 'more than willing to assist somebody else to breach theirs'. Magnusson believes that the zealous commitment to source protection is problematic in that it 'encourages journalists to run the risk of providing a haven for crooks and charlatans' (1999, p. 38). However, others argue that any dilution to the commitment to confidentiality is untenable and would impede journalists in doing their job. The MEAA maintains that journalists must respect confidences because disclosure could put their source at risk of reprisal. Also, and possibly more importantly, the failure to guarantee confidentiality would, in all probability, undermine continuity in the supply of information. Without access to such material, the MEAA claims its members would be unable to do their job.

The MEAA has been vociferous in its demands for **shield laws** to protect journalists' confidential sources. The Senate Standing Committee on Legal and Constitutional Affairs has also lent its support for such laws. In 1994, the committee recommended that the law be amended to allow journalists qualified privilege (Senate Standing Committee on Legal and Constitutional Affairs 1994). The committee argued that such laws would oblige a court to weigh up competing public interests on a case-by-case basis, and to order disclosure if, in the opinion of the court, it would frustrate the administration of justice (Butler & Rodrick 2004, p. 331). So far, only NSW has taken steps to incorporate such protections into statute although it seems likely that the remaining states and territories are close to announcing the establishment of a network of national shield laws (Merritt 2007).

It would seem that there are serious legal constraints that impact upon journalists. It is these problems, among others, that have resulted in Australia achieving a poor ranking in the fourth annual worldwide index of press freedom, published by **Reporters without Borders**. The report puts Australia 35th, well behind comparable countries such as New Zealand (19th), Canada (16th) and the UK (27th) (Reporters without Borders 2007).

> **shield laws** laws that protect the right of journalists to keep their sources private

> **Reporters without Borders** an international organisation that fights for the freedom of the press and freedom of expression, and ensures protection of journalists by denouncing human rights breaches

OFFICIAL GOVERNMENT OBSTACLES

While the doctrine of 'freedom from restraint' hinders the ability of Australian governments to directly regulate the activities of journalists, and print journalists particularly, this is not to suggest that governments are utterly powerless. Over the years, Western governments developed various strategies and techniques, both overt and covert, to thwart journalistic scrutiny.

This is seen clearly in relation to the administration of freedom of information (FOI) legislation. FOI legislation was introduced federally in 1982 and adopted by state and territory governments in 2003. The intent behind the legislation is to create a public right of access to government information in the interests of transparency and governmental accountability (Pearson 2004, p. 261).

The statistics show that FOI has been successful in facilitating public access to official documents. In 2004–05, 72.4 per cent of applications for information under FOI were granted in full, with only 6.4 per cent rejected. In practice, however, the attempt by journalists to use FOI for the purpose for which it is intended is frustrated by the requirements and conditions imposed by the legislation. The information can be hard to access as a result of blanket exemptions applied to information, and the (over) use of conclusive certificates, which allows a minister to block information that they believe is contrary to the public interest. There can be delays in receiving information (a problem for journalists who have deadlines to meet), and oftentimes unrealistic requirements for identification of some official documents. One of the biggest disincentives is the excessive fees for service. The costs of following through on a FOI request can be exorbitant, running into thousands of dollars per request (Herman 2005, p. 96). In one case, a newspaper was told it would cost one million dollars to process an application for information regarding travel for Commonwealth parliamentarians (Australian Press Council 2002).

While it is unclear whether the obfuscations are malicious or legitimate, what is certain is that journalists are reluctant to use FOI as an information-gathering tool. Journalists continue to rely on information from unofficial leaks and off-the-record briefings, and not official material. One critic claims that this state of affairs renders journalists 'vulnerable to being manipulated and misled', making it 'easier for government officials to manage the news' (Herman 2005, p. 97).

MEDIA OWNERSHIP CONSTRAINTS

Declining levels of media ownership are also thought to place fetters on jour-nalists. The Australian media has become increasingly **oligopolistic**; dominated by a handful of media corporations. While the trend to concentrated owner-ship has occurred across all sectors of the media, it is particularly apparent in the newspaper industry. As it presently stands, five media companies own all of the country's capital city newspapers. Moreover, two of the five companies (Fairfax and News Ltd) have acquired an 80 per cent market share of the daily capital city newspaper market and a 100 per cent stake in the national daily papers (Communications Law Centre 2003, p. 21; Windschuttle 1988, p. 86).

> ▶ **oligopolistic** refers to a situation in which there are only a few competitive firms operating in a market; while competition between the different sellers can sometimes lead to lower prices, in some contexts the firms may collude to raise prices and restrict production, thereby leading to higher prices for consumers

It is generally recognised that there are some advantages associated with the rise of large media organisations. Namely, it is credited with having allowed journalists to realise a modicum of professional distance from the media owners. Yet, some fear that the benefits are superficial and ultimately conceal a more insidious side effect. Any diminution in the number of media organisations is likely to produce a corresponding reduction in employment opportunities. This, some claim, may well have the effect of making jour-nalists timid and pliable, and unwilling to challenge the views of their employers if it threatens their job security (Nash 2004, p. 7).

DEMANDS OF THE JOB

Journalists are constrained by the highly commercialised environment in which they operate. The Western media's independence from government comes at a price; namely that news is a commodity—'simply the content which attracts audiences', which in turn attracts sponsorship dollars (Ward 1995, p. 101). This has important implications for news content. It means that newsworthiness is not driven solely by its perceived relevance and significance, but by the content's potential to attract advertising revenue. Survey evidence shows that Australian journalists are conscious of the need to be responsive to audience demands, with 34 per cent reporting that their work was altered in order to increase its audience appeal (Schultz 1998, pp. 146–7).

Not only does the commercial nature of the media have implications for decisions about what is 'newsworthy', but it also affects the process of gathering information and determining production schedules. Media companies are ultimately 'businesses', and their internal management and operational structures reflect this. Most journalists work in large- to medium-sized bureaucratic organisations, with clear hierarchical divisions of labour. Journalists are rarely afforded the final say on which stories are selected and how they are delivered. Much of their work is 'supervised and directed' by editors and senior management (Ward 1995, pp 101–2). They are also subject to time constraints and the pressure to meet deadlines. A significant number of Australian journalists (56 per cent) have indicated that the pressure of deadlines affects their ability to do their job, and a further 66 per cent indicated that space and time constraints were also salient (Schultz 1998, p. 147).

Moreover, the nature of the medium affects conceptions of newsworthiness, thereby influencing how journalists approach their daily tasks. Media such as television rely heavily on visuals and are constrained by the half-hour timeslot in which they typically appear. Decisions made about which stories will go to air and how they will be presented are influenced by their visual aspects. As a general rule, the television medium subscribes to the mantra of 'no pictures, no story' (Ward 1995, p. 105). In contrast, the 'natural rhythm' of the print media is such that it 'prefers to print stories that occur within a period of a day, or where those events take longer to unfold, only the climaxes are reported' (Windschuttle 1988, p. 268). Print is ultimately less dependent on visuals and able to carry significantly more factual detail than its television counterpart (Ward 1998, p. 105). This provides print journalists with slightly more time to investigate a story, and to provide more background information. It seems that the medium itself circumscribes the way in which journalists see and report a story.

It is not unreasonable to conclude that news is 'not what happens but is the end product of a process'. Although the content of news may be unpredictable, the manner in which journalists approach the task is not (Ward 1995, p. 108). Journalists do not always have full discretion to pursue stories according to their whims or at their own leisure. They are ultimately 'captive of their daily work practices and creatures of the organizations that employ them' (Ward 1995, p. 101).

Debates and controversies: Declining levels of public trust

Various surveys show that Australian journalists believe they have an obligation to serve the public good, and a responsibility to disclose the truth. Schultz's study of Australian journalists shows that 95 per cent of journalists said that uncovering and publicising information was either 'quite' or 'very important' (Schultz 1998 pp. 247, 258).

While most Australian journalists clearly think they have a responsibility to defend the public interest, it is less clear that the public has confidence in their abilities and motivation for doing so. Public cynicism of journalists is high. A poll undertaken by Roy Morgan Research in 2005 revealed that only 11 per cent of Australians believe that newspaper journalists had high or very high ethics. When ranked alongside 28 other professions, journalists finished in the 25th position behind lawyers, union leaders and parliamentarians.

The negative public perception of journalists turns on three broad areas of grievance: sensationalism, bullying and dishonesty. Journalists are oftentimes criticised for publishing or broadcasting material of a relatively trivial nature, which does not genuinely advance the public's right to know. The news is sensationalised, ostensibly in the interests of attracting audiences and sponsor interest. It is frequently claimed that stories about celebrities, salacious gossip, lifestyles and infotainment dominate at the expense of hard news and serious analysis. To make matters worse, the public believes (63 per cent) that journalists often get their facts wrong (Roy Morgan Research 2005).

Concomitant with concerns about the decline in news quality is growing public disquiet about the behaviour of journalists. Surveys show that around 74 per cent of people believe that television journalists unnecessarily invade people's privacy, and 69 per cent of newspaper journalists are guilty of the same (Roy Morgan Research 2005). Journalists are widely perceived as bullies who are unmerciful and unrelenting in the pursuit of a story. At worst, journalists have been accused of gross cruelty and negligence. As recently as 2005, some journalists were implicated in a suicide attempt by the then-leader of the parliamentary Liberal Party in NSW, John Brogden. Brogden quit the leadership of the Liberal Party following revelations he had made racist slurs against the Premier's wife. Following Brogden's resignation, claims surfaced in the *Daily Telegraph* that he was also guilty of sexual misconduct. Not long thereafter, Brogden attempted to take his own life. While the *Daily Telegraph* claimed it had an obligation to print the story about the sexual misconduct, others believed that because Brogden had resigned there was no reason for the matter to be made public, particularly because the new allegations were unsubstantiated (*Media Watch* 2005). The media's bad taste was brought even further into sharp relief when photos were published of Brogden being taken away by ambulance drivers following his suicide attempt.

The third category of complaint is that some journalists are dishonest and untruthful about relationships that might influence their objectivity and compromise their ability to remain impartial. Journalists are perceived to lie to obtain information, omit important details, occasionally plagiarise and buy (rather than investigate) news stories in order to beat their rivals to an exclusive (see Box 4.3). There has also been considerable unease about the failure of some journalists to disclose influential relationships, such as commercial agreements with sponsors. This issue was brought to the public's attention in 1999 when it was revealed that a number of high-profile radio announcers had accepted payment for advertising services. The scandal, referred to as the 'cash for comments' affair, saw Sydney broadcasters Alan Jones and John Laws, and others, failing to disclose to their audience that they had received payment in exchange for favourable coverage of certain subject matter. This prompted 'renewed debate about the blurring line between editorial and advertising which results from commercial pres-sures and unrestrained self-interest' (Hart, cited in Gordon-Smith 2002, p. 283).

> ### Box 4.3   Douglas Wood and chequebook journalism
>
> In 2005, Douglas Wood was paid by the Ten Network for an exclusive interview about his kidnap ordeal in Iraq. Wood, a building contractor, was beaten and held for 47 days in captivity by Iraqi insurgents until he was eventually rescued in a military operation. On his eventual return to Australia, a battle broke out between the networks to buy his story. Within hours of his plane touching down in Melbourne, the Ten Network managed to beat its rivals to secure an exclusive with Douglas Wood for the 'bargain basement' price of $400,000.
>
> Public opinion was divided about the ethics of Wood selling his story and the Ten Network for buying it. Some commentators argued that the money Wood received was legitimate compensation because he was forced to endure media intrusion both during his capture and following his release. They claimed that Wood had a legitimate right to benefit financially in much the same way the Ten Network and other media outlets had profited financially from his misfortune. It was also suggested that Wood's decision was sensible because by signing an 'exclusive' deal he would be in a better position to retain some control over how his story would be told.
>
> However, others proffered that Wood should not be allowed to profit personally from his ordeal given the $10 million price tag paid by Australian tax payers to rescue him. They argued that Wood had an obligation to share freely his story with his fellow citizens. Others raised concerns about the broader consequences associated with the practice of chequebook journalism. It was suggested that the high price tag puts a financial strain on a newsroom's resources—eating into finite newsroom budgets. This tends to result in fewer resources to investigate and report other news stories.
>
> **Should there be laws preventing journalists from purchasing 'exclusives'? What are the pros and cons of 'chequebook' journalism?**

While such criticisms of journalists clearly weigh on the public mind and appear to have some basis in fact, to what extent is this a cause for concern? It is important to note that the allegations are not new. Mayer argues that claims about declining journalistic standards are as old as the profession itself. Negative claims against the conduct of journalists found expression in Australia as early as 1795. He suggests that one of the great myths of journalism is the 'decline in standards' thesis (Mayer 1964, p. 21). Contrary to popular belief, the early Australian press dedicated a 'high proportion of editorial space to crime, sport and salacious human interest stories' (Lumby 2002, p. 321). It is nonsensical to believe there has ever been a golden age of journalism (Gordon-Smith 2002, p. 279).

It is also unclear who is at fault for low journalistic standards, should they indeed exist. One could quite easily make the argument that the fault lies with the media owners who push journalists to write sensationalist articles and take short cuts in order to gain exclusives for the sake of financial gain. Alternatively, fault could be laid at the public's feet. There are good grounds to argue that the public appetite fuels the demand for salacious gossip, and that journalists are simply responding to market signals. However, it is just as easy to claim that this problem results from the failure of self-regulation to rein in the conduct of journalists. That is, the problem lies not with the individuals or the media organisations but with 'weak' mechanisms to hold journalists to account.

Even if we are able to narrow the source of the problem, how do we solve it? If we assume the fault lies with the proprietors' narrow interest in money over quality journalism, does this mean we should consider disbanding private ownership of the media and return it to government control? If the problem is a function of consumer demand, can it be fixed by simply ignoring the audiences' wants and desires? This would require handing over control for determining media content to faceless bureaucrats. But if the problem lies deep within the culture of journalism, then the obvious solution would be to replace self-regulatory mechanisms with more stringent statutory controls. Whichever way it goes, the antidote entails some form of government intervention, and it is probably fair to say that the cure is likely to be worse than the disease.

It is also important to take a minute or two to remember that journalists also do good work. While the public is not always happy with their conduct, it nonetheless relies on journalists for information and news. Moreover, there is also the hope that new media platforms, such as the internet, might go part of the way to improving the quality of information. Not only is the internet fast emerging as a vehicle for non-journalists to participate in the making and distribution of news, but is also provides opportunities for journalists to offer their opinions, facts and thoughts free from the burdens that typically constrain them; such as deadlines and ratings. In doing so, the sovereignty of conventional journalism as the sole contributor of facts to public debate is challenged, opening up the possibility of more transparent, competitive and pluralistic journalism (Radio National 2005a).

SUMMARY

This chapter has shown that in Western societies, such as Australia, journalists are regarded as critical to the operation of a free and dynamic media. While journalism was originally regarded as a trade, over time it has managed to acquire many, but not all, of the accoutrements of a profession. This has raised questions about what should be done (if anything) to elevate the profession on a par with medicine or law. The chapter has also shown that journalists operate under a number of constraints. Key among these are the legal system, obstacles erected by governments, media ownership constraints and the demands of the job. These considerations hinder journalists in fulfilling their public service obligations. However, one of the biggest issues to confront the profession is growing public disillusionment with their conduct, precipitated by concerns about sensationalist reporting, bullying and dishonesty. While it is unclear who is ultimately at fault for the low regard in which journalists are held, there is no escaping the fact they remain an indispensable element of Australia's liberal democratic media.

Questions

1 Do you think journalists can lay claim to professional status, given that anyone who writes or publishes is entitled to call themselves a journalist? Should there be strict entry requirements, as in law or medicine, and, if so, what should these be?

2 What do you think accounts for the low regard in which the public hold journalists, and who is to blame for this state of affairs? What, if anything, can be done to remedy this problem?

WEBSITES

ABC Media Watch—An ABC television program that analyses the activities of the Australian media (http://www.abc.net.au/mediawatch/).

Australian Press Council—The self-regulatory body of the print media (http://www.presscouncil.org.au/).

Committee to Protect Journalists—An independent, non-profit organisation dedicated to the global defence of press freedom (http://www.cpj.org/).

Media, Entertainment and Arts Alliance—The peak union organisation that covers media, entertainment, sports and arts industry employees (http://www.alliance.org.au).

Walkley Magazine—An Australian media publication dedicated to exploring media issues (http://magazine.walkleys.com/).

FURTHER READING

Hirst, M. & Patching, R. 2005, *Journalism Ethics: Arguments and Cases*. South Melbourne: Oxford University Press.

Lumby, C. 2006, 'Media ethics'. In S. Cunningham & G. Turner (eds), *The Media and Communications in Australia*, 2nd edn. Allen & Unwin: Sydney.

Merritt, C. 2007, 'Privacy laws hit press freedom', *The Australian*, 22 March.

THE POLITICS OF SPIN

5

This chapter will:

- outline the evolving relationship between politicians and journalists and the changing demands of each profession
- show how politicians attempt to manage the way their image and messages are presented in the media, and their strategies to bypass the press gallery through talkback radio and government advertising
- consider the ways in which journalists must now deal with a large media management infrastructure operated by governments, which makes it more difficult for them to hold politicians accountable for their actions.

Throughout this book, we have assumed that the most important role of the media is to keep a critical watch on the government. Naturally, governments find this media scrutiny tedious. They would prefer that some of their exploits remain secret—particularly the various blunders to which politicians are prone. An equally important role of the media, however, is to allow communication between citizens and their representatives. Naturally, governments wish to ensure that any such communication puts them in a positive light. This chapter deals with a number of issues arising from the increase in public relations techniques in Australian politics: the triumph of image over substance in political debate, the use of government advertising for partisan purposes, and the advantages for incumbent governments provided by various taxpayer-funded media units.

More journalists are employed by Australian governments than by all the newspapers that cover Australian politics. All levels of government now employ a host of communication professionals. More than 4000 trained journalists work for state and federal governments. Not so long ago, only the prime minister received this kind of assistance—a lonely press secretary. Now every member of the federal Parliament has a part-time or full-time **media adviser**; state and federal ministers employ a number of media advisers, speechwriters and other political advisers; and government departments have well-resourced public affairs sections to advise them on communications strategy. This is part of a worldwide trend towards the professionalisation of political communication, sometimes referred to as the PR state.

Public relations is the attempt to garner favourable media coverage of a client organisation. The aim of public relations professionals is to achieve this favourable coverage by exploiting opportunities in the free media, through press releases and conferences, and through contacts with journalists and editors (Turner 2002, p. 219). Public relations professionals tend to exclude paid advertising from their methods, since getting the media to carry your message for nothing is both cheaper and more effective. Government and political party communications strategies, however, tend to integrate advertising and PR methods, since the cost of advertising is not a major concern of governments, which are now the nation's biggest advertisers. The idea of a PR state suggests that politics has come to be as much about presentation and **spin** as it is about public policy. Critics of the PR state concept suggest that this is a narrow view, and that consideration of the policy outcomes of democratic politics should not be obscured by an obsession with process.

> **media adviser** an employee of a politician, often with experience in journalism, whose job it is to manage the politician's relationship with the media

> **spin** an effort to persuade individuals or the public of a given proposition; the term is usually used pejoratively to suggest that the proposition in question is an unlikely one

Government and the media: a changing relationship

The liberal view of a natural antipathy between government and the media is incomplete. In fact, the two institutions are highly interdependent: both get something they need from the relationship. The media has a vested financial interest in the activities of government. Part of what the media does is report the news, and government activity is often an important source of this news. The more controversial the government is, and the more blunders that politicians make, the more likely it is that people will turn on their radios and televisions and buy newspapers. Reporters need a constant supply of stories. They depend heavily on access to government sources since it is governments that make policy decisions. Getting that access often depends on politicians' perceptions of the reporter and their employer. More broadly, the media depends on the government to ensure a stable economic climate, enforce legal contracts, and guarantee its rights and property. Without the media, it would be very difficult for modern governments to inform the public of increasingly complex policy changes. While politicians have many avenues of communication with voters, including advertising and direct mail, there is no substitute for widespread media coverage when it comes to getting a message out effectively. In this way, the media provides the oxygen that politicians need to win elections.

While the liberal view of the media's watchdog role assumes some sort of balance between the relative influence of government and the media, in recent decades the relationship has become asymmetrical. That is, the government, through its extensive communication resources, has the whip hand. Government communications strategy includes everything from timing announcements to maximise (or minimise) coverage to the expensive advertising campaigns that now accompany major policy changes. Often, the PR state strategy is not simply about influencing what is reported, how and when, but also aims to bypass journalists altogether. Veteran press gallery journalist Michelle Grattan observed that this leaves a politician like John Howard 'simultaneously over-exposed and under-available' (1998, p. 38). In other words, by utilising PR strategies, senior politicians manage to get their image and message in the media without being accountable to the press gallery. However, while there is little doubt that the professionalisation of political communication has shifted the balance between the government and the media, Eric Louw points out that good journalists can use the proliferation of media advisers to their own advantage (2005, p. 149). Particularly when governments are divided about a course of action, the spin merchants can be played off one another in their desire to have their own version of events reported.

| Box 5.1 | Can public figures have private lives? |

One of the perennial questions in the media's coverage of politics is the extent to which politicians' private lives are of legitimate interest to the public. During his short-lived leadership of the Australian Labor Party (ALP), Mark Latham berated the media for speaking to his ex-wife about their marriage and speculating about information supposedly about to become public. Latham received little public sympathy, however, since he was a combative politician and had used his family in photo opportunities to promote himself when he first became leader.

When Cheryl Kernot published her memoirs in 2002, veteran press gallery journalist Laurie Oakes broke the story on Channel Nine that a crucial part of her story was missing. Oakes revealed that Kernot and senior ALP figure Gareth Evans had had an affair. Oakes defended his action by arguing that the affair would put Kernot's defection from the Australian Democrats to the Labor party in a completely different light from the way Kernot had described it in her book. While many journalists disagreed with Oakes's decision, it did not stop them discussing the matter at great length once the story was in the public sphere.

Federal Liberal MP for Parramatta, Ross Cameron, also found his private life in the public sphere in the lead-up to the 2004 election. On this occasion, however, Cameron calculated that it was better for him to break the news about his extra-marital affair to a sympathetic journalist well before the election than to have it make front-page news in the run-up to polling day.

Is there ever a justification for the media to reveal details of the private lives of politicians?

Another trend, strongly associated with the rise of television, is the importance of images in the media, and in the reporting of politics in particular. This trend has been criticised for lowering the tenor of public debate. You have no doubt heard references to the 'dumbing down' of our culture. With fewer people getting news from broadsheet newspapers, and many more (if they follow the news at all) from television, politicians tailor many of their strategies and activities to the demands of television. That medium has also changed the way it reports politics, favouring image over substance, and giving participants in political debate only a brief opportunity to make their case. Even the prime minister may only have ten seconds or so to get his message across on the nightly news. Politicians have thus become adept at the pithy sound bite, which is not a sound basis for detailed policy debate in our society.

Habermas (1989) argued that television represents the 'closure of the public sphere'. In other words, television distracts us from, and trivialises, politics. Reporting of politics is often criticised for focusing too much 'on the close infighting and the personality contests, and too little on the contest of ideas over policy' (Waterford 2005, p. 158). Yet, the media are obsessed with stories about leadership and party infighting because that is what obsesses politicians. Stories about leadership tension are usually the result of politicians **backgrounding** journalists. Of course, whether such political gossip needs to be reported so extensively is another question. Television also amplifies personal attributes or characteristics that print and radio do not, as demonstrated in the following examples:

> ▶ **backgrounding** involves journalists seeking information from political actors without naming them in the resulting story

- *Kim Beazley's girth*—When Beazley was initially selected to lead the Federal Parliamentary Labor Party following the 1998 poll, there was considerable discussion of his weight. He made a habit of walking to the top of Mount Ainslie in Canberra to become fighting fit for his second stint as leader of the opposition.
- *Peter Costello's smirk*—It is widely claimed that Costello is unpopular with the public owing to his combative countenance and, more particularly, his smirk. Paul Keating faced similar problems in the inherently difficult Treasury portfolio. Trying to create a softer image upon becoming leader can be difficult.

- *Carmen Lawrence's fashion*—When she became Premier of Western Australia in the 1980s, her dress was attacked. With a bit of help from a stylist, she went from 'dowdy' to 'respectable'.

Thus, attempts to manage political communication have two related strands—the image and the message.

The dominance of television images has coincided with (and helped bring about) an emphasis in politics on the two major party leaders, to the exclusion of other cabinet ministers. It is sometimes surprising which politicians are the most successful at image management. John Howard and former New South Wales premier Bob Carr, two of the less charismatic politicians of their era, were very adept media managers. They succeeded because they were disciplined, providing regular television images and sound bites, making few blunders to distract attention from their message, and leading strongly disciplined parties that stuck to the script of the leader. Carr's background in journalism gave him a keen understanding of the demands of the news cycle, and how to time and present announcements in a way guaranteed to maximise his intended image and message.

Two parallel developments have made the modern spin cycle of particular interest to us. As politics has become more professionalised, news management has become a major preoccupation of governments. It consumes a lot of resources, and ensures that political saleability has become one of the most important considerations in policy development. As Michelle Grattan has written, 'spin requires a very good filing system, and a very good monitoring procedure' (Grattan 1998, p. 41). There is a growing view that the media are succumbing to government manipulation. Schultz claims that up to half of all articles published in major Australian newspapers began as press releases (1998, p. 56). Both Tiffen (1989, p. 83) and Ward (1995) argue that this reflects inherent weaknesses in the production of news, which make the media vulnerable to manipulation. Ward has suggested that the routinisation of the news places governments in a particularly good position to manipulate stories to their own advantage (1995, pp. 115–16). This is because the media require stories to go to air or print every day of the week. Without stories, there is no audience, and without an audience, there is no advertising revenue. Journalists often look to official government sources for their stories and information, which governments are more than happy to provide.

Governments employ a number of techniques to foster journalistic dependence on them as a media source:

- *Employing journalists who were formerly part of the press gallery*—They still have contacts in the press and are familiar with the demands of editors.
- *Selectively leaking stories*—State and federal budgets are the best example of this process. Early in the budget process, examples of policies under consideration are leaked to gauge the public reaction to them. Since the budget is a big document with many policy changes, leaking its contents in the week or so leading up to budget day ensures that any good news is spread over a number of news cycles instead of just one. Regular leaking in this way puts journalists in a more dependent relationship with politicians, particularly ministers. Often, the leak is made only on the condition that no opposition figure is quoted in the resulting story, undermining the journalistic commitment to balance.
- *Blacklisting journalists who dare to challenge the government's agenda and rewarding those who do the government's bidding with exclusive stories*— Former Prime Minister Paul Keating (1991–96) was the master of this particular technique. According to one member of the Canberra Press Gallery, in his first ever conversation with Keating the then Treasurer offered to put him on a 'high grade drip' if he covered economic policy favourably, and left no room for doubt what would happen if he did not (Stekette 1996, p. 409).
- *'Hijacking' reporters*—Tiffen claims one strategy is to invite journalists on overseas trips. Once a reporter has been assigned a story, they are required to produce one. Tiffen suggests that this often leads a journalist inflate a story so as to justify their time away (1989, p. 83).

As a consequence of these media management techniques, defenders of the role of the media in our democracy fear that the media has been neutered and is now captive to government. The *Sydney Morning Herald*'s state political reporter, Anne Davies, commented on her craft:

> Exclusives that set the agenda are important in boosting circulation. But simply running the government's announcement before it is made, without any serious critique, comes perilously close to being advertising for political parties. It may be of mutual benefit to newspapers and politicians, but it's certainly not in the public's interest (Davies 2006).

In turn, the ability to manage media coverage is beginning to affect the selection of candidates and the choice of party leaders. Candidates need to be presentable, well spoken (no speech impediments), affable and not entirely unattractive. Ideally, they should have no obvious physical imperfection. If they do, they are set upon by a team of stylists to remedy the problem. John Howard received an eyebrow trim and a new pair of glasses for his second run at the prime ministership in 1995. At the same time, journalists and audiences are aware of the trend toward political PR, and have changed their reporting and consumption of news about politics as a result. Often, journalistic scepticism of diversionary tactics on the part of politicians becomes the focus of a story.

Building the PR state

Communications professionals are found throughout our political institutions. Some work directly for politicians, while others are public servants employed by government agencies.

MEDIA ADVISERS

Formerly known as press secretaries, and sometimes called 'minders', media advisers are now common throughout all levels of government (as well as the private sector). Since the 1970s, the number of media advisers attached to ministers' offices has grown rapidly. The Federal ministry employs dozens of media advisers. The prime minister's staff of 18 includes a senior adviser (communications), a senior adviser (media) and a press secretary. One in every ten ministerial advisers is a media adviser. In addition, the leader of the opposition and shadow ministry all employ media advisers. Most members of Parliament also employ a media adviser, at least on a part-time basis. Funding for advisers is less lavish at the state level, where media advisers tend to be limited to the ministry and the leader of the opposition. Former Premier of New South Wales Bob Carr, a journalist himself before entering politics, valued staff with journalistic or PR backgrounds. He employed such people in other advisory roles in addition to his media advisers in order to ensure his entire office was attuned to the demands of the news cycle.

Media advisers have a number of roles: keeping up with the news to ensure their employer is in touch with how various issues are being reported; writing press releases and speeches; providing photo opportunities; acting as a buffer between journalists and politicians by being available to the media 24/7; liaising with other arms of the government to ensure messages are consistent with the official party line; and providing friendly journalists with a constant supply of information. Often, quotes from politicians that we read in the newspaper come not from the horse's mouth but directly from media advisers with the authority to speak on their employer's behalf.

MEDIA UNITS

The role of media units is to coordinate communications strategy within and between various agencies. More controversially, these taxpayer-funded bodies engage in partisan political behaviour. It is the ability of these units to act as a conduit between government departments, party leaders, party organisations and grassroots politicians that make them essential to the PR state. By contrast, the federal leader of the opposition employs a seven-person media unit, but it lacks access to sensitive information available only to the government. Media units have been controversial for successive governments because they not only promote the government's message, but also monitor and discredit opposition parties.

The Hawke and Keating governments' National Media Liaison Service (NMLS or aNiMaLS) attracted a good deal of controversy by pointing journalists towards errors made by the opposition. The Howard Government abolished aNiMaLS, but quickly replaced it with its own partisan media: the Government Members Secretariat (GMS). Special Minister of State Eric Abetz explained that the GMS 'provides information and resource support to private members' (Abetz 2004). While this is true, in the context of the government's overall communication strategy, and the importance of local marginal seat campaigns that complement the national election campaign (as the next chapter will show), the GMS is a crucial organisation. Responsibility for the GMS was transferred in 1998 from the Department of Finance and Administration to the Chief Whip's Office, effectively making it unaccountable to the Parliament. The importance of the GMS lies in the way it connects the government's national communications strategy with individual members of Parliament, most notably those members in marginal seats. This allows government policy releases, advertising and other communication on behalf of the executive to be made timely and relevant to the grassroots House of Representatives campaigns that help win elections.

The GMS is a prime example of the way that government and party communication strategies have become inextricably linked. One of the reasons that government media units do not attract the attention that aNiMaLS did is that their functions are now diffused throughout the executive and legislative arms of the government. The GMS has a coordinating rather than a monitoring role. The **media monitoring** function of aNiMaLS has been contracted to commercial operators such as Rehame and Media Monitors (Barns 2005 p. 2). Although relatively small in terms of resources and staffing, the GMS plays a central role in the Coalition Government's communication strategy. It is the centrality of the GMS, combined with its access to senior government operators, which makes it function so successfully.

> **media monitoring** transcripts of radio and television programs that are made available to politicians and government departments so that they can keep track of what is making news and check on the results of their media management techniques

PUBLIC AFFAIRS DEPARTMENTS

In addition to media units with an explicitly partisan function, there are also public affairs departments and officers attached to every government agency. The people employed in these offices are generally public servants, meaning that officially they work for the government rather than for the party in power. Public affairs units are designed to promote policies and strategies, and to answer routine media and public inquiries about matters relevant to their department. For this reason, these units are not particularly controversial (however expensive), although there is a concern that their resources can be harnessed for party-political benefits.

We see the fruits of their labour on the nightly news, when ministers make policy announcements at prearranged locations, standing in front of hoardings bearing government slogans, as the reporter quotes impressive statistics from the carefully tailored media pack. It is difficult to separate this kind of routine policy announcement from the wider communications strategy of the government, and interests of the party in government. Public affairs units do not operate in a political vacuum. Their strategy is influenced by higher-level bodies such as the Government Communications Unit (GCU) and, of course, by ministerial direction.

Governments have also been making greater use of media consultants. In addition, all sorts of research done by the public service (or by private companies at taxpayers' expense) is made available only to the party in government. This includes media monitoring, polling and focus-group analysis. It can be difficult to extract exact figures, but the amount tends to run into the millions. Locating these functions in each government department makes them less visible than a large centralised organisation such as aNiMaLS.

The growing strategic importance of media units is evidenced by the fact that since the 1980s, governments have attempted to coordinate the activities of the various entities very closely. One specific mechanism designed to achieve this has been the establishment of a Ministerial Committee on Government Communication (MCGU). This kind of committee has been used in various forms since the 1980s. The committee in the Coalition Government is chaired by the Minister of State and consists of four other permanent members. Its fundamental purpose is to ensure that all government information campaigns conform to the government's needs. Moreover, there is a growing trend to locate entities such as the media units and the MCGU in Prime Minister's or Premier's Department (rather than Finance). The situation (or location) of media units in the departments of heads of government indicates the strategic importance of good media. It also ensures that the leader of the government, or their office, can exercise a significant degree of control over communications output (Ward 2003, p. 10).

Debates and controversies

ACCOUNTABILITY

The media's watchdog role has been made more cumbersome by the host of government media units and advisers that have been placed between politicians and journalists. Further, the large and increasing numbers of ministerial staff who appear to have an important influence on public policy play an opaque role in the political process. These developments have made it easier for government ministers to claim **plausible deniability** when controversy erupts. It is difficult for the public to assess exactly what ministers have been told and when. Combined with a narrow interpretation of ministerial responsibility, which argues that ministers should only be held accountable for their personal actions and not for the misdemeanours of their departments, we have reached a point where few ministers are forced to take responsibility for government mismanagement.

> **plausible deniability** when no official records exist of what a minister was or was not told of a given matter, the politician is said to have plausible deniability of any knowledge of that matter

Political advisers, considered part of the private staff of politicians, fall outside the normal chain of accountability. Since the mid 1990s, governments have evoked what is known as the McMullan Principle. Keating Government minister Bob McMullan refused to allow his ministerial staff to appear before a Senate committee on the grounds that 'ministerial staff are accountable to the minister and the minister is accountable to the Parliament and ultimately the electors' (Holland 2002, p. 15). The Senate has the power to call before it any Australian resident, backed by the threat of imprisonment. The principle of ministerial staff not appearing before parliamentary committees is a bipartisan one. Opposition politicians wish to have their own ministerial staff at some point, so do not give the Senate the full extent of its power, even when the activities of government advisers becomes a point of political controversy.

Media advisers are partisan political actors. Many journalists resent the role they play in contemporary politics. After being frustrated at her newspaper's inability to find out details of a visit to Australia by the President of the USA, Margo Kingston complained that: 'Howard's press secretaries now saw their job as preventing the flow of information to the Australian people—as information blockers, not information providers' (2004, p. 19).

Box 5.2   Children overboard or truth overboard?

In the run-up to the 2001 elections, the number of boats carrying asylum-seekers between Indonesia and Australia became a matter of political controversy. Shortly before the formal campaign commenced, the Coalition Government prevented the MV *Tampa* from completing its journey to Australia after picking up asylum seekers whose boat was sinking. In the first week of the campaign, another vessel carrying asylum seekers got into trouble and HMAS *Adelaide* was sent to provide assistance. What happened next became a matter of great controversy. The Immigration Minister, Philip Ruddock, announced that some refugees had thrown their children into the water. 'I regard this as one of the most disturbing practices I have come across' (Weller 2002, p. 1), he said. The Prime Minister chimed in: 'I don't want in this country people who are prepared, if those reports are true, to throw their children overboard' (pp. 1–2).

During the 'children overboard' affair, then Defence Minister Peter Reith claimed that he was unaware of reports from the Navy that contradicted the view that the children had not been thrown into the ocean. The Department of Defence was subject to 'media clearance rules' that required all media releases to be vetted by the minister's office. Official information regarding both the earlier MV *Tampa* episode and the events during the campaign was thus very tightly controlled. When a Senate inquiry looked into the matter, Reith's media adviser, Ross Hampton, accepted full culpability. However, Parliament had no opportunity to question Hampton because the Minister refused to allow him to appear before the Senate inquiry. Reith did not contest the 2001 election, so ministerial responsibility was not in effect.

Subsequently, Mike Scrafton, having moved on from his position in the Defence Minister's office, publicly contradicted the Prime Minister's account of the affair shortly before the 2004 election. When he was told by reporters that Scrafton had passed a lie-detector test on current affairs television, Howard asserted that he was about to submit himself to 'to the great lie-detector test in Australian politics, and that is the collective judgment of my fellow Australians' (cited in Uhr 2005, p. 123). The government, then, claimed that its accountability to the people at an election trumped any concerns about the democratic processes during the children overboard affair.

In what sense are ministers accountable to the Australian people? Should ministerial staffers be accountable to Parliament for their advice and actions?

We have already seen a number of methods used by politicians in their relationship with journalists. More troubling from the point of view of political accountability are strategies for bypassing journalists altogether. One of the most popular of these is talkback radio. Some talkback hosts are journalists, and others are not. Since talkback radio is first and foremost an entertainment medium, it brings a different atmosphere to the discussion of politics than other sources of news. Politicians like live radio because their comments go to air unedited. They can get their message out without the fear that the news organisation will selectively edit their comments to show them in a poor light. The importance of talkback radio is difficult to measure. Opinionated hosts such as Sydney's Alan Jones are thought by politicians to be crucial in swinging public opinion. Yet, talkback audiences tend to be older and more conservative than the average voter. They often listen to have their views reinforced rather than challenged (Ward 2002).

Political parties are also acutely aware of the importance of local media during election campaigns. These regional or suburban outlets can be particularly useful for reaching voters who do not normally follow state or national politics very closely. Often, local and community newspapers have few resources for news gathering. They are therefore susceptible to public relations methods, both commercial and government.

Another way of bypassing journalists and therefore avoiding accountability is only available to one side of the political debate—the extensive and growing use by governments of information campaigns.

THE ROLE OF GOVERNMENT ADVERTISING

While the resources required to staff and operate the various government media units is considerable, most controversy about government communication centres on a much more visible issue—the cost and nature of government advertising. Government advertising campaigns that provide information about policy changes, promote public health, or discourage dangerous activities such as speeding, do not arouse too much controversy. It is when advertising is perceived to be promoting the policies of a political party that concerns are raised. Working out where to draw the line between essential information campaigns and party propaganda, however, is not easy.

Spending more than a billion dollars in its first decade in office, the Coalition Government is the nation's biggest advertiser. Some campaigns, including the biggest (Defence Force Recruitment) are not politically contested. The most controversial campaigns have been those that used large amounts of government money to advertise changes that were yet to be legislated. This occurred in the cases of the goods and services tax (GST) in 1998 and changes to industrial relations laws in 2005. The New Tax System campaign was the largest in Australian history. Of a total of more than $100 million, $30 million was spent shortly before the 1998 election campaign. State governments, too, are spending increasing amounts on advertising. The Victorian Government's $6 million 'Building a world-class Victoria' campaign was slammed by the opposition as government self-promotion (Martin 2005).

While the trend of increased government expenditure on advertising began under the Hawke and Keating governments, spending has been consistently higher under the Howard Government. The concern is that governments are using the public purse to fund campaigns it possibly should not. That is, political advertising is not really being used to inform the public about changes to policy, but to advertise or sell the government itself. What compounds this problem is that it is often very difficult to differentiate political campaigns from election campaigns, and that governments are deliberately blurring the distinction between the two—which is, essentially, unethical.

It is difficult to disagree with this assessment from John Howard: 'There is clearly a massive difference between necessary government information for the community and blatant government electoral propaganda. Propaganda should be paid for by political parties' (cited by ABC *Media Watch* 2004). Howard made that comment as opposition leader in response to the Keating Government's $9.4 million Working Nation campaign. At the time, Howard declared the Working Nation campaign 'a disgraceful sham'. The Howard Government has since accelerated an existing trend towards increased government spending on advertising. Spending increased from $61 million (in 2004 prices) in 1991–92 to $103 million in 1995–96, and peaked at $240 million in 1999–2000 when the Howard Government introduced the GST (or 'A New Tax System' as the propaganda preferred to put it). Leaving aside the GST campaign, the Howard Government has spent more than $100 million on advertising every year since 2000–01, a mark the Hawke and Keating governments reached only once (Grant 2004). Figures on advertising spending do not include the costs of market research, campaign design and distribution. A leaked cabinet document reflected government concerns over the 'danger that if [advertising] is perceived as a promotional campaign for the government, it could heighten existing negative views of the system' (cited in Koutsoukis 2004.). Harry Evans, Clerk of the Senate, was heavily criticised by Coalition Senators when he suggested that the government's $20 million 'Work Choices' campaign was party-political.

The evidence appears to support the contention that governments are inclined to play fast and loose with advertising expenditure prior to an election. It is typical to find fairly major pre-election spikes in political advertising. Grant shows that there are sharp increases in government spending outlays just prior to an election. For example, in the four months prior to the 2001 polls, the government spent $78 million. Between January and July of that year, the government spent $40 million, with just over half of this in the first two weeks of July (*Australian* 2004). To spend money on advertising, the Commonwealth Government must, as with all financial matters, ask Parliament's permission. However, sometimes governments exploit loopholes in the system, spending money on advertisements that have not been approved by Parliament. They are able to do this courtesy of s. 81 of the Constitution: to 'raise money for the purposes of the Commonwealth'. This is normally done through a contingency fund of up to $390 million for the government's use under specified conditions. The High Court ruled in 2005 that such contingency funds could be used for purposes such as the government's Work Choices campaign, even though the relevant legislation had not reached the Parliament.

POLITICAL PARTIES AND THE PUBLIC INTEREST

The activities of the PR state are controversial partly because all of the activity described in this chapter requires large amounts of taxpayers' dollars that could arguably be better spent on government programs. It is also controversial because it is very difficult for observers to distinguish between the legitimate use of government information campaigns and the use by political parties of the resources of the state for their re-election. For example, there are any number of reasons a government might wish to spend public money on advertisements. Most people would agree that an advertising campaign aimed at pubic health or safety is reasonable. What if the motivation for the campaign, however, is not simply that of raising pubic awareness of a problem, but rather to demonstrate that the party in power cares about that problem and is doing something about it? This criticism was made by women's groups of the Howard Government's advertisements on domestic violence, for example. In practice, it is impossible to draw a clear line between the need for the state to promote awareness of social problems and solutions, and the interests of the party or parties in power.

It may be that the problem with government advertising is not so much some pernicious effect on public opinion, but that the money could be spent much more effectively on government services. The money spent on advertising policies would arguably be better served by redirecting the money spent on advertising a service into the service itself. For example, it has been claimed (by the opposition) that the $21 million the government spent on advertising changes to the Medicare system would have funded 450 000 bulk-billed Medicare visits and 85 000 dental procedures (*Australian* 2004a).

Box 5.3   Work Choices

In late 2005, the Howard Government embarked on an advertising blitz in support of its industrial relations legislation, given the name Work Choices. Yet, the same clear majority of voters opposed the changes as had been the case before a one-month period where the government spent around $50 million promoting their policy (*Sydney Morning Herald* 2005, p. 7). This largest-ever monthly spend for an Australian advertiser seemed to amount to nothing in political terms. Earlier advertisements paid for by the Australian Council of Trade Unions (ACTU) had a greater effect on political debate, not necessarily because voters accepted their anti-reform message, but because they raised the profile of an issue inherently unpopular for the government. Through judicious use of the media, the ACTU brought the industrial relations issue onto the political agenda before the government was ready with the detail of its proposals. Part of the problem for the government was that once again the advertisements themselves became a matter of political controversy. For example, the pulping of more than $100 000 worth of pamphlets because the word 'fair' had been omitted from their cover was used by the opposition as an example of government profligacy in its information campaign on industrial relations in 2005–06.

Look carefully at the government advertising you come across. Can you make a distinction between ads in the public interest and those promoting a government or political party?

Ideally, Parliament could lay down clear guidelines to prevent the misuse by political parties of public money. However, separating the roles of the government of the day and the interests of the political party or parties in power is not easy. As we have seen, this issue comes up in all aspects of government communication: the employment of media advisers across all levels of government, advertising by government agencies, and public affairs sections in government departments. Information campaigns are not in contravention of the Constitution if their political advertisements contain material of an 'electoral matter'. It might be unethical for them to do this, but it is apparently not illegal (or so says the Government Solicitor). The only restriction on the government is that the advertisement must be for the 'purposes of the Commonwealth' (ANAO 1998). The present government has been reluctant to tighten the regime to ensure that political advertising funds are not misused (or used as an extension of a government's election campaign). There have been a couple of attempts to introduce legislation into Parliament that would restrict uses of political advertising (for example, the *Government Advertising Bill 2000*). However, the government has not been supportive of these bills. The Auditor-General has recommended that the government undertakes a parliamentary review of the matter, and even went as far as suggesting draft guidelines to ensure that the boundaries between political advertising and electoral advertising remain relatively fixed.

In a submission to a parliamentary inquiry into government advertising, political scientist Sally Young made a series of recommendations on the regulation of government advertising. These include annual reports on advertising in addition to the departmental reports required in the budget; annual reports on public opinion research; publication of advertising contracts; and comprehensive guidelines on when government advertising is in the public interest. As we have seen throughout this chapter, many aspects of government communications strategy are heavily criticised by opposition parties, who promptly find that when they win government, they simply cannot do without all the expensive bells and whistles of the PR state. The prospects for reform, then, are bleak.

SUMMARY

Australian governments are spending increasing amounts of money on media units, media advisers and political advisers more generally. Politicians have learned to bypass journalists in their public communication by appearing on live radio and rapidly increasing the amount of money spent on government information campaigns.

This process undermines the accountability of politicians by limiting the extent to which they are questioned by journalists. Journalists and media audiences are aware of these problems and attempt to compensate for them. Voters are aware of attempts by politicians to manipulate their image, and are becoming increasingly sceptical of them. It is far from clear that expensive government information campaigns achieve anything other than irritating the electorate, and, while legal, may not be ethical.

Questions

1   How have governments in recent decades changed the ways in which they deal with journalists? Have modern methods of political management given politicians an advantage over journalists?
2   Do we pay too much attention to political images instead of political substance? How does our obsession with image affect the way that female politicians are covered by the media?
3   Is there a need for governments to spend millions of dollars a year on advertising? Where would you draw the line between necessary information campaigns and party propaganda?

WEBSITES

Crikey—Keeps track of the links between governments, media outlets and PR firms by publishing lists of those who have worked for one or more relevant organisation (http://www.crikey.com.au/).

FURTHER READING

Barns, G. 2005, *Selling the Australian Government: Politics and Propaganda from Whitlam to Howard*. UNSW Press: Sydney.

Grattan, M. 1998, 'The Politics of Spin.' *Australian Studies in Journalism*, vol. 7, pp. 32–45.

Kingston, M. 2004, *Not Happy, John! Defending Our Democracy*. Penguin Books: Melbourne.

THE PERMANENT CAMPAIGN 6

This chapter will:

- trace the changes in the conduct of Australian election campaigns and the consequences of these changes for public participation in politics
- assess the impact of the media on election results
- discuss the media's focus on political leaders during election campaigns
- discuss the role of elections as mechanisms of political accountability.

Election campaigns bring about a number of challenges for the media in fulfilling its watchdog role. Part of the media's job in a liberal democracy is to hold governments to account for their actions. Election campaigns are not ideal times for this to happen. Political parties release masses of election promises in a short period of time, making serious analysis of the detail virtually impossible. This chapter is about the way political parties communicate with voters in order to win elections, not only during campaigns but also over the entire electoral cycle. The concept of permanent campaigning, where politicians try to influence voters between elections, raises a number of questions about democracy in Australia. In this chapter, we examine further the advantages of incumbency in political campaigning—the various actors in our democracy do not have equal access to the media, and the major parties receive the lion's share of news coverage during election campaigns. We also look at the influence of the media in deciding who wins elections in Australia, and question how effective elections are in holding governments accountable for their actions.

Politics for professionals

Making his first speech to Liberal Party MPs after his victory in the October 2004 Australian federal election, Prime Minister John Howard said that he was 'a great believer in perpetual campaigning', and that the government campaign to win the next election had already begun. The concept of the **permanent campaign** is important to understanding modern political communication. While the formal campaign period remains important, and an increasing number of voters claim to be making up their mind who to vote for in the week leading up to the election, they are influenced in their decision by political messages received in the months and years prior to polling day. Politicians are therefore highly conscious of the way they are portrayed in the media at all times.

> **permanent campaign** the use of the resources of government to promote a political party over the entirety of the parliamentary cycle

We still have formal campaign periods during which rules surrounding balanced reporting and editorial comment come into force. Yet, political parties have long since expanded their efforts at election and re-election beyond this relatively short window.

Modern campaign methods include **focus groups**; the use of mobile phones, email and internet; and the strategic use of the office resources of MPs. These methods are used on a permanent basis to build a complete communications strategy. The resources of the state, including government advertising, postal and office entitlements of members of Parliament, are used to research and communicate with the electorate. While many of these techniques have been in use for some time, it is only recently that they have been successfully coordinated to the extent that we can now say that the permanent campaign has reached Australia.

▶ **focus group** a small group of people, usually swinging voters, on whom political parties test policy ideas and slogans

Changing campaign techniques in Australia

The effort to professionalise campaigning in Australia began with the Australian Labor Party (ALP). South Australian Premier Don Dunstan's 1967–68 re-election campaign was the first to utilise advanced opinion polling and extensive television advertising. Similar techniques were used successfully by the federal Labor opposition at the 1972 election, led by Gough Whitlam. The 'It's Time' campaign, complete with celebrity-studded television advertisements, hit the right note for Labor after 23 years in opposition. It hit the right note, of course, because it had been extensively market-tested (Young 2005, p. 8). One of the oldest sentiments in democratic politics—it's time for a change—was given an upgrade by the marketing professionals. The 1972 campaign brought together a number of strands of professional communication with which Australian political parties had been experimenting for some time. Incorporating techniques developed overseas, particularly in the USA, is now regular practice for Australian political parties. During the 1980s, for example, then NSW ALP Secretary Stephen Loosely visited Canada to inspect the direct mail system used there (Mills 1986, p. 196). Stephen Mills's pioneering work on the professionalisation of Australian campaigns traced the ALP's development of opinion polling, focus groups, targeted advertising and direct mail-outs. Their Coalition opponents were not far behind.

The structure of political parties and the nature of their election campaigns tend to reflect each other. When political parties had tens of thousands of active members, campaigns would consist of volunteers distributing leaflets, organising meetings and debates, and candidates knocking on the doors of as many voters as possible. Large numbers of people could become involved because the campaign lasted for a defined period. At the local level, many of these activities continue, although the membership of the major political parties is much smaller today. Now, these local campaigns are dwarfed by an emphasis at the state and national level on the political parties and, increasingly, on their leaders. One consequence of this more professional approach to campaigning is that local party branch members feel disconnected from the campaign, giving them less incentive to continue their party membership. Under a compulsory voting system such as Australia's, major parties are largely assured of their core supporters' votes on polling day. The communications strategy of the big parties is therefore based on convincing **swinging voters** to support them. Both major parties in Australia contest the middle ground, leading to the suggestion there is a convergence of major party positioning in the centre of Australian politics.

Australia has a long history of **negative campaigning**. This technique seeks to accentuate the differences between the two major parties. Commentators noted the way in which fear triumphed in the 2004 campaign: opposition leader Mark Latham, days before the election, referred to Howard's campaign centring on fear (*Sydney Morning Herald* 2004). There is nothing new about a successful tactical use of fear in a political campaign. Negative advertising is regarded by political strategists as a more effective campaign tool than positive advertising. The party faithful tend to want their political representatives to focus on their achievements in government; however, the strategy of fear and negativity is the more effective method of appealing to swinging voters concerned about bread-and-butter issues such as rising interest rates, unemployment or economic downturn (see Young 2004, pp. 262–6). The sort of campaign that suggests quality of life will be adversely affected by a change of government therefore requires a negative campaign.

swinging voters voters who are prepared to change the party for whom they vote between elections

negative campaigning a campaigning style that highlights the bad things about the opposing party and its leader

The trend towards professionalisation in politics has coincided with a greater focus on party leaders in Australian campaigning. This is often referred to as a presidential style of campaigning, another influence from the USA. The rise of presidential-style contests between party leaders has increased the personalisation of negative attacks. However, while the media focus of campaigns is firmly on the party leaders, successful campaigns require extensive coordination between the leader's office and the wider party organisation. Political parties have become adept at quickly cobbling together advertisements that respond to controversies raised during the campaign. Political advertising is thus often very simple, consisting of still images, shots of newspaper headlines and voice-overs. This allows parties the flexibility to change tactics at the last minute.

A number of other techniques are used to complement messages in the mass media. The Liberal Party used telephone messaging for the first time in a federal election in Australia in 2004. Usually associated with 'getting out the vote' in non-compulsory voting nations like the USA, telephone messaging is a questionable form of campaign advertising in Australia. Its use by the Liberal Party did not carry an authorisation tag as required under the *Commonwealth Electoral Act 1918* (Miskin 2005). Another strategy of political parties to influence electors is direct mail, which aims to draw the attention of voters to policy announcements throughout the life of the Parliament. Through efficient use of their voter databases (each of the major political parties has a list of voters in each electorate and attempts to gather data about their voting intention), the parties can send these messages only to those voters likely to be interested in them, saving on cost and the risk of over-selling. All parties use direct mail extensively, taking advantage of the increasingly generous mail and office allowances Parliament awards MPs. Even if only a tiny percentage of the electorate does in fact make up their minds in the final days of the campaign, the parties work in seats with such fine margins that it is worth their while trying to influence those people up until the last minute. While this type of coordination is available to both government and opposition, successful Australian governments have gained the added advantage of enmeshing their campaigns into the apparatus of government.

Box 6.1   Election campaigns and new media

One of the earliest attempts to use the internet to influence Australian voters was Jeffed.com, a site maintained by a disgruntled former employee of then Victorian premier Jeff Kennett, which received much media attention during the 1999 state election campaign. The key to the site's success, however, was the fuss it caused in traditional media sources. Sites such as howardlies.com have received similar publicity. However, the internet in its own right has yet to prove an indispensable part of election campaigns in Australia.

In the USA, by contrast, the internet can be an important tool for fundraising, particularly for those candidates (such as Howard Dean in 2004) portraying themselves as outsiders. Similarly, minor parties who find it difficult to break the major parties' stranglehold on mainstream media coverage use new technologies to reach younger voters. In Australia, the Greens lead the way.

During the 2004 US presidential campaign, a group named Swift Boat Veterans for Truth attacked the military service record of Mr Bush's opponent, John Kerry. They placed television advertisements in a small number of markets, but their claims were initially ignored by the mainstream media. Conservative bloggers promoted the story, and the availability of the advertisements online allowed easy access. The claim and counter-claim about the credibility of the group only ensured that their message penetrated even further, neutralising any political advantage from Kerry's record of military service.

Note the way that the examples above show the online world interacting with the mainstream media to have an effect. For the 2004 federal election, the majority of Australians still nominated television as their main source of information about news and current affairs. Well into the information age, just three per cent of people nominated the internet (Ward & Stewart 2006, p. 194). Thus far, political parties have mostly used the web as another platform for advertising, rather than exploiting the interactive features of the medium. We discuss the possibilities for a more interactive media and political system in Chapter 10.

Would you use the internet to communicate with a politician or find out more about their policies?

The advantages of incumbency

Professional campaigning techniques have been used in Australian politics for some decades. The permanent campaign refers to the coordination of campaign techniques throughout the machinery of government, and the ruthless effort to seek partisan advantage at every opportunity. While the concept of the permanent campaign incorporates the activities of interest groups, opposition parties and journalists, it is in the communication strategies of governments that the technique is most clear. According to Ornstein and Mann, 'the line between campaigning and governing has all but disappeared' (2000, p. vii). In Australia, cabinet ministers receive an increasing proportion of their advice from political staffers rather than bureaucrats. The public service has adopted public relations techniques to promote new policies (and, of course, the relevant minister). The Howard Government has been the beneficiary of the culmination of these trends to be the first Australian government to be in perpetual campaign mode.

While professional campaign techniques have been practised in Australia for some decades, it is only recently that the degree of coordination between government agencies, the prime minister's office and the **party organisation** have been refined to the extent that we can now say that the Australian public is subjected to a permanent campaign. The permanent campaign offers extensive political advantages to the government over opposition parties. By coordinating the activities of government agencies and party activities through the political offices of the executive, governments can award themselves extensive resource advantages over the opposition, through government advertising and public relations strategies.

> **party organisation** a complex set of official structures common to all parties, ranging from local branches to national secretariats that support their members of Parliament

While all Australian political parties are becoming more professional, some elements of the permanent campaign are available only to the party or parties in government. The official campaign period, then, is used by the parties to reinforce, rather than change, the perceptions about politics that voters have developed over longer periods of time. For the government, having peppered the airwaves with official information advertisements, the path is well laid for a set of political advertisements during the formal campaign period. In contrast, the opposition is required to match its rhetoric and media releases during the permanent campaign period with paid advertising during the official campaign in the lead-up to election day.

Crucial to any government's communications strategy are the media units outlined in the previous chapter. As we saw in Chapter 5, there are numerous organisations involved in government communications. At the hub of the Howard Government's permanent campaign has been the Government Members Secretariat (GMS). While the GMS has a relatively small number of staff, it plays an important role in keeping government members informed of communication strategy. It is through the offices of the prime minister and other ministers that the GMS finds out about key government communications decisions, rather than through the public service agencies themselves. The prime minister's office, the party secretariat and the GMS then develop party tactics—such as the time and place of announcements, campaign literature and advertising—to complement the official government strategy. In turn, these party tactics feed back into the decisions of the Ministerial Committee on Government Communication. The GMS is then responsible for ensuring that all government members and candidates have the information and resources to take advantage of official government communication in their own campaigns as they see fit.

Box 6.2   The permanent campaign in action

The Howard Government's communication strategy for the 2004 federal election maximised the coalition party's resources by coordinating messages from a range of sources. This was achieved by directing government advertising to the promotion of changes in policy in areas considered weaknesses, such as Medicare. In turn, the messages carried by this advertising were used in party election material.

Party election strategy was clearly linked to the wider government communications strategy. For example, generic pamphlets including the line 'Strengthening Medicare' were distributed during the 2004 campaign, shortly after a controversial and expensive government advertising campaign designed to ensure the public that changes to the Medicare system were indeed 'Strengthening Medicare'. The brochure was electronically sent to all Liberal MPs across the country. By pre-determining the statements and quotes in the brochure, the GMS ensured that individual electorate offices did not overcommit their electorate to, for example, statements that may have embarrassed the government. This is one aspect of a wider professionalisation of political practice in Australia, and again illustrates the blurring of the line between government and party.

Incumbent parties thus benefit from a host of resources: as the largest parties in the Parliament, they receive the biggest slice of public campaign funding; governing parties find fundraising easier because they can provide access to decision-makers; and tens of millions of dollars in additional benefits flow from government advertising.

How aware do you think voters are of these incumbency advantages? Are we reaching the point where the public resents this use of public resources by political parties?

Generic brochures circulated by political parties have sections that can be customised to ensure individual electorate offices can sell their local message in addition to the state-wide or nationwide campaign message. For example, a generic brochure used by the Liberal Party in 2004 had sections provided for the MP to be mentioned as part of 'John Howard's Liberal team', as well as room for the name of the particular electorate to be inserted. It also had a section on the left-hand side of the brochure for candidate particulars, with the order and content predetermined by the party. Such content includes community organisation involvement and length of time spent living in the electorate. Of course this micro-managing of the distribution of campaign messages cannot entirely guard against errors at the local level.

Opposition parties face a difficult balancing act between putting out detailed policies too early—and thereby subjecting them to close analysis by the government (courtesy of the resources of government departments)—versus not putting them out early enough and being accused of having no policies and/or putting them out too late to be fully understood by the public (particularly where the policy is complex). In 2004, Labor's most expensive policy, Medicare Gold, came out of the blue in the final two weeks of the campaign. When detailed policies are announced during the campaign period, the public find it difficult to fully absorb them. The government effectively ran negative media as to the effect they would have on the economy and the budget.

At the federal level, there have only been a handful of changes of government since the Second World War. It is difficult enough for the opposition to make a case for a change of government. Extensive use of the resources of the state to improve the public's perception of the governing party makes the task of opposition that much harder. It is therefore important that the media reports on any transgression of the line between government communication strategy and party election strategy. This is, unfortunately, easier said than done, particularly when a governing party is permanently in campaign mode.

Figure 6.1 **Role and relationship of the GMS within government and party**

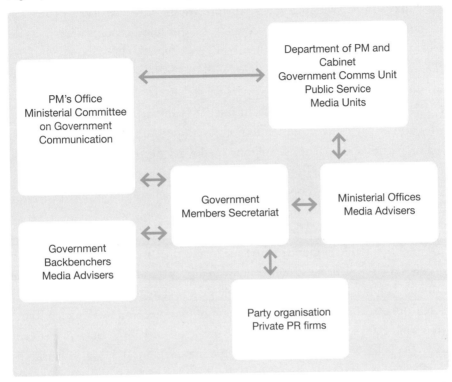

Source: Errington and van Onselen (2005, p. 29).

Debates and controversies

TO WHAT EXTENT DO THE MEDIA INFLUENCE ELECTION RESULTS?

We tend to assume that the media has an enormous impact on politics. We would not be writing this book if we did not think the media is important to the way we are governed and to the results of elections. In Chapter 3, we saw a range of opinion on media effects, but little consensus over the extent of those effects. Long-time ALP polling guru Rod Cameron suggested that 'the people who determine elections in this country are the least interested and the least informed about politics ... They vote on instinct for superficial, ill-informed and generally selfish reasons' (cited in Tiffin 1989, pp. 138–9). Cameron's claim is consistent with research around the world suggesting that those of us who pay most attention to politics and political news are the least likely to be swinging voters. In turn, those with low levels of interest in politics are in fact more susceptible to the few messages that they do receive during election campaigns than those with higher levels of interest (Denemark 2002). We can see, then, with this information on media effects in mind, why it is that political parties try so hard to identify and influence a relatively small number of people during their campaigns: the swinging voters who do not pay much attention to politics under normal circumstances. The major parties spend tens of millions of dollars during election campaigns using a range of tactics from mass media advertisements to carefully tailored personal letters in the hope of influencing the small proportion of people who change their vote from election to election.

A Newspoll survey after the 2004 election found that 30 per cent of respondents decided whom to vote for in the final week of the campaign, a number that has been steadily increasing over recent decades (*Australian* 2004b). While many of these late deciders don't actually change the way they vote from election to election, the number of swinging and weakly identifying voters has been steadily increasing since the 1960s. In 1967, only 11 per cent of voters failed to identify with one of the major political parties. That number had increased to 30 per cent in 1990 (Chaples 1997, p. 358). Impressions of the leaders and their parties may have been formed well before the campaign began, but those impressions need to be solidified into a clear voting intention. Hence the large sums of money spent during election campaigns, and the increasing sums spent between elections in the permanent campaign.

Box 6.3 A day in the life of an election campaign

Election campaigns have changed dramatically in recent decades. Rod Tiffen cited a journalist's observation of the campaign during the 1980s: 'Election campaigns are real killers. You go from 6am to midnight seven days a week for three weeks' (1989, p. 131). Even back then, media-savvy politicians had begun to revolutionise campaigning. Today, journalists following the leaders during campaigns are more likely to be bored than frazzled. Political parties have stripped back the public face of their campaigns in an attempt to control which images and sound bites are broadcast by television and radio. A typical day for the prime minister or leader of the opposition will start with a live radio interview, move to a photogenic location (child-care centres are popular) to make a policy announcement and that's about it for the day. Other events, such as private party fundraising functions and interviews with individual journalists, take place behind closed doors.

Walks through shopping centres or other public locations with the media pack used to be popular for politicians. However, these events are unpredictable. Not all members of the public are pleased to see their political leaders. Campaigning in South Australia in the lead-up to the 1990 election, then Prime Minister Bob Hawke was heckled by a local, whom Hawke dismissed as a 'silly old bugger'. This comment was highlighted by all the nightly news broadcasts, and threatened to reinforce public perceptions that the government was out of touch with the electorate. During the 1993 campaign, then opposition leader Dr John Hewson held a series of public rallies to promote his 'Fightback!' policy platform. It was easy for his opponents to turn up at these rallies and promote an atmosphere of division, playing on public concerns that a change of government would have been a risk.

The paradox of the micro-management of the modern election campaign is that media outlets seize upon the smallest of mistakes, simply to show something a bit different in their stories. Thus, pictures of a party leader tripping on some stairs (which happened to John Howard in 1996), or being badgered by protesters in animal suits, are often featured in news broadcasts and newspapers, much to the chagrin of the media minders who sit up all night planning the day's events down to the smallest detail. There is something deliciously subversive about the way these incidents are used to upset the rhythms of the permanent campaign.

Think about the sorts of images that we see on television news broadcasts during election campaigns. How much planning do you think goes into the images that we get to see? Has the importance of getting the right image over-shadowed our political leaders' engagement with the general public?

Notwithstanding the ongoing debate about media effects, politicians certainly behave as though the media make a difference. They continually attempt to influence the way they are portrayed in newspapers and electronic media. Apart from the prime minister, though, few politicians gain media attention simply by appearing in public. They have to generate news by making announcements or through public relations strategies. Whether or not news organisations think those activities are worth reporting is a matter of editorial judgment. These decisions are driven by the values of the journalists who gather the news, the priorities of the editors who have to fill papers or broadcast time, judgments about what consumers will think is important, and the political effects of certain stories. It is difficult to get around the fact that government policy announcements make bigger news than almost anything the opposition has to say. Government policy is about what will happen, not what should happen. Of course, governments make plenty of announcements, perhaps responding to the claims of the opposition or interest groups, which are mere political argument rather than policy substance. Nevertheless, government ministers find it easier than their shadow counterparts to grab headlines.

We are left with the aphorism that the media may not tell us what to think, but it does tell us what to think about. As much as journalists like to think of themselves as neutral observers of politics, they are as much a part of election campaigns as the politicians (Tiffen 1989, p. 127). Newspapers play a particularly important **agenda-setting role**, as radio and morning television fill much of their programs with stories broken by newspapers. While politicians go to great lengths to set the news agenda using the techniques we discussed in the previous chapter, journalists and editors have an enormous body of material that they need to prioritise on a day-to-day basis. There is, of course, plenty of incentive for both the political parties and the commercial news media to pay attention to those issues most concerning the public. There is also a tendency, however, for the public to view as important those issues to which the media pay a lot of attention. Within a framework set by their proprietors, then, journalists and editors make crucial decisions about the political news agenda. Feeding into these decisions about what is newsworthy about politics is a near-obsession with the competitive aspects of politics. Stories about policies or legislation usually run a poor second to stories about leadership tension, the latest polling or speculation about election results. The parties like to stress the differences between them, when those differences are often slight.

During the formal campaign period, in particular, some issues will receive front-page treatment, while others just a paragraph or two. Tiffen nominates three intersecting factors in the news coverage of election campaigns. The first

> **agenda-setting role** the power of senior journalists to make choices about which news items make the front page of a newspaper, or the lead story on broadcast news, to shape the agenda in politics

is the sheer intensity of the campaign. Journalists run as a herd because they do not have time to reflect on the events of each day's events. There are not many 'scoops' to be had in this environment. They are forced to digest large amounts of policy detail on a range of subjects in a ridiculously short space of time (this is to say nothing of the ability of voters to digest that information). Second, journalists have little choice but to make news out of the various set pieces and publicity stunts staged by the political parties. There are few other sources of information during the campaign period. Finally, the campaign intensifies our perception of politics as a competitive contest. Newsworthiness is determined primarily by judgments about how various events may affect the outcome of the election (Tiffen 1989, p. 130).

With such a complicated picture, it is difficult to determine who is setting the agenda in political news. Why is it, for instance, that political debate in this country centres on the economy? Is it because that is what is on the minds of mortgage-strapped voters? Does the government like to see the economy, rather than the environment, at centre stage? Why do journalists and editors see the economy as 'hard news' to the exclusion of other issues? Politicians are often accused of being poll-driven. Yet, they often make decisions that go against what opinion polls tell us is popular, such as sending troops to Iraq. Media outlets often do the same thing, often reporting what they think is important rather than commercially appealing. They hope that they will be rewarded in the long run for their judgment. All of this assumes that we as citizens wish to consume news about our political system.

IS AUSTRALIA DEVELOPING A PRESIDENTIAL-STYLE SYSTEM OF GOVERNMENT?

The dominance of television has sharpened a number of trends in Australian politics that emphasise the importance of the prime minister. The decline of important elements of the Australian political system, such as **cabinet government** and ministerial responsibility, have coincided with the rise of television to produce a political system that in some respects resembles the

American presidential type. Prime ministers have the resources (through their own department) to dominate both policymaking and communications strategy. The extent of such trends varies depending on the style of the particular prime minister. There remain, however, important institutional differences between the Australian and American systems. For example, the highly disciplined political parties in Australia and the formal **separation of powers** in the USA can make Australian prime ministers comparatively more powerful than their American presidential counterparts. On the other hand, prime ministers can be deposed by their own party without reference to the electorate. This happened to Bob Hawke when Paul Keating took over the prime ministership in 1991.

> ▶ **cabinet government** the system where all important decisions are made by a group of senior ministers, for which they take collective responsibility
>
> ▶ **separation of powers** the separation of government responsibilities into executive, legislative and judicial realms

News coverage of Australian election campaigns tends to centre on the leaders of the major political parties—the two leaders with a chance of becoming prime minister. Why, for instance, does the leader of the Australian Greens not share the stage in the televised leaders' debates? The Greens leader is not a chance to become prime minister, of course, but such logic is self-fulfilling. In the USA, candidates for president who receive support in a series of opinion polls above a threshold of about five per cent are allowed to participate in presidential debates. A number of independent and minor party candidates have participated in these invaluable media opportunities in recent decades, although none has gone on to become president. Australia's major parties would never allow this to happen. Leadership debates are a relatively recent import into this country, and their format is by default decided by the prime minister, since the leader of the opposition always wants as many chances as possible to spend some time on prime time television. As prime minister, John Howard has limited leadership debates to one per campaign, pointing to Parliament as the true forum for political debate, but in reality acknowledging that televised debates are not his strong suit. The 'debate over the debates', after the formal campaign has been announced, has become another of the trivial rituals of Australian politics.

While leadership debates are a hallmark of modern political campaigns, there is not much evidence that they affect election results. John Howard's defeat in debates with Beazley and Mark Latham (according to polls of swinging voters) did not stop him winning the 2001 and 2004 elections. This is, perhaps, because these set pieces are less important to leaders well established in the public mind. For less well-known opposition leaders, the hour or so of concentrated media attention is an enormous opportunity. Regardless of his performance in those debates, the public had already had plenty of time to make their mind up about Prime Minister Howard.

ARE ELECTIONS SUITABLE MECHANISMS FOR POLITICAL ACCOUNTABILITY?

One of the most important roles of the media in our democratic system is helping to keep governments accountable for their actions. The ultimate form of political accountability is an election, where a government stands to lose power if voters believe election promises are broken. However, the media and the public may have vastly different ideas about what it means to keep a government accountable. The media have a strong sense of their role as a watchdog on government corruption; however, swinging voters are often more concerned about issues that affect them directly. They have a low opinion of politicians and are not surprised by corruption scandals, regardless of whether individual ministers have been held accountable.

Politicians are keenly aware of the short attention span of both voters and the media. Election promises are often broken shortly after an election. Governments use their first **budget** and first session of Parliament to make difficult decisions, hoping that the public has a short memory. It may be two or three years before the next election campaign. Is it realistic to expect the media to dredge up old issues during an election campaign in order to hold governments accountable for things that happened years before?

> **budget** all of a government's taxation and spending plans for the year combined in a single statement

The limit of the media's power to hold governments accountable was illustrated in both the 2001 and 2004 federal election campaigns. The 2001 campaign was dominated by a series of events that tipped the emphasis towards immigration and national security—traditional strengths of the Coalition parties. In spite of this emphasis on issues favouring the Coalition, opposition leader Kim Beazley had won the televised leaders' debate, and the Labor party was preferred to the government in areas such as health and education. During the last week of the campaign, journalists seeking to hold the government accountable for its actions during the 'children overboard' affair (see Chapter 5 for details) appeared to play into the government's hands, even though they were doing precisely what they were trained to do. *Lateline's* Tony Jones even interviewed the prime minister twice in one day as events unfolded. The fact that the prime minister gave *Lateline* a second interview suggests that he was happy to keep the issue of asylum seekers in the headlines. The increased majority for the government on election day showed why.

One of the best recent examples of agenda-setting by a politician during an election campaign was John Howard's press conference to announce the date of the 2004 election. Howard had been under the hammer for weeks over truth (or lack thereof) in government with regard to the war in Iraq and the children overboard affair. As speculation about the date of the election intensified, and opinion polls continued to show the opposition in the lead, the eventual announcement of the election date for 9 October proved to be a circuit-breaker for the government. Howard's press conference on the day he called the election was one of the more deft exercises in media management in recent memory. Had Howard sought to change the subject completely from Iraq and children overboard to economic management (as his advisers were likely recommending), the media would not have been particularly accommodating, particularly as Senate hearings into the children overboard affair were to be held during the first week of the campaign. Instead, the Prime Minister emphasised trust. Who do you trust to manage the economy? Who do you trust to keep interest rates low? Newspapers responded with headlines the next day about trust. Even reporters hostile to the Prime Minister's tactics in changing the subject, and his record on telling the truth, found themselves following Howard's agenda. Given the election result, the Prime Minister's rhetoric about trust appeared to strike a chord with highly geared voters in the mortgage belts of the capital cities.

Does this mean that the electorate got it wrong in 2001 and 2004? In a democracy, voters make up their own minds what is important. The media does its job by giving the electorate as much information as possible. Elections are held every few years. They are a blunt instrument where accountability is concerned. Governments do not lose office very often. Usually, the trigger for a government losing office is a recession rather than a scandal. This makes the ongoing role of the media in exposing the activities of government particularly important. They may be able to force resignations by ministers and changes of government policy. If elections are clumsy instruments of government accountability, then Parliament and a free media become even more important in the effective functioning of our democracy.

SUMMARY

This chapter has described the links between the government communications infrastructure outlined in Chapter 5 and the efforts of political parties to win elections. Australian political parties are becoming increasingly professional in their operation. They no longer rely on large membership or face-to-face engagement with voters in order to win elections. Managing the media is an important part of this strategy, although bypassing the media in communicating with voters is also important. These developments bring into question the fairness of our democratic system. Incumbent governments have an advantage over their opposition by using public resources in a permanent campaign. In becoming increasingly sophisticated in the way they target small numbers of key voters, political parties may be taking for granted their long-time supporters. The ability of the media to hold governments accountable for their actions is also compromised by the methods used in the permanent campaign.

Most of what we know about the platforms of the parties competing for office is presented to us through the mass media. It is difficult, though, to conclude that the media play a decisive role in election results. Political parties and interest groups are constantly seeking to influence what is reported. Careful attention is paid during the formal campaign period to balance between candidates. Political professionals are never certain which way voters may turn at the last minute and what may influence them. Most importantly, those voters who make up their minds at the last minute are frequently influenced by the barest impression of politics gained through advertising instead of the nightly news. All the expense and clamour of an election campaign may well be a complete waste of time. The margins in elections are simply so small that the major parties leave nothing to chance.

Questions

1 What are some of the advantages that governing parties have over opposition parties in Australian election campaigns?

2 Think about a recent federal election campaign. Do you think that individual media corporations are powerful enough to influence the results of a federal election?

3 Why is it difficult for the media to keep political parties accountable during election campaigns?

WEBSITES

Sites for individual political parties include some archived campaign material:

Australian Labor Party (http://www.alp.org.au/)

Australian Democrats (http://www.democrats.org.au/)

Australian Greens (http://www.greens.org.au/)

Liberal Party of Australia (http://www.liberal.org.au/)

The Nationals (http://www.nationals.org.au/)

FURTHER READING

Errington, W. & van Onselen, P. 2005, 'Public servants or partisan dirt diggers? Inside the Government Members Secretariat'. *Australian Journal of Communication*, vol. 32, no. 2, pp. 25–39.

Mill, S. 1986, *The New Machine Men*. Penguin Books: Melbourne.

Young, S. 2005, *The Persuaders*. Pluto Press: Melbourne.

THE PROSCRIPTION AND PRESCRIPTION OF MEDIA CONTENT

7

This chapter will:

- explore the rationale for content regulation and control, and the guiding principles that underpin it
- examine how the rules pertaining to content regulation evolved
- provide an overview of the institutional and legal framework of content regulation
- highlight the difficulties that arise from the application of the regulatory regime.

Control over communications—whether it involves speech, text or images—is a sensitive issue in most societies, but particularly within Western liberal democracies where the citizenry typically hold strong views about their right to express and exchange ideas and information. While Australia's political system is bedded in liberal democratic values, this does not necessarily translate into unqualified support for the principle of free speech. It is generally accepted that restrictions on communications are required in order to prevent chaos in the streets. Important liberal thinkers, such as J.S. Mill, argued that while free speech was an inalienable right, it could only remain so if it did not cause 'harm' to others. He believed that free speech was essential, provided a person's words did not directly violate the rights of others (van Mill 2002, p. 5).

While this notion of 'harm' remains the guiding principle in most liberal democratic societies, there is considerable disagreement about what constitutes 'harm' and how extensive any resultant restrictions on speech or other forms of media content should be. Some liberal thinkers believe that the basis for limiting speech should be the harm caused to others. That is, restrictions should be imposed only when the dissemination of particular content presents the risk of clear and imminent physical danger. Scholars, such as Joel Feinberg, reject this notion and argue that more serious restrictions on one's right to free speech are needed that recognise the potential for free speech and free ideas to cause 'offence'. Here, the argument is that the emotional and psychological harm caused by exposure to certain ideas or images is as damaging as any physical act of aggression that might arise as a result of the publication of particular views. The 'offence' principle, as outlined by Feinberg, suggests that ideas or images that are offensive or distressing, and that cannot be easily avoided, should be censored. Others, however, believe that both approaches are too conservative. Some writers contend that certain material should be banned if it undermines the ability of an individual to participate equally in democratic life. They argue that it is legitimate for government to silence any content that denigrates a person and undermines their equal status as citizens (van Mill 2002).

In Australia, as elsewhere, these kinds of arguments are often invoked to justify the **censorship** of material. Australian governments typically defend their right to censor communications, based on three sets of concerns. First, censorship ensures that children, and to a lesser extent 'vulnerable' adults, are not exposed to unsolicited material that is obscene. That is, censorship serves to protect defenceless members of society from inappropriate and socially harmful material. Second, some material is **proscribed** on the grounds that it has the potential to cause physical or psychological harm. It is generally thought that exposure to certain images or ideas is not only harmful to those who are directly exposed to them, but that it can also have a negative impact on 'innocent' or 'unsuspecting' third parties. Finally, certain information is censored in order to protect the physical integrity of the state. Sensitive government records that relate to the defence of the nation and important cabinet documents are concealed from the public and the media in the national interest.

> **censorship** the prohibition, control and suppression of ideas, speech and other forms of human expression

> **proscribe** to prevent or exclude something from use or mention

Evolution of Australia's censorship regime

Historically, Australia has operated one of the most zealous censorship regimes in the Western world, 'proud to ban what was acceptable in London, Paris and New York' and seeing itself as a 'bulwark for Anglo-Saxon standards' (Moore 2005). As has been noted elsewhere in this book, the colonial authorities had initially declared it illegal for newspapers to publish without governmental approval. Fortunately, the courts refused to approve the relevant Act, thereby liberating the industry from the government's yoke (Pearson 2004, p. 33). This established a precedent for the treatment of the press, resulting in a situation whereby print content was controlled post-publication, mostly via the law of libel.

> **libel** a false and malicious publication that injures someone's reputation or defames them

Whereas the newspaper sector managed an early escape from the clutches of tight government control, books and magazines were not so fortunate. In 1901, the Commonwealth government assumed responsibility for the importation of books and films into the country. The passage of the *Customs Act 1901* enabled the Commonwealth government to confiscate and ban imported material, although locally produced publications remained within the policy remit of the states. The *Customs Act*, along with a complex web of state and Commonwealth laws and agencies, established a regime that classified and prohibited literature without 'reference to public opinion or legal and expert advice' (Moore 2005).

However, in the first 28 years of the Commonwealth's foray into these matters, it was loath to ban imported publications. Only three books were prohibited during this time and, in the case of two of the books, it was only cheap editions that were outlawed (Coleman 2000, p. 13). However from the late 1920s onwards, the Commonwealth became more zealous in its suppression of imported texts. The catalyst, according to Coleman, was the **Great Depression**. Against a backdrop of great economic uncertainty, the Commonwealth caved in to public demands for tighter restrictions and controls on printed matter (Coleman 2000, pp. 18–19). During this period, there were occasions where customs authorities impounded books because the title of the publication was considered raunchy (Butler & Rodrick 2004, p. 390). Sometimes books were banned merely on the basis of the reputation of the importer, or because of a letter of complaint from a member of the public (Coleman 2000, p. 26). Thousands of books were banned or edited. It is estimated that as many as 5000 books, excluding political publications, were interdicted by customs authorities in the period between 1929 and 1936 (Coleman 2000, p. 19).

> ▶ **Great Depression** a period during the 1930s in which Australia, along with a host of economies throughout the world, experienced high unemployment and stagnant economic growth

In the late 1930s, there was a slight relaxation of controls following the creation of the Book Censorship Board. The board was devised in response to concerns about the arbitrary nature of the government's censorship practices. The board, a three-man team that had the task of advising the minister as to the suitability of imported publications, examined those titles that laid claim to some kind of literary merit. The board was regarded as a major improvement on the existing regime, relieving public servants and, more particularly, customs officers (who often had little to no training in such matters) of the responsibility for making decisions about the suitability of material. Fewer books were banned following the commencement of the board, although it was not uncommon for the minister to ignore or reverse its advice (Coleman 2000, pp. 30–5).

In the 1950s, the board became the pre-eminent authority in classifying books. The minister stopped overriding the board's decisions or banning publications without prior discussion, although retaining the legal right to take such action. From this point on, a period of 'qualified liberalism' prevailed. This trend, as we will see a little later in this chapter, gained momentum in the 1960s and the 1970s, and was extended to the Film Censorship Board, originally established in 1917 to examine imported films under Commonwealth customs regulations, and to register and classify films for public exhibition under state legislation (Griffith 2002, p. 9). In 1988, both the Book and Film Censorship boards were transferred to the Office of Film and Literature Classification (OFLC), and in 1996, following the establishment of a uniform classification scheme, the Classification Board was created (Libertus.net 2001).

Much like the print and film media, the government has taken an active interest in controlling the content that appears in the broadcast medium. Some of the early prohibitions imposed by the government were, by today's standards, quite petty. For example, radio licensees in the 1930s were required to ensure that their announcers were of good education, style and personality, and possessed of a clear enunciation, as far as possible free of characteristic dialect (Given 2003, p. 48). Also, up until the 1950s, radio stations could not broadcast jingles on a Sunday for reasons of religiosity. However, some of the restrictions were of a more serious nature. In 1923, there was a sweeping prohibition that 'all matters broadcasted shall be subject to such censorship as the Minister determines'. That meant that the minister could ban any program he chose. Similarly, up until the 1980s, a condition of licences was that licensees could not dramatise matters relating to any 'real' political event within five years of event or matter taking place (Given 2003, p. 49).

In 1992, a co-regulatory system was introduced to regulate the broadcasting industry, which replaced a more prescriptive government scheme. Under the new regime, responsibility for monitoring content, language and scheduling of transmissions was transferred from the Australian Broadcasting Authority (now the Australian Communications and Media Authority; ACMA) to the relevant industry bodies. While the system has been trumpeted in some quarters as a victory for greater liberalisation of the broadcasting media, others are concerned that self-regulation has produced a decline in programming standards. Opponents of the scheme were quick to point out the perils of self-regulation when in 2005 episodes of the reality television program *Big Brother* were found to have contained material that exceeded the appropriate classification standards. This, along with other instances, has prompted concerns that self-regulation is failing; a problem that many believe is amplified by the limited powers afforded to ACMA to discipline broadcasters for breaching standards.

Prescribing content

In addition to prohibiting certain types of media communications, the Australian government also requires that certain content must be made available to the public. That is, the government insists that certain ideas and images must be shown in the public interest. While most of us would not regard this as a form of censorship, some writers have argued that content prescription is censorship under a different guise. They argue that the compulsion to show particular material results in a situation whereby content that the public would otherwise have selected cannot be shown in order to create opportunities for the **prescribed** content to be viewed. To this way of thinking, censorship and prescription are merely the opposite side of the same coin.

> **prescribe** in this context, to issue an order or command that something must be done or shown

While Australian governments have a long history of prohibiting material, they have demonstrated a certain reticence to prescribe content. This has been particularly true in relation to Australian content. The first Act to regulate the broadcasting sector, the *Broadcasting Act 1942*, did not impose specific Australian content requirements, but rather exhorted licensees to give encouragement to Australian talent. This was supplemented with restrictions on the importation of foreign television programs and advertisements (Sinclair 1992, p. 24). Up until the 1960s, there had been little necessity for government to do more in this respect because television operated largely as a 'live medium', consisting of locally made programs. However, when the Australian Broadcasting Control Board (now ACMA), noted the displacement of live programs in favour of imported programs, a quota on Australian content was introduced (Sinclair 1992, p. 24). Moreover, the requirement to show particular content has been an obligation imposed almost exclusively on the broadcast media. The official rationale is that the broadcasting sector's dependence on radio frequency spectrum gives legitimacy to the imposition of quotas. Because of limited market entry (that is, restrictions on the number of broadcasting licences that are allocated), those who hold broadcasting licences do so in the knowledge that their privileged status carries public interest responsibilities in the form of obligations to make and show particular types of programs.

The arguments advanced in support of content prescription are slightly different to those used to justify the proscription of material. These include: nation building and preservation; the creation and preservation of Australia's cultural and social industries; and the protection of consumers.

NATION BUILDING AND PRESERVATION

Over the years, Commonwealth governments have maintained that the public's access to certain types of content was vital to the task of nation building. With the advent of the broadcasting medium, in particular, governments argued that it was important to show programs that would unify Australian society, and elevate its public both culturally and intellectually. Initially, governments took the initiative by creating a publicly funded broadcaster that produced programs that ostensibly catered to such objectives. However, in the 1960s, the government came under increased pressure to lift quotas on Australian content in order to defend the national identity from the onslaught of foreign programs, and US programs especially (see Sinclair 1992). In the case of the commercial radio sector, the government lifted the quota on Australian content while also specifying when that music must be played. The Australian content quota for radio was increased dramatically from five per cent (established in the 1950s) to 15 per cent in 1975 (Miller & Turner 2002, pp. 138–9). Under the present regime, the quota for Australian content varies depending on the genre of music played by the station, with current quotas ranging between five per cent and 25 per cent. Australian content requirements are underpinned by a desire to enable Australians to develop national confidence, pride and sense of community, and to have access to content that reflects the Australian experience.

THE CREATION AND PRESERVATION OF AUSTRALIA'S CULTURAL AND SOCIAL INDUSTRIES

Another objective served by content prescription is to assist in the creation and preservation of Australia's cultural industries. It is generally recognised that Australian commercial television broadcasters, in particular, will be tempted to buy cheap foreign imports rather than produce and license local material. Local content is expensive and carries a high degree of financial risk.

Australian broadcasters pay $50 000 per hour to license a new US drama, but upwards of $200 000 to $300 000 to license local content. Moreover, there is some uncertainty as to whether the broadcaster will be able to recoup the cost of the domestic program through advertising revenues. Whereas foreign programs that have proven popular in their local market are quick to attract a loyal following in Australia, first-release domestic programs struggle to attract similar levels of audience support (Productivity Commission 2000, pp. 166–7). Given the financial disincentives to create local content, the government imposes Australian content standards that require broadcasters to transmit local content. The current regime requires that 55 per cent of all programs shown between 6am and midnight must carry Australian content, with additional requirements for Australian first-release documentaries, children's television programs and Australian drama. In doing so, one of the government's aims is to provide opportunities for Australians to develop strong, viable creative industries.

THE PROTECTION OF CONSUMERS

The imposition of content requirements also reflects the concern that unless expressly directed by government, the commercial media are unlikely to accommodate the needs of all groups in society. Children's programming is a case in point. In the late 1970s, the 'C' (children's) classification and 'C' time were introduced to improve the quality and quantity of children's programming as a result of fears that the commercial media was failing to provide suitable children's content. The initiative was largely justified on the grounds that children had a right to programs that are geared to their needs, and that commercial broadcasters had a public interest responsibility to produce content appropriate for children. The current children's standard requires commercial television licensees to show 260 hours of children's programs, at least 130 hours of which must be **first release** per annum (25 hours of the 130 hours must be children's drama). In addition to this, broadcasters must show eight hours of repeat Australian 'C' drama and 130 hours of pre-school programs (Australian Communications and Media Authority 2007).

▶ **first release** programs that have not been televised and that are no more than two years old

Institutional and legal framework of content regulation

Unlike many of their Western counterparts, Australia's governments have few formal legal restrictions on their ability to regulate information flows and media content. This is because the federal Constitution does not carry an explicit right to free political speech or a free press. Australia has no equivalent to the first amendment found in the US Constitution, which protects American citizens from laws that attempt to abridge freedom of speech, or of the press.

In 1992, the Australian **High Court** did recognise a limited right to free political speech. The High Court found an implicit right to free speech contained within the Constitution on the basis that the text sets out a system of **representative** and **responsible government** (ss. 7 and 24). The High Court took the view that free political communication is essential in order to give effect to the system of democracy outlined in the Constitution. The High Court's ruling was a watershed in Australian law. In recognising that the Constitution carries an implied right to free political communication, it has imposed some constraints on the ability of Australia's governments to pass laws that hinder the individual's freedom to discuss political matters. However, it is still uncertain how much protection this ultimately affords to the individual or media organisations. In part, this is because the right is heavily qualified; that is, the right is limited and is not absolute. It appears that the right is restricted to discussions of a political nature only (federal, state or territory). This is thought to include discussions about the conduct or fitness of elected members; political parties, public bodies and officers; those seeking public office; government conduct, policy and legislation; and political views about persons who are engaged in activities that are the subject of political debate. Moreover, there appear to be limits when this right can be invoked as a defence in a defamation suit. It seems that the implied right to free political communication can only be used as a defence where it can be established that the defendant had reasonable grounds for believing the information was true; took proper steps to establish the veracity information; and was not motivated by malice (or an improper motive) (Spry 1997). As it stands, the media typically do not use this as a defence in legal proceedings (political qualified privilege), relying on it as a 'back-up' defence only (Pearson 2004, p. 211).

The absence of explicit constitutional protections essentially gives the government a broad hand to legislate as it likes, with few formal restrictions (see Box 7.1). The government mostly regulates media content through **statute**. 'Statute' refers to laws made by and in Parliament, and is the most direct expression of the government's ability to restrict and regulate content in Australia, as well as other politically sensitive information. As we will see in Chapter 11, the government has at its disposal various laws that it can invoke to prevent the distribution of material it believes would undermine the national interest if made public. However, the most important laws for purposes of this chapter can be grouped loosely under one of two broad headings: censorship laws and broadcasting laws.

▶ **High Court** the highest legal body in Australia, which, among other things, is charged with the responsibility of interpreting the Australian Constitution

▶ **representative** a form of democracy wherein voters choose representatives to act on their behalf

▶ **responsible government** a form of government wherein the party or parties that win the most seats in the lower house of Parliament, or have the support of a majority of members in that house, form the government of the day

▶ **statutes** laws that have been devised and sanctioned by Parliament

CENSORSHIP LAWS

Censorship laws apply to film, printed material, videos and video games. While both the Commonwealth and the state governments have their own censorship legislation, the Commonwealth is largely responsible for classifying material, and the states enforce and police the classification. Since the mid 1990s, Australia has operated under a uniform classification regime. There are, however, some lingering variations in that: Tasmania and WA have retained the right to classify publications; Queensland has the power to classify both publications and computer games; and most of the states and territories have some provision contained within legislation that allows them to override classification decisions made by the Classification Board (Griffith 2002, p. 15).

The Commonwealth principally regulates film and video, publications and video games using the *Classification Act 1995*. The *Classification Act* requires that material of a commercial nature, with some exceptions, must be classified before it can be displayed or sold legally in Australia. This gives rise to restrictions on:

- *What can be viewed*—Australians do not have a right to view and access material just because it exists, or because the material is of personal interest. Some content is denied to the public because it is regarded as inappropriate for consumption. The justification for banning material is that the content is so obscene that it is likely to offend the sensibilities of the average person. This can result in the material being banned or, in some cases, the offending section or parts deleted from the media product.
- *Who can view particular content*—Some content is legally available to adults but restricted to children, or persons under the age of 18 years; that is, certain content is classified and subject to graded access.
- *The conditions under which certain content can be accessed*—Certain content can be accessed provided it is done so under particular conditions. This generally requires the consumer to actively seek out and request the material, as in the case of certain types of magazines. Not only is the circulation of the material limited to certain places (or times), but it is often packaged in a particular manner. Classification of material is justified on the basis that the material is not so offensive that it should be banned, but that it is sufficiently offensive that it should not be displayed openly or be easy to access.

The task of classifying content falls to the Classification Board, which consists of a Director, Deputy Director, two senior classifiers and five full-time members, with some provision for part-time members also. The *Classification Act* limits the number of members to a maximum of 20, and an appointee can only serve on the board for a maximum of seven years. The **Governor-General** selects the board on the advice of the Attorney-General. In effect, this means that the Attorney-General determines board appointments. When considering new appointments to the board, the law requires the minister to consider applicants who are 'broadly representative of the Australian public' and to consult with his/her counterparts in the states and territories before appointing permanent members.

▶ **Governor-General** the Queen's representative in Australia; the formal head of the Australian state

Once appointed, the board is nominally independent from the minister. While the board assumes full responsibility for the classification of materials, it is not permitted to classify material according to the private views of its members. As Griffith explains: 'The classifiers play a dual role, as experts who are also representative of the community at large, who are charged with the task of interpreting and applying th[e] normative schema on the community's behalf' (2002, p. 8). The 'normative schema' is set down in two documents. The first of these is the Classification Code. The code establishes the available ratings that the board can assign to relevant media content. In addition to the code, the board is required to heed the Classification Guidelines. These guidelines describe the criteria for assessing material. There is a separate classification schema for each of film and video, computer games, and books and magazines.

Box 7.1 Censoring suicide

In 2006, the federal government amended the law to criminalise certain types of internet usage. More particularly, the Act (*Criminal Code Amendment: Suicide Related Material Offences*) makes it an offence to use the internet to incite, counsel or propose suicide.

The government justified the Act on the grounds that it was seeking to protect vulnerable internet users who may be targeted and encouraged to take their own lives (especially teenagers), citing the trend in Japan of strangers arranging suicide pacts over internet suicide chat rooms. The government claimed that its intention was not to stifle debate about euthanasia, but to make it unlawful to publish any information that encouraged an individual to take their own life. The Act, according to the government, simply seeks to 'recognise the harm that can be done by those who use the internet with a destructive intent' (Hansard 2005, pp. 4–5). The Australian Federation of Right to Life Associations, the peak body of pro-life groups, also supported the Act, concerned that 'do-it-yourself suicide has become a cult movement' and a 'simple' solution to what is an essentially complex problem (Woolfe 2006).

A number of groups oppose the Act. The journalist's union, the MEAA, is worried that the new legislation will undermine press freedom and the ability of journalists to report on politically sensitive matters, such as euthanasia. Electronic Frontiers Australia, a non-profit organisation concerned with online freedoms and rights, has complained that the new Act is poorly constructed, with the capacity to 'chill freedom of political communication'. Barnes argues that the Act is problematic in that it criminalises 'the conduct of thousands of humane and compassionate Australians' who 'genuinely believe that dying with dignity is a fundamental human right of us all' (Barnes 2006). His concern is that the Act will not simply punish unscrupulous individuals who target vulnerable teenagers, but also those members of the community who, for genuine reasons, are wishing to explore different methods for terminating their life, and those who wish to assist them.

Is the government right to make it unlawful for people to use the internet to discuss 'incite, counsel or provide instruction on suicide'?

BROADCASTING LAWS

Whereas censorship laws apply to the regulation of film, print and computer games, the commercial and community broadcasting sector is subject to broadcasting laws. The broadcasting sector is regulated by the Commonwealth government under the *Australian Broadcasting Services Act 1992*. This Act also regulates the internet. Both SBS and the ABC are regulated under their own Acts.

There are a number of mechanisms that regulate the broadcasting sector that arise from the *Australian Broadcasting Services Act 1992* and other relevant Acts. These include:

- *Licence conditions*—This is a list of 'dos' and 'don'ts' for licence holders that are mandatory conditions attached to broadcasting licences. Conditions vary depending on the category of broadcasting service, and licensees face prosecution for breaching licence provisions. One example of a licence condition is the requirement that licensees must broadcast items of national interest without charge if directed by the minister.

- *Codes of practice*—All media sectors and licence holders are required to develop codes of practice that they must make publicly available by lodging them with ACMA. The codes should address the twelve general principles set out in s. 123 of the *Australian Broadcasting Services Act 1992*. Examples of the matters that may be addressed by the codes include such things as ensuring that methods for classifying programs reflect community standards; promoting accuracy and fairness in news and current affairs programs; and captioning of programs for the hearing impaired.
- *Program standards*—These are intended to supplement the codes of practice, and relate mostly to requirements for children and Australian content that must be shown on commercial broadcasting services. Examples of program standards are the *Broadcasting Services (Australian Content) Standard 1999 (ACS)* and *Television Program Standard 23*, both of which regulate the Australian content of advertising on commercial television (Butler & Roderick 2004, p. 526).

Box 7.2   X-rated material

There are many things that are either prohibited or required content under Australian law. The list is quite long. Essentially, a person cannot display, possess or sell printed material that has been 'Refused Classification' (banned). To do so in Western Australia, for example, can result in fines of up to $15000 and 18 months' imprisonment. Similarly, showing a film that has not been classified can result in a $10000 fine.

One issue that has proven contentious is the treatment of adult pornography, or X-rated films. 'X-rated' is defined as material that is sexually explicit, but which is consensual and not accompanied by depictions of certain fetishes and violence. In all of the Australian states, it is illegal to purchase such material. While X-rated material cannot be bought in any of the Australian states, it can be lawfully purchased in the Australian Capital Territory and the Northern Territory.

Do you think Australia is too strict in relation to regulation of adult material? Is there a case to be made for allowing X-rated films to be legally sold in all Australian states and not just the territories?

Debates and controversy: from the morality test to the reasonable adult test

The laws devised by governments to regulate media content are, understandably, of importance to the public. It is the material that the government prohibits, rather than the material that it prescribes, that draws heated public discussion. Over the years, various groups have sought to lobby the government on the issue of content prohibition. On one side of the debate are the pro-censorship groups: typically groups with strong religious affiliations, such as Media Standards Australia and the Lyons Forum. On the other side is the anti-censorship lobby: groups such as Libertus that are strongly opposed to restrictions on the grounds that it infringes important civil liberties.

It is the government's responsibility to reconcile the interests of pro- and anti-censorship groups. The government must strike a balance (or at least be seen to) between the right of adults to see and watch what they wish, against the right of those who do not wish to be confronted by material they believe to be injurious to the social good. This is a difficult task due to the zero-sum nature of the demands made by the two groups. Any gains made by one group will inevitably come at the expense of the other, ultimately making it difficult for government to develop policy that satisfies either camp.

As explained at the beginning of this chapter, content restrictions and censorship are justified in terms of a public benefit argument (for example, to protect the innocent) and to maintain public standards. For a long time, the test of whether something was obscene as to warrant censorship was the morality test. The morality test was predicated on the view that offensive and obscene material could be identified on the basis that it possessed the power to deprave and corrupt the individual exposed to it—it was obscene because it induced sinful and immoral thoughts (Butler & Rodrick 2004, p. 390).

This definition of obscenity was used up until the early 1980s to prohibit the importation of certain material and to ban locally made items. However, the 'morality' test was considered unsatisfactory by many because it was always a little unclear whose moral code was being applied in such circumstances (Butler & Rodrick 2004, p. 390). That is, just because certain material might induce sinful and immoral thoughts in one person, it did not necessarily follow that it would engender the same response in another. Quite apart from this, it took away the individual's right to decide these matters for themselves, shifting the responsibility to government officials.

It was the courts that were the first to begin the revolt against this definition of obscenity; that is, the power to deprave and corrupt. In the late 1960s, Justice Barwick of the High Court took to task the meaning of both obscenity and indecency. He argued that material could only be construed as indecent if it offended the modesty of the average person in sexual matters. A colleague, Justice Windeyer, was to later suggest that obscenity was better defined as material that 'transgressed the contemporary standards of decency of the Australian community' (Williams 1997a, p. 7). In proposing that the test of obscenity should be offence to the modesty of the average person, it opened up the possibility that obscenity was not inherent in the subject matter, but dependent on both the context and audience to which it is shown (Gaze & Jones 1990, p. 382).

In the late 1960s, the federal Australian Labor Party adopted a new party platform on censorship. It basically stated that, as a general principle, adults should be entitled to view and see what they wished. Eventually, parliaments around the country began to also question the usefulness of the 'morality test'. They largely turned to the standards or ideas being expressed by the courts, which is a principle referred to as the 'reasonable adult test'. The 'reasonable adult' test is simply that decisions about the suitability of material for public consumption should be based on what a 'reasonable (moderate) adult' is willing to tolerate, even if they do not wish to view the material. By the 1970s, most, if not all, states had enshrined the 'reasonable adult test' in legislation, with the Commonwealth following suit in 1984 (Williams 1997, p. 7). One of the advantages of this new test is that it gives authorities a greater array of options when dealing with sensitive material. It is now possible to 'classify' material rather than simply banning it, deleting the offending sections or parts, or, in some cases, dealing with the problem by simply attempting to ignore the existence of the material.

The concept of classification essentially allows the government to better balance the rights of those who wish to view certain material against those who do not want to be exposed to unsolicited material, but who do not care if others wish to view it. It essentially permits consenting adults to access certain types of pornography while simultaneously ensuring that the abstainers do not have to worry about seeing that material displayed openly on their television or supermarket shelves.

It is the Classification Board that is largely required to give effect to the 'reasonable adult' test when classifying films, videos and DVDs. Essentially, the *Classification Act* delegates the responsibility for determining whether material is fit for public consumption to the board. Under the *Classification Act*, the board is provided with guidelines before making a decision about material.

According to the Classification Code, all decisions of the board are to be guided by four basic principles:

- Adults should be able to read, hear and see what they want.
- Minors should be protected from material likely to harm or disturb them.
- Everyone should be protected from exposure to unsolicited material that they find offensive.
- There is a need to take account of community concerns about depictions that condone or incite violence, particularly sexual violence; and the portrayal of a person in a demeaning manner.

In doing this, they are required to take into account a range of factors such as:

- standards of morality and decency accepted by a reasonable adult
- the literary, artistic or educational merit of the material
- the general character of the material; that is, a depiction of an explicit sexual act is acceptable if it is for a medical textbook, but a similar picture in a different type of publication might have to be sold under special conditions
- the intended audience to whom the material is marketed.

While the reasonable adult test is viewed as an improvement on the 'morality test', it is not devoid of problems. The weakness of the test is that, like its antecedent, it is highly subjective. There is the problem of identifying the qualities a reasonable person can be expected to possess. Is a person who is opposed to soft-core pornography any more or less reasonable or moderate than a person who is not? Second, how does one determine prevailing community standards, which is the second aspect of the test? It is questionable whether there is such a thing as a uniform 'community' standard, or a common set of values shared by all people living in Australia. It has been argued that one's 'standards' are heavily conditioned by race, gender, geography and even age. Given Australia's diverse and scattered population, can we expect that Australians are able to reach consensus on such matters? There is the further problem of knowing who should assume the responsibility for determining such matters. Who is most competent at sketching the profile of a reasonable adult or assessing the community standard? Are the courts best suited to this task, or bureaucrats, psychologists, community panels or politicians? While the 'reasonable adult test' has provided improved access to material that would have ordinarily been censored, it has not necessarily lessened the inherent subjectivity of the test. It remains the case that those who are left to administer the law have little to guide them other than some nebulous notion of what is 'reasonable' to the community at large.

While the 'reasonable adult' test fails to remedy all the problems associated with the preceding regime, there was a relaxation of censorship following its adoption. A summary glance of the Classification Board's decisions in 2005–06 indicate that it is not overly censorial—only a small proportion of material was refused classification. The board refused classification to seven out of 1106 commercial publications; 30 out of 6516 commercial films and three out of 759 computer games submitted for classification (OFLC 2006). This shows, despite flaws in the system, that Australians have reasonable access to all forms of media, with the censors largely operating in the spirit of the liberal democratic ethos.

SUMMARY

This chapter has illustrated that Australia has a long history of censorship, a practice that is not inconsistent with liberal democratic values. Liberals recognise the benefits of censorship, although they often disagree about what content should be denied and the objectives that should be served in doing so. The chapter also discussed the role and importance of content prescription, noting that the broadcasting sector, unlike other media industries, is required by law to show Australian content. The government justifies content prescription on a number of bases, key among them the preservation and maintenance of Australia's cultural identity and creative industries. More specifically, the chapter has attempted to demonstrate that while the subject of content prescription is not without controversy, it is the issue of censorship that has the greatest capacity to polarise public opinion. Policymakers have, historically, erred on the side of caution, suppressing any material that they believed had the power to deprave and corrupt. Today, the 'reasonable adult' test forms the basis for classifying most forms of Australian content. While the 'reasonable adult' test is generally regarded as an advancement on the previous regime, it is problematic nonetheless. Whereas some groups regard the prevailing system as too liberal, others argue that it is not liberal enough. Despite the best efforts of Australia's policymakers to devise a system that satisfies all members of society, it has ultimately proven a near-impossible task.

Questions

1 What kinds of communications should be prohibited, and what criteria should be used when making such determinations? Is it illiberal to ban communications because certain content is likely to be offensive or undermines an individual's standing in the broader community?
2 Is there a strong case for the abolition of Australian and children's content for the broadcasting sector?
3 Would Australians necessarily benefit from the inclusion of a guarantee of a free press within the Constitution?
4 Do you think the criteria and principles contained in the Classification Code are 'reasonable'?

WEBSITES

Electronic Frontiers Australia Inc (EFA)—A non-profit national organisation representing internet users concerned with online freedoms and rights. EFA was formed in 1994 to protect and promote the civil liberties of users and operators of computer-based communications systems (http://www.efa.org.au/Issues/Censor/).

Libertus.net—Provided and maintained by Irene Graham, it has information about the history and state of censorship of films, publications and computer games in Australia. This website is opposed to censorship (http://libertus.net/).

Media Standards Australia Inc—Formerly the National Viewers and Listeners Association of Australia, it aims to influence the media to adopt more conservative policies, particularly in relation to sex and violence (http://www. mediastandards.org/).

Office of Film and Literature Classification (OFLC)—A federal government website that contains information relevant to Australian censorship law. It includes information on the Classification Board, Classification Review Board and the OFLC, as well as other aspects of the National Classification Scheme (http:// www.oflc.gov.au/special.html).

Chopping list: banned and censored movies in Australia—Provides an unofficial list of movies that have been banned by Australian censors (http://www.cosmos.net. au/~hologram/chopping/list_home.html).

FURTHER READING

Coleman, P. 2000, *Obscenity, Blasphemy, Sedition: The Rise and Fall of Literary Censorship in Australia*. Duffy and Snellgrove: Sydney.

Jackson, K. 2001, 'Censorship and Classification in Australia'. *E-Brief.* Australian Parliamentary Library: Canberra.

NEW DEVELOPMENTS IN MEDIA OWNERSHIP

8

This chapter will:

- trace the history of media ownership regulation in Australia and the development of privately owned media corporations
- critically analyse government policy towards broadcasting policy, the relationship between political parties and media corporations, and the importance of incumbent media owners in the development of media policy
- discuss the relevance of new technology to issues of media ownership and diversity.

The diversity principle

A free and independent media is crucial to our conception of democracy. Our democratic institutions cannot flourish without considerable freedom for the media to scrutinise the operations of government. Media outlets promote the notion of the media as the 'fourth estate' to argue against government intervention in their work. However, this ideal of a free media at the heart of democracy does more than provide a rationale for allowing the media to remain as free as possible from government control. It has also, particularly in the twentieth century, served as a justification for the state to make sure that the media are equipped to do their job properly—regulating or owning media outlets if necessary. Media regulation is therefore a balance between intervening for the public good and ensuring that media outlets, including those owned by the government, are free to criticise government policy. Government intervention in commercial media ownership rests heavily on the promotion of diversity. As unobjectionable as the concept of diversity may seem, there is much debate over how best to achieve it. Further, high-minded principles about the role and importance of the media often come a poor second to the machinations of political and corporate power when media policy is implemented.

One role of an independent media is to provide a marketplace of ideas. The marketplace metaphor works on a number of levels. Like any market, competition is important to the efficiency and vitality of production. We expect governments to intervene in markets to limit the power of any single player. The Australian Competition and Consumer Commission (ACCC) plays this role in the wider economy, approving mergers and takeovers under the *Trade Practices Act 1975*. Of course, the media are, as Schultz points out, 'not just another business' (1994a). The media are often referred to as the consciousness industry. In recognition of this importance, extensive legislation governing media ownership is now a crucial arm of public policy across the industrialised world. Diverse ownership of the media is important to ensure the expression of points of view antagonistic to the government and the prevailing orthodoxy on any given issue. This helps to ensure 'informed decision-making, cultural pluralism, citizen welfare, and a well-functioning democracy' (Napoli 1999a, p. 9). As you can see, democracy has quite a lot riding on the principle of diversity. It's worth, then, thinking critically about some of the assumptions underpinning the relationship between a diverse media and a healthy democracy.

Box 8.1 A diversity of diversity

Napoli (1999a) divides the concept of diversity into content diversity, source diversity and exposure diversity. There's not much point in having a diverse range of sources of information if they are all catering to the same segment of the market. We also need to pay attention to who it is that produces radio and television programs, not just who it is that broadcasts them. The number of production houses might be greater or smaller than the number of distributors. The people employed by the media might be drawn from a narrow segment of society—out of touch with the concerns of the rest of us. Exposure diversity refers to the range of views to which any individual might be exposed. A well-rounded citizen should be exposed to a range of points of view on any given issue.

Providing a diversity of sources does not, however, guarantee a diversity of ideas. The television series *Frontline* brilliantly satirised the banality and similarity of supposedly competitive commercial television current affairs programs. This lack of genuine choice comes about because different media outlets are often trying to appeal to the same audience demographic.

Think about the concept of diversity. What types of diversity do you value as a consumer of media, and as a citizen in a democracy?

Another question mark over the relationship between diversity and democracy stems from the potential of new technologies to provide much more diversity in broadcasting. We might be impressed by the availability of hundreds of channels through digital pay television, but that content diversity may actually narrow the rate of exposure diversity. Having a number of 24-hour news channels might increase the availability and range of news on television, but that is meaningless if we choose to watch the 24-hour drama, comedy, sport or music channels instead. By contrast, the much narrower choices available on free-to-air television obliges most viewers to watch the news in the evening. In a digital environment, then, society could become polarised between those who consume lots of news and those who consume little or no news. Lamenting the lack of serious news and current affairs on commercial broadcasters, John Doyle (2005) has argued that 'commercial radio is so slight because it is under-resourced; so, too, is television. And if more channels are allowed then the resources will be even further stretched'. Expensive programming, such as news gathering and drama, may be un-affordable in a more competitive market.

We might also question the value of a diverse newspaper market. Londoners have a much larger choice of newspapers than Australians. British newspapers therefore appeal to a smaller segment of society than papers such as the *Australian* and the *Sydney Morning Herald*. While this facilitates newspapers that are distinctly left or right wing in their orientation, regular readers of such newspapers are exposed to a more limited range of views than readers of Australian broadsheets, which must appeal to a wider segment of the market. Australian newspapers are more likely to act as a 'forum' for a range of ideological viewpoints than their British counterparts due to the differing nature of the two markets. In our discussion of diversity, then, we need to recognise that a diversity of media sources does not mean that each citizen is being exposed to a range of political views. Further, ensuring a diverse range of media content and sources may not have much impact if most of us choose to consume only a fraction of that diversity (Napoli 1999a, p. 28). All of this will, in turn, have consequences on the level of political awareness in our society. Diversity is not an end in itself.

Moguls, mates and ministers

Politics is all about power, its effects and its distribution. Parliaments take an interest in what media outlets get up to because they believe that those outlets have power: the power to project images of politicians, set the political agenda, debate important issues and influence the outcome of elections. The large and growing companies that dominate the Australian media today have their roots in private family ownership of metropolitan newspapers. The Packers, the Fairfaxes and the Murdochs are the most famous of these. These newspaper families had a strong ethos about the proper role of the media in society. Newspapers have historically led passionate campaigns for or against governments and the major issues of the day. In turn, politicians have always been very conscious of the power of media moguls. Look at this quote from Eric Beecher, a former editor of the *Sydney Morning Herald*:

> The issue is power. Real raw power that derives from owning or controlling the most effective instruments of influence within a democracy, outside the parliamentary system—newspapers. For it is the nature of this power, were it ever to be more widely understood, that would turn the debate about newspaper ownership … into a mainstream polemic about the instruments of democracy and whether or not they are functioning properly. If you have ever

seen, as I have, the sweating palms and shaking glass of one of Australia's most senior politicians after an unsatisfactory audience with a powerful newspaper proprietor, you would begin to understand something about why Australian politicians will never enter into this debate unless it is forced on them (cited in Schultz 2002, pp. 106–7.).

This is a compelling portrait of power. Australian history is replete with stories of media moguls intervening in Australian politics. Unhappy with the election of the Scullin Labor government in 1929, Sir Keith Murdoch, then proprietor of the *Melbourne Herald*, encouraged Joseph Lyons to break from Labor to form a new conservative party, the United Australia Party (Ward 1995, p. 125). The modern ALP has the memory of the dismissal of the Whitlam government ingrained in its culture. Part of that Labor mythology is the role of Rupert Murdoch using his newspaper to campaign against the government (Tiffen 2002, p. 43). Former Liberal Prime Minister Malcolm Fraser described the pressures from media proprietors as 'conversations and lobbying and the sorts of activities that politicians are very much aware of … [I]f that pressure is coming from one or two extraordinarily dominant media owners, it can get very difficult' (cited in Schultz 1998, p. 82).

Politicians, then, are only too aware of the power of the media. Of course, there are always constraints on media owners that give us reason to question the veracity of such stories. For example, the scale of the loss of the Whitlam government in 1975 suggests that many factors were at work. It is necessary for us to consider the **structural power** of the media, in addition to the power of individual media barons. Part of that structural power is the ability of the media to filter debate about itself and its future.

> **structural power** a consequence of the inherent importance of a particular section of society, such as the role of the media in reporting on politics

What about Beecher's claim that media ownership would become a potent political issue if the public knew of its importance in shaping political debate? We have limited evidence of what the pubic thinks about media ownership, but most of it tells us that Australians are as suspicious of media power as they are of other powerful institutions. According to the Australian Attitudes Survey, 81 per cent of Australians agree that media ownership is too concentrated, and 70 per cent agree that the mass media has too much power (Denemark 2005, p. 233). Nevertheless, it is difficult to think of an election where media policy figured prominently. Issues such as national security, the economy, health and education tend to dominate election campaigns even when the parties are divided over media policy, as is frequently the case.

Some argue that media elites enjoy a good deal of autonomy, both from the owners of the corporations that employ them, and from the wider society. Former *Media Watch* host David Marr's claim that journalistic culture is 'vaguely soft left' (2004) stands in stark comparison to the often conservative views of media proprietors. In a similar vein, if media owners and journalists are drawn from a narrow section of society, they will inevitably have similar points of view on a range of issues. Lord Beaverbrook, then proprietor of London's *Daily Express*, told the 1948 Royal Commission on the Press that while he owned the paper 'purely for propaganda and for no other object', its utility for that purpose was dependent on its being in 'a thoroughly good financial position' (cited in Murdock 1982, p. 137). Further, regardless of who owns or edits a newspaper, incumbent owners inherit a culture, including a group of journalists and readers with a set of expectations of the purpose of the newspaper. While concentration of ownership may give greater weight to any single media outlet, it also forces each outlet to appeal to a wider cross-section of the population. Too much barracking for one side of politics inevitably alienates part of the audience.

We can think of power in our society as a series of structures that both enable and limit the power of any given actor. The structural power of the media lies in the direct access it gives to millions of readers, listeners and viewers. This access is important to advertisers, politicians and interest groups, and gives power to those who can control that access. Structural limits on corporate power in the media include consumer sovereignty (our ability to change the channel or buy a different newspaper), the need to attract advertisers, the more general need to make profits and, more generally still, the desire for a supportive business environment. We should not expect to see many newspaper owners promoting the virtues of socialism, although **Karl Marx** had a long career as a newspaper columnist. Neither of these views about autonomy and limiting structures can be entirely correct, and media owners, editors and journalists naturally make choices every day within certain constraints (Murdock 1982, p. 125).

> **Karl Marx** a key nineteenth-century thinker and co-author (with Frederick Engels) of *The Communist Manifesto*

These constrained choices are always on display in the way that media outlets cover politics. For example, News Corporation newspapers have been very supportive of the Howard Government, in particular its agenda of freeing business from government regulation. All News Corporation newspapers editorialised in favour of re-electing the Howard Government at the 2004 election. Yet, the *Australian* continually hounded the Howard Government to release documents under the *Freedom of Information Act*. In particular, the paper sought a series of documents from the Treasury that contradicted government claims over taxation and industrial relations reform. This apparent contradiction comes about because, regardless of the editorial position of the newspaper or its parent company, owners wish to sell as many of their papers as possible. One of the best ways to ensure this is to break big news stories. Journalists have a role to play in reporting politics regardless of the editorial position of their employer. Members of the public, whichever way they intend to vote, expect the media to scrutinise the operations of government. Indeed, the *Australian* itself is the product of a media proprietor paying attention to values other than the corporate bottom line. Rupert Murdoch, steeped in the fourth-estate values of his father, established the paper in 1964 and ran it at a loss for many years with an eye towards the prestige and influence available only through a national daily newspaper.

Box 8.2   Playing politics

There are a number of ways for media owners to influence politics other than through their media outlets. Lobbying politicians, either directly or through peak organisations such as Free TV Australia, is one option. Another is to donate money to political parties. This enables, at the very least, access to ministers responsible for developing media policy.

Disclosures for the period including the 2004 federal elections, published by the Australian Electoral Commission (www.aec.gov.au), include many donations by media companies to both the major political parties. Donations to the Liberal Party from individual members of the Stokes, Murdoch and Fairfax families totalled tens of thousands of dollars. Village Roadshow, owners of the Austereo radio network, donated close to half a million dollars, split between the major parties. Network Ten gave the big parties $75 000 dollars each. APN News and Media gave $75 000 to the Labor Party. Harold Mitchell, who places advertising for Labor, donated $25 000 to the party's Victorian Branch. Evan Thornley, with interests in Looksmart and Pluto Press, donated $35 000 to the ALP in Victoria. Thornley entered the Victorian upper house at the 2006 election. The Packer family donated to both parties through companies such as Burswood Casino and Channel Nine. Just how much influence such donations buy in the context of the tens of millions of dollars raised by the major parties is difficult to assess. It's hard to imagine any minister refusing to meet executives of media companies regardless of what political donations they make, due to the structural power of the media. That might explain the absence of News Corporation from the AEC disclosure list. Not surprisingly, donations to political parties, particularly those by media companies, are rarely front-page news.

Media owners are inherently interested in the machinations of politics, but also become directly involved in political parties. James Packer has long been a member of the Liberal Party in Sydney. He played a role in the elevation of former Packer employee Malcolm Turnbull to Parliament in the blue-ribbon seat of Wentworth. Politicians find their way into the media, too. Former Treasurer of the federal Liberal Party, Ron Walker, became chairman of Fairfax in 2005. ALP powerbroker Graeme Richardson worked for PBL after retiring from politics. This is all part of the interdependence of politics and the media.

Do you think media companies should be allowed to make donations to political parties? What do the media companies get in return?

Another reason for the decline in overt political partisanship in recent decades is the fading influence of the politically connected families of the old media barons. For various reasons, privately owned media companies have almost all become public companies. Corporations take a pragmatic approach to politics, not wishing to offend any political party if doing so could damage their bottom line. Just as importantly, one of the features of the professionalised modern Australian Labor Party has been a greater willingness to forge links with corporate Australia generally, including media companies.

In contrast to the ethos of media-owning families, corporations tend to look first and foremost to their economic bottom line. Australia has been slower than other parts of the world to follow the trend towards exclusively corporate ownership of the media. Hence, the debate about media and politics in this country still tends to revolve around families such as the Murdochs and the Packers.

The evolution of media ownership law in Australia

When newspapers were the dominant media well into the twentieth century, restrictions on their ownership were deemed unnecessary, given the competitive nature of the market. Compared with today's newspaper market, where the twelve major capital city and national papers are owned by four companies (ten of them by two companies), the situation a century earlier, where twenty-one such papers were shared between seventeen owners, looks quite diverse (Ward 1995, p. 126). Regulation of the print media remains for the most part a state government function. The emergence of wireless broadcasting in the early part of the twentieth century saw the federal government take an interventionist role. (Section 51(v) of the Australian Constitution gives the federal government power over 'postal, telegraphic, telephonic, and other like services'.) Australian governments have chosen to intervene in the broadcasting market in a number of ways. The Commonwealth's trade and corporations powers (ss. 51(i) and 51(xx) of the Constitution) give the federal government the power to regulate commercial activity, including the ownership of all forms of media.

The airwaves are a scarce public resource. The government therefore has an obligation to ensure that there is a public benefit from any utilisation of that resource (Brown 2000, p. 49). At the very least, governments need to ensure that broadcasting spectrum is allocated in an orderly manner to prevent signals interfering with each other. Therefore, broadcasting from the very beginning has been regulated in a quite different way from newspapers. In the electronic media, Australia has a system of mixed public and private ownership. European countries tend to have a higher level of public broadcasting, while the USA provides a model for predominantly private broadcasting.

Most countries restrict foreign ownership of the media in some way. There are a number of arguments for restricting foreign ownership. First, the idea of foreign entities being able to influence domestic elections worries many people. Second, strategic assets such as finance, manufacturing and infrastructure have been historically protected from foreign ownership for reasons of national defence. In recent decades, such arguments have lost out to the worldwide trend towards free capital markets, although many restrictions persist. When News Corporation bought the Fox television network in the USA, Rupert Murdoch was forced to relinquish his Australian citizenship. News's subsequent shift of its corporate headquarters to the USA makes it an essentially American company. Australia's laws limiting foreign ownership prevented *new* acquisitions by foreign companies, allowing existing holdings to persist.

One of the most important decisions on media regulation in Australia was that of the Menzies government's distribution of commercial television broadcast licences in the late 1950s. A Royal Commission on Television recommended that issuing television licences to existing media interests was a logical step, given the existing expertise of these companies. The fact that many of these interests were supportive of the government no doubt was an important consideration as well (Griffen-Foley 2003, p. 64). By the 1960s, ownership of licences in Sydney and Melbourne allowed the creation of de facto networks for Seven and Nine, owned by the Fairfaxes and the Packers respectively. The pattern of broadcasting policy favouring the interests of incumbent media companies instead of potential competitors (to say nothing of the public interest) was well established. Not a single commercial radio licence was issued in metropolitan areas in the three decades before the introduction of FM in the 1970s (Papandrea 2001, p. 66).

Cross-media laws

The main feature of private media ownership in Australia in recent decades has been the restriction on **cross-media ownership**, introduced in the *Broadcasting (Ownership and Control) Act 1987*. As the then Treasurer Paul Keating put it, proprietors could either be 'queens of the screen, or princes of print, but not both'. This was the first instance of the federal government intervening in newspaper ownership, through its trade practices power.

After an industry shake-up caused in large part by the new laws, a few big companies now dominate the industry. Virtually every television and radio station in the capital cities changed hands. PBL sold Channel Nine to Bond Media for a billion dollars—buying it back after the 1987 stock market crash for considerably less. News Ltd acquired the Herald and Weekly Times group after promising the competition regulator to sell a newspaper in each of those cities where the merged entity would have a monopoly. However, when two of the papers concerned, the Brisbane *Sun* and Adelaide *News*, were subsequently closed down in controversial circumstances, Murdoch had sidestepped the regulator and retained his monopoly. As it turned out, Rupert Murdoch emerged as a king, rather than a prince, of print. (Schultz 2002, p. 110)

cross-media ownership laws that until 2007 limited media companies to one type of platform—television, radio or newspapers—in each market

The *Broadcasting Services Act 1992* maintained the cross-media restrictions, but relaxed some of the market concentration and foreign investment rules. Removing foreign ownership restrictions on commercial radio allowed British company DMG to bid for new FM licences and develop the Nova and Vega networks. The entry of this foreign competitor into the market has shaken up a concentrated and complacent industry. Ownership of two radio licences are now allowed in each capital city. Combined with the shift to industry co-regulation of content, the development of national networks in a hitherto localised industry marked a major change (Miller & Turner 2002, p. 142). As we saw in the case of media content, media laws need to be interpreted by government regulators. Where ownership is concerned, the issue of who controls the company is all important. A Canadian company, Canwest, took a controlling interest in Channel Ten in the 1990s, apparently in contravention of laws restricting foreign ownership of television licences. Numerous inquiries by government regulators have accepted Canwest's argument that it does not have control of the board of Channel Ten, allowing smaller shareholders additional voting rights.

The Keating government attempted to increase diversity in the Australian media by restricting some pay-television licences to new owners. Incumbent free-to-air licence holders had successfully lobbied against the introduction of pay television in Australia (it began in the USA in the 1950s). Restrictions on advertising and content in the new medium affected profitability, and most of the new operations failed. This episode supports one of the arguments in favour of allowing incumbent players to lead the way in new platforms, since they have experience in the media industry. The most important decision surrounding pay television was to allow the owners of infrastructure to also provide content (allowing Telstra and Optus to own the dominant providers). This misguided attempt to let the market decide how pay television would operate allowed the owners of the infrastructure to dictate terms to content providers such as the failed C7 sports channel (later the subject of prolonged legal action). The pay-television industry settled down to a comfortable monopoly when Optus agreed to reduce its role to that of a reseller of Foxtel programming. With Foxtel co-owned by Telstra, News Corp and PBL, the notion that pay television would be a competitor to the incumbent media interests was nowhere to be seen.

Some new technologies are difficult for the government to delay because they have an impact not just upon the media that provides our news and entertainment, but also communication across the economy. **Digitisation** of television and telephony has the potential to reduce the scarcity of broad-casting spectrum, and therefore put the profitability of incumbent licence holders at risk. Unfortunately, the legislation to regulate digitisation provides an example of public policy at its worst. Incumbent networks were divided over multi-channelling (using the allocated spectrum to broadcast more than one signal). The market leader, Channel Nine, receives a premium for delivering a mass audience to its advertisers. It had no interest in segmenting its own market, or doing anything with free-to-air television that would undermine its investment in pay television.

▶ **digitisation** the use of digital technology to replace analogue technology; digital signals can be compacted and therefore carry more channels than the single, continuous analogue signals

When the government's policy was announced in 1998, digital spectrum was issued to existing free-to-air networks without charge, and multi-channelling was banned, with the spectrum to be used instead for high-definition broadcasts and datacasting (the definition of which specifically excluded television services). Licence conditions for datacasting were so restrictive than their auction was shelved due to lack of interest. The then Communications Minister, Senator Richard Alston, defended the government's decision:

> Australia has a world class TV system, with a strong local content component and a highly skilled production sector. This could be threatened if the existing networks had to battle a new competitor at the same time as paying huge sums to transfer to digital broadcasting, or if the Pay TV networks found themselves with significantly stronger free-to-air opponents while still trying to find their feet (cited in Papandrea 2001, p. 70).

Naturally, those media interests that had lobbied for a different outcome saw the matter quite differently. Incumbent interests have a strong incentive to defend any advantage that government policy brings them. It is when incumbent media interests are divided over their preferred position on policy changes that we see public debate about media policy through those media outlets. However, it is in this situation that the status quo is the most likely outcome, since governments try to avoid alienating any powerful media company. This probably explains why governments have been so slow to license new technology in Australia. In the case of digital television, the government made the smallest changes possible without ignoring the new technology altogether. By the close of the twentieth century, Australia's media ownership was among the least diverse in the developed world (Brown 2000, p. 50).

Debates and controversies

TECHNOLOGY AND DIVERSITY

Privatisation and deregulation have been central policy planks for consecutive Australian federal governments. The Australian telecommunications sector was deregulated in the 1990s, and its biggest company, Telstra, privatised. Phone companies are anxious to become content providers through their mobile networks and the internet. The ideological disposition towards deregulation also influenced media policy. Attempts to change media laws cause intense debate because they affect our culture as well as our politics.

Debates surrounding technology and deregulation have become intertwined, as advocates of deregulation point towards the potential of digital networks, with the capacity to quadruple channel capacity without compromising on transmission quality, to allow a more diverse range of media voices.

'Serious journalism,' says former *Sydney Morning Herald* editor Eric Beecher, 'has never been profitable in its own right' (2005b, p. 9). Newspapers have in the past subsidised journalism with the revenue from classified advertising. With online advertising revenue growing at more than 50 per cent per annum, traditional newspaper revenue is under threat. As media companies turn into global conglomerates, the ability of serious news reporting to justify its existence is increasingly coming into question. 'Journalism no longer retains its place at the centre of media power' (Beecher 2005b, p. 10). Of course, the onset of television in the mid twentieth century saw entertainment replace news as the main currency of the media. Newer technologies are simply speeding up that process. Newspaper circulation is in decline as more and more information outlets spring up. In response, newspapers have attempted to shift their classified advertising online, and acquire successful online advertisers (such as News Corporation's purchase of *Career One*). The market for online advertising, however, will undoubtedly be much more competitive than the newspaper classified market. This will eat away at the revenue of existing media companies.

Duplication of some of the features of newspapers online is an example of **convergence**. For more than a decade now, communications analysts have been talking up the prospects of convergence, where media platforms become less distinct, and outlets differentiate themselves by their content. New technology, then, may be bringing the era of mass media to an end. Digital technology does not just allow new market entrants; it also changes the way broadcasting works by allowing a flow of information from the consumer to the producer. We will discuss the potential of new media in Chapter 11. While it may be too early to regulate the media as though convergence has already arrived, the potential is real. As we will see, this argument about technology and diversity has been used by the Howard Government to justify deregulation of media ownership.

▶ **convergence** the use of the internet to replace separate media platforms such as television, radio and newspapers

Many people (journalists in particular) are sceptical that the internet can be a reliable source of information. They fear that we will lose the established sources of information crucial to the operation of our democracy without gaining anything substantial in return. What we see on the internet is the proliferation of opinion. Anyone with a keyboard and an internet connection can publish their view of the world. The ratio of opinion to hard facts is increasing every day. This has the potential to undermine the quality of debate in our democracy. But it may also cause us to rediscover the value of serious news sources. In making sense of the internet, we often fall back on the brands that we already know. Thus nine.msn, Fairfax and ABC have established popular websites. Making money out of this presence is a different challenge altogether in such a competitive environment.

The extent to which the internet poses a challenge to media companies used to comfortable market positions is still unclear. As new communication technologies emerge, existing corporations are in a good position to exploit them. They can buy start-up firms brimming with new ideas, use public familiarity with their brand to differentiate themselves in a competitive environment, and promote their online activities through their traditional outlets. As well, large firms are in a position to wait out some of the short-lived trends in a fast-changing environment (Herman & McChesney 1997, p. 124). Constructing a web page is easy. Providing content that people might want to pay for has proved to be much more challenging. Very few newspapers are able to turn a profit from online access. Those that do, such as *The Wall Street Journal*, tend to have a well-heeled and loyal audience. In any event, our ability to read newspapers online does not of itself increase diversity.

If incumbent media companies can grapple successfully with new platforms, globalisation may simply be the process by which national media monoliths become global media monoliths. This provides new challenges for governments charged with regulating media industries. The uncertain status of News Corporation in Australia was illustrated when it launched a new giveaway newspaper in Sydney in 2004. Foreign ownership laws then prevented foreign companies, which News had by then become, from starting newspapers here. The regulator, however, interpreted the law in a way favourable to News. This may be a sign of things to come as media corporations get bigger, with their audiences residing in a host of countries with different laws about ownership and content.

CHANGING LAWS IN AUSTRALIA

When the cross-media ownership laws were introduced in 1987, the coalition parties voted against them in the Parliament. Kerry Packer publicly endorsed John Howard for the prime ministership on his Nine Network in 1995 (Schultz 2002 p. 84). After gaining office in 1996, the Howard Government sought on a number of occasions to introduce legislation to remove the cross-media ownership restrictions. One of their key arguments for doing so was that technology was quickly rendering media ownership restrictions anachronistic. The government was not alone in making this argument. Media regulation was under attack from a number of quarters as outdated and too restrictive of Australian companies competing in a global economy. Australian Press Council chief David Flint argued that 'we are soon going to have more sources of news down the super highway than any of us will be able to handle ... far from achieving diversity, media regulation has held us back' (Flint 1995). Most importantly, the Murdoch press supported government policy. Fairfax, without a dominant shareholder, was the logical takeover target if the cross-media restrictions were dropped. Fairfax journalists in 1997 began a pubic campaign against the proposed changes, fearing the consequences of the Packer family acquiring papers such as the *Sydney Morning Herald* and Melbourne's *Age*. Government backbenchers nervous about concentration of media power derailed the legislation.

With the two most powerful media companies in the land lobbying to have the cross-media laws changed, however, the issue was never going to go away. In 1999, the Treasurer referred broadcasting policy to the Productivity Commission. Unsurprisingly, given its ideological orientation, the Commission recommended that:

> ... the cross-media rules prevent mergers among 'old' media companies, and will impose increasingly severe constraints on them. The rules' effectiveness will decline as convergence proceeds. The cross-media rules should be removed once a more competitive media environment is established (Productivity Commission 2000, p. 3).

Note the importance of only removing the cross-media rules in a more competitive environment. The Commission suggested that such an environment should include a specific media public-interest test in the *Trade Practices Act*. However, the Productivity Commission, being pro-competition, was not interested in protecting the interests of incumbent broadcasters. The Commission's report relied heavily on the concept of convergence, arguing that:

- Diversity of sources of information and opinion is most likely to be served by diversity in ownership of media companies, and by competition.
- Broadcasters should be able to provide their services using whichever platform (over the air, cable or satellite) is most efficient.
- Rapid and certain conversion to digital television is the key to unlocking the spectrum. It will create opportunities for new players and new services. (Productivity Commission 2000, p. 2)

Naturally, the concept of creating opportunities for new players in broadcasting alarmed the owners of free-to-air television licences. The government readily accepted the Commission's advice on removing cross-media restrictions, but wilted under lobbying from free-to-air television licence-holders when it came to new market entrants. Without new market entrants, the effect of removing the cross-media laws could be significant (depending, of course, on the number of assets that were for sale or vulnerable to takeover). In Melbourne and Sydney, the minimum number of commercial media owners (assuming that no new newspapers were launched) would drop from twelve to seven (Papandrea 2002, p. 261).

The government's prescriptive approach to digital technology was repeated when arrangements for the digital radio spectrum were finalised in 2005, when a five-year moratorium on new licences was announced. The Minister explained that 'the incumbent commercial broadcasters clearly need to drive' the switch to digital (Radio National 2005b). The incumbent broadcasters, however, have no incentive to innovate when their profits are protected by government regulation. The analogue television signal was due to be discontinued by 2008—never a realistic prospect. The restrictions on content prevented digital television becoming attractive to consumers. In turn, low take-up rates give no incentive for investment in digital content. In Britain, by contrast, digital television has been used to open up the market for broadcasting. The 'Freeview' digital television platform offers over thirty free-to-air channels. Combined with the lack of restrictions on pay-television programs in Britain, this has led to a much faster take-up of digital television there than in Australia (where penetration had reached only 15 per cent by 2006). Such a liberal policy may only be viable in the larger British market, but the contrast with the Australian policy is striking.

Meanwhile, the cross-media issue never left the Coalition Government's agenda. Legislation aimed at deregulating the ownership of Australian media companies was introduced in 2002. The government argued that restricting foreign ownership reduces the diversity of media in this country. For instance, a Spanish company had expressed interest in setting up a newspaper to rival the monopoly papers in Brisbane and Adelaide. The Minister for Communications, Senator Alston, believed that changing technology was rendering existing laws useless. Deregulation, he argued, would put Australian media companies in the best position to deal with the infinite competition provided by broadband internet technology. He also pointed out that the internet provided a large number of voices in debates about politics, reducing the concern that removing the cross-media laws would allow further concentration of ownership.

In spite of these arguments from Alston, the government's bill to deregulate media ownership failed to pass the Senate. Some senators accepted the government's argument about foreign ownership, but were not prepared to accept the changes to the cross-media laws. The government was unwilling to compromise. Margo Kingston provides a lively description of the lobbying of senators over this issue in her book *Not Happy, John! Defending our Democracy* (2004).

After the Howard Government won a majority in the Senate from 1 July 2005, new Communications Minister Senator Helen Coonan played down the prospect of a fourth commercial free-to-air channel on *The Media Report*: 'I think we have to be very careful about fragmenting the existing both advertising market and the existing free-to-air market and industry for just repeating something else when there is so much other diversity, both on Pay and on other media platforms' (Radio National 2005b).

There are not many segments of the economy where the government frets about fragmenting the market. There has been a trend towards more competition across the economy for three decades. However, the Howard Government has been consistently transparent in its efforts to please the incumbent owners whenever they change media law. Clearly sensitive to criticism about the government's approach to media policy formulation, Coonan argued that 'to suggest that the views of the media industry in Australia are not legitimate when we are contemplating far reaching and comprehensive reforms is not justified' (Coonan 2006). Of course, nobody had made such a suggestion—only that the interests of the incumbent licence-holders be measured against the public interest. After the Minister consulted with the major media players for a year or so, the public was given a month to respond to her issues paper. The Minister pointed to 'an ever-increasing number of new sources of information and entertainment ... [so that] ... news is now available from hundreds of unmediated sources in addition to the news available on the regulated platforms.' (Coonan 2006)

In the consultation phase before the most recent legislative changes, the major media companies were still in consensus about the need to lift the cross-media restrictions, but divided over issues regarding digital television, anti-siphoning and free-to-air multi-channelling. This time, however, the government could not afford to do nothing because Australia was falling so far behind the rest of the world in broadcasting policy, and analogue television broadcasting was due to be switched off in 2008. As well, existing broadcasters were beginning to feel the impact of new technologies on their advertising markets.

In 2006, the government finally achieved its goal of deregulating media ownership. Foreign ownership restrictions were relaxed. The cross-media rules were weakened rather than abolished, with companies restricted to ownership of two out of the three traditional platforms of newspapers, radio and television. The legislation also contained an ownership diversity test on media mergers, with a minimum of five 'voices' in metropolitan areas and four in smaller markets. The National Party also insisted on additional pro-tection of news production in rural media markets. While the changes to media ownership laws were not due to take effect until 2007, injections of foreign capital into companies such as PBL and Seven following the passage of the legislation suggested that a bout of takeover activity was inevitable.

SUMMARY

This chapter has outlined the main features of the regulation of media owner-ship in Australia. Underpinning any framework of media ownership law is the importance of diversity of opinion in a liberal democracy. Incumbent media owners play a crucial role in the development of legislation governing media ownership. New technologies and the convergence of media platforms have opened up new debates over the role of laws restricting concentration of media ownership.

The Howard Government used the supposed diversity of information provided by the internet as justification of its abolition of the cross-media ownership laws. In the long term, new media platforms may indeed provide a good deal more diversity of opinion, news sources and ownership. However, it is not certain that the role of newspapers, radio and television in holding governments accountable will be upheld by these new media outlets. Indeed, the government's own policies restricting the diversity of ownership of digital television licences provided another example of incumbent media owners protecting their own interests. In the short term, the most likely outcome from the abolition of the cross-media ownership rules will be a concentration of power in the Australian media.

Questions

1 What advantages do incumbent media owners enjoy in the development of new policies and legislation surrounding the Australian media?
2 How will the convergence of communications technologies affect the structure of the Australian media?
3 What reasons did the Howard Government give for abolishing the cross-media ownership laws in 2006? Was this decision justified?

WEBSITES

Media and broadcasting—The Commonwealth Government's broadcasting and online regulation site (http://www.dcita.gov.au/media_broadcasting/).
Broadcasting—The Productivity Commission's report into broadcasting (http://www.pc.gov.au/inquiry/broadcst/finalreport/broadcst.pdf).

FURTHER READING

Beecher, E. 2005, 'The Decline of the Quality Press'. In R. Manne (ed.) *Do Not Disturb. Is the Media Failing Australia*? Black Inc. Agenda: Melbourne.

Brown, A. 2000, 'Media Ownership in the Digital Age: An Economic Perspective'. *Media International Australia*, no. 95, May.

Griffen-Foley, B. 2003, *Party Games: Australian Politicians and the Media from War to Dismissal*. Text Publishing: Melbourne.

PUBLIC BROADCASTING:
Wither the ABC and SBS?

9

This chapter will:

- outline the nature and operation of public broadcasting in Australia
- set out the objectives and principles that underpin public broadcasting
- describe the historical circumstances that gave rise to the creation of Australia's public broadcasting sector
- examine the key debates and controversies associated with the Australian public broadcasting sector and the ABC particularly.

Government ownership of media is typically viewed with some trepidation in most Western liberal democratic societies. Beginning in the nineteenth century, there emerged the view that government could not be trusted to own media lest it be used against society to ill effect. The provision of media services, it was felt, was best left to private commercial operators, with the government's role limited to 'light-touch' regulation of the sector in the public interest. However, the advent of new broadcasting technology in the 1920s prompted a reassessment of this position. It was regarded as acceptable and even desirable for governments to own broadcasting services. Since this time, public broadcasters became an established fixture in many liberal democratic countries such as Canada, the UK, South Africa and Australia.

The concept of public broadcasting in the Western liberal tradition was developed in Britain (Jacka 2003, p. 330). While public broadcasting was moulded to suit the particular needs of the domestic setting (see Harding 1985), the justifications for the creation of the sector were predicated on similar types of arguments. In Australia, the provision of public broadcasting services was designed to achieve three interrelated objectives. First, it was envisaged that public broadcasting would help to correct **market failure** by ensuring the supply of broadcasting services on an equitable and efficient basis throughout the country. It was expected that commercial providers would concentrate their efforts on the lucrative metropolitan mass audience, ignoring less profitable sectional and minority viewers. Through the establishment of a public broadcaster, obvious discrepancies in service provision could be minimised. Second, the government was aware that broadcasting had significant political and social applications. If used judiciously, the new medium could enhance the level of education among the populace; facilitate cultural improvement of the masses; inform Australian audiences; and form a literate citizenry. In essence, a public broadcasting service could bring ideas, culture and information to the masses, regardless of their geographical location or financial circumstances (Semmler 1981, p. 18). Finally, it was hoped that a public broadcaster could help foster nation building. At the time of the establishment of the public broadcasting sector, Australia had been a **federation** for little more than 30 years. The majority of Australians mostly identified with their home state, and did not have a strong attachment to the 'national' government, or a strong conception of what it meant to be an 'Australian'. A public broadcaster that promoted an Australian identity would help unite Australians and build a cohesive nation (Craik & Davis 1995, p. 119; Jacka 2003, p. 331).

> **market failure** the inability of the market to achieve an efficient allocation of resources due to incomplete or asymmetric information

> **federation** the unification of the six colonies that formed the Commonwealth of Australia in 1901; the process resulted in a new political arrangement whereby powers and functions were divided between the federal (or central) government and each of the states

What is publicly owned broadcasting?

Public broadcasting is, as its name suggests, broadcasting services that are owned and controlled by the citizenry. Public ownership is typically differentiated from the commercial broadcasting sector on the basis of three key attributes:

- It is a public asset that is theoretically owned by all members of society.
- Taxpayers principally underwrite its costs, rather than revenue dollars earned from the sale of advertising time.
- It is a non-commercial activity. Whereas the commercial sector produces programs in order to make money, public broadcasters do not create programs for reasons of profit. Programs are produced and aired to serve a public interest rather than a private profit motive (Tracey 1992).

According to Michael Tracey (1992, pp. 17–18), the concept of public broadcasting is informed by eight principles, which have implications for the organisation and operation of publicly owned media. These include:

- *Universality of availability*—Broadcasting services should be available to all people in the interests of serving the public good and not to maximise customers.
- *Universality of appeal*—A public broadcaster has a responsibility to provide programs that cater to different tastes in society in a way that does not pander to populism. In serving the diversity of society, a public broadcaster should not simply give the public 'what they want'. Rather, its goal is to provide good-quality programs that serve tastes that might be dormant in society.
- *Provision for minorities*—A public broadcaster provides a forum in which certain groups and subcultures in society can communicate with like-minded persons and voice issues of importance to members of their community.
- *Enhancement of knowledge in society*—Services should educate the public and raise levels of knowledge and understanding in order to enable individuals to fully participate in democratic society.
- *Maintenance of distance from all vested interests*—Funding should be independent of both advertising and government. While it assumed that public broadcasters should be financed out of government coffers, there

should be restrictions on the ability of government to allocate such funds as it chooses.

- *Provision of programming that encourages 'good programming' rather than chase audience ratings*—A public broadcaster should create programs that are good in their 'own' terms and not on the basis of their ability to attract large audiences. By maintaining high programming standards, public broadcasters should serve as a benchmark against which the commercial stations can be judged.
- *Support for innovative and creative programs*—New and original programs should be funded and supported, even if these ultimately fail to attract a large audience. That is, a public broadcaster should encourage and nurture program makers and be prepared to take 'creative' risks.
- *Nurturing of the public sphere*—Services should motivate viewers as 'citizens', gently reminding the public that citizenship carries both rights and obligations. To this end, public broadcasting helps to socialise the individual into the ways and customs of the society in which they belong.

A brief history of public broadcasting in Australia

Public broadcasting in Australia has evolved and changed considerably over the years. Initially, the government showed little interest in establishing a dedicated government-funded public broadcaster. Although mindful of the perils of 'market failure', the government opted to address such concerns by offering two different types of commercial licences: radio 'A' and 'B' licences. Radio 'B' licence-holders were expected to be self-funding, while radio 'A' licensees operated in a highly protected market, with the number of such licences restricted to two per state, and were financed mainly from the revenue of listener licence fees (Semmler 1981, p. 6). In exchange for public funds, radio 'A' licensees were obliged to establish additional stations at their own cost if so directed by government. It was hoped that this measure would extend the availability of broadcasting services to areas outside of the capital cities (Committee of Review of the Australian Broadcasting Commission 1981, p. 56).

While this system was a partial success, the arrangement ultimately did little to correct market failure. Radio stations sprang up in the profitable urban centres, but few were established in the more sparsely populated regional and rural areas. The scheme did little in real terms to encourage broadcasters to extend services to areas where profits were likely to be both uncertain and low (Harding 1985, p. 236; Inglis 1983, p. 11; Semmler 1981, p. 6). At the same time as disparities in service provision between the rural and urban centres became more acute, those in government became increasingly aware that broadcasting would be 'more potent … in exerting an influence for good or evil than any other agency' (Semmler 1981, p. 10). In combination, both events were to drive the government's decision initially to nationalise all radio 'A' licenses and, in 1932, to pass legislation establishing Australia's first public broadcaster, the Australian Broadcasting Commission (ABC).

The ABC began transmission on 1 July 1932 at 8pm with responsibility for the provision of 'adequate and comprehensive programs'. Over the next four decades, the Australian Broadcasting Commission grew and expanded. In the 1940s, the ABC was granted permission to create an independent news service. This ended the ABC's reliance on the commercial press for the supply of news on a fee basis and established the broadcaster as a news service of repute (Committee of Review of the Australian Broadcasting Commission 1981, p. 65; Inglis 1983, pp. 129–30). In 1957, the ABC became a national television broadcaster, even though it was to take a number of years before such services were available throughout the country on a uniform basis. In the late 1960s, reforms were implemented that sought to increase the ABC's independence from government. While the government ultimately retained the power to direct the ABC on certain matters, when it exercised this authority it was now required to inform Parliament, thus injecting an important new layer of transparency in the relationship between broadcaster and government (Committee of Review of the Australian Broadcasting Commission 1981, pp. 63–4).

In the 1980s, a major review of the ABC was undertaken, entitled *The ABC in Review: National Broadcasting in the 1980s*, but known colloquially as the **Dix review**. Initiated by the Fraser Government, the Dix review recommended a number of significant changes to the operations of the ABC, changes that persist to the present day. Importantly, the Dix review, and the reforms undertaken in its aftermath, represented an attempt to recast the very foundations of the ABC. The ABC was given greater responsibility for its own management and budget, and was required to be more cost-effective, an obligation which was enshrined in legislation. As Craik and Davis (1995,

p. 122) explain, 'reorganisation and consolidation occurred at every level, supported by information systems designed to provide a detailed check on costs and performance. The ABC moved to contract out some services, and into aggressive entrepreneurial marketing activity. Employment conditions changed dramatically'. Moreover, a new board structure was implemented, replacing the old commission system. While the responsibilities of the new board changed little, the mode in which it was expected to operate did. No longer would the board run the ABC as a public utility, but 'like any commercial enterprise' (*Australian Broadcasting Corporation Act* 1983). In recognition of its new 'corporate' direction, the ABC was renamed the Australian Broadcasting Corporation.

> **Dix Review**   a major review of the ABC in 1981, named after Alexander Dix who chaired the review

The ABC dominated public broadcasting for more than 50 years. In the 1970s, a second public broadcaster was established, the Special Broadcasting Service (SBS). SBS was introduced by the Fraser Government in 1978 (Jakubowicz & Newell 1995, pp. 13–15) in response to the perceived failure of the ABC to live up to its obligation to provide a universal service—one that catered for all Australians regardless of their country of origin. It initially began as a radio service, designed to meet the needs of non-English-speaking people, and in 1980 was granted a television licence (Jacka 2003, p. 334). SBS is lauded as 'unique' because it 'broadcasts in more languages than any other network in the world' (SBS 2002).

The anatomy of Australia's public broadcasters: the ABC and SBS up close

Both SBS and the ABC are governed by their own legislation. The ABC is established by the *Australian Broadcasting Corporation Act 1983* and SBS is created under the *Special Broadcasting Services Act 1991*. The legislation is important for a number of reasons. It outlines the objectives of each organisation, describing the purpose of the public broadcasters and the functions they are intended to fulfil in Australian society. The Acts also detail the organisational structure of each entity, conveying important information about who is responsible for their management, and the limits and reach of those who exercise authority within both agencies.

As would be expected, there are a number of differences as well as similarities between the ABC and SBS. This is reflected in their holdings, mission statements, funding, and organisational structure.

MISSION STATEMENTS

Both the ABC and the SBS are governed by a mandate or mission statement set down in their respective Acts. According to the ABC's mission statement, its function is to 'provide within Australia innovative and comprehensive broadcasting', which among other things will 'contribute to a sense of national identity and inform and entertain, and reflect the cultural diversity of the Australian community' (*Australian Broadcasting Corporation Act 1983*).

The ABC's mandate has two important consequences for how it operates. The first is that there is an expectation that *all* Australians should have access to the ABC. As a result, one of the priorities of successive governments has been to ensure that the ABC reaches all Australians, regardless of where they reside. At present, ABC television reaches 98.13 per cent of all the population via ordinary analogue means. The second effect that results from the wording of the mandate is that a significant proportion of the ABC's programming consists of Australian content. While this has not always been the case, today more than half all programs broadcast on the ABC are made in Australia.

In contrast, the SBS mission statement states that its role is to: 'Unit[e] and enrich our society by creatively communicating the values, the voices and the visions of multicultural Australia and the contemporary world' (*Special Broadcasting Services Act 1991*). The wording of the mission statement indicates that SBS is not intended to deliver a comprehensive service in the same way as is expected of the ABC. The function of SBS is to fill a very specific gap in the market, catering to Australia's diverse ethnic population. As a result of this, SBS has never been subject to pressure to develop a large and loyal audience in order to justify its existence (Jacka 2003, p. 335). This is reflected in SBS's programming choices and audience reach. It broadcasts in more than 60 languages, and around half of its programs are in a language other than English. Only a small percentage of its content is Australian made, approximately 20 per cent of the total (SBS 2000). Moreover, while SBS is received in all the major capital cities, many of the regional centres are unable to access it using traditional analogue technology. While the government is trying to rectify this situation, it is not a high policy priority.

Box 9.1   Charter of the ABC

The functions of the Corporation are to provide within Australia innovative and comprehensive broadcasting services of a high standard as part of the Australian broadcasting system:

- broadcasting programs that contribute to a sense of national identity and inform and entertain, and reflect the cultural diversity of, the Australian community
- broadcasting programs of an educational nature
- to transmit to countries outside Australia broadcasting programs of news, current affairs, entertainment and cultural enrichment that will:
  - encourage awareness of Australia and an international understanding of Australian attitudes on world affairs
  - enable Australian citizens living or travelling outside Australia to obtain infor- mation about Australian affairs and Australian attitudes on world affairs
  - to encourage and promote the musical, dramatic and other performing arts in Australia

  In doing so, the ABC shall take account of:
- the broadcasting services provided by the commercial and public sectors of the Australian broadcasting system
- the standards determined by the Australian Broadcasting Authority in respect of broadcasting services
- [the need to] to provide a balance between broadcasting programs of wide appeal and specialised broadcasting programs
- the multicultural character of the Australian community
- the provision of broadcasting programs of an educational nature ...

Source: *Australian Broadcasting Corporation Act 1983.*

Do you think the ABC's Charter is too broad? Is it possible for the ABC, or any broadcaster, to perform the roles outlined in the charter?

ORGANISATION

Both the ABC and SBS are statutory bodies. A statutory body is a particular type of public sector entity that is run by a board of directors that reports directly to Parliament. This is unlike other public sector bodies, which typically answer to a minister. One of the purposes this arrangement serves is that it minimises the extent to which the government is able to interfere with the activities of both broadcasters.

The boards of the ABC and SBS comprise part-time directors and a full-time chairperson. The board sets the overall strategic vision of the broadcaster and ensures that it operates within the limits of its Act. The board also appoints the managing director, the individual charged with the responsibility for overseeing its day-to-day activities. The board is assisted by a secretariat (which offers administrative support to the board) and a board-appointed advisory committee (which provides 'grassroots' or community advice to the board).

While the legal status of the ABC and SBS limits the government's capacity to control the activities of both boards, the government does retain some discretion over its operations. The boards are legally bound to consider the government's policy statements, and to notify the government of any significant change to their corporate plan. This entitles the government to be 'heard' by the board, even if there is no obligation on the board to 'obey'. The government's control over the 'purse strings' and ability to determine the composition of the board affords them considerable indirect influence over the broadcasters.

HOLDINGS AND SERVICES

Over the years, both broadcasters have managed to acquire various holdings and expand the range of services they offer to Australian audiences. The ABC and SBS each has interests in radio, television, online services and retail activities. The ABC employs a little over 4000 people. It has four national radio stations, 51 regional stations, a national television network and two digital channels. The organisation also has online broadcasting services that host more than 1.7 million pages of web content. There is also an international broadcasting service that transmits into Asia and the Pacific. In addition to this, the ABC has 39 dedicated shops around the country. As one would expect, SBS has significantly fewer capital holdings. This reflects, in part, a difference in age of the broadcasters. SBS is little more than 20 years old, whereas the ABC has existed for over 70 years. SBS employs around 800 people and its holdings consist of a national television network, a national radio network and nine capital and seven regional stations. It also has two digital stations as well as a majority stake Pan TV Ltd, a company that supplies world movies to pay-television channels.

FUNDING

As has been mentioned previously, the ABC and SBS are largely funded from disbursements received from the federal government. While both broadcasters are funded substantially from the public purse, their funding models are different. ABC receives more funding than SBS. In 2004–05, the ABC had an annual operating budget of $959 million. The bulk of its funds, around 79 per cent, come directly from government appropriations. In addition to funding from government, the ABC also raises revenue from independent sources, which is typically the sale of goods and services. The ABC generates around $200 million from its own sources, such as program and merchandise sales (ABC 2004–05, p. 56).

SBS operates on a budget less than one fifth of the ABC. Its annual operating budget in the 2004–05 period was $162.4 million. Like the ABC, the SBS obtains most of its income from government appropriations. Around 78 per cent of its total budget is government sourced, while the remainder is self-generated. However, one of the significant points of difference between the two organisations is that SBS is permitted to raise money through advertising. In 1991, the Hawke Government legislated to allow SBS to accept advertising. SBS is permitted five minutes of advertising per hour, compared with 15 minutes for commercial stations. In the 2004–05, SBS grossed $30.9 million in advertising revenue (SBS 2004–05, pp. 44, 50). Recent changes, namely the decision to permit advertising throughout its programs and not just during 'natural breaks', is expected to enable SBS to raise an additional $10 million in revenue a year (Murray 2006a).

The ABC is prohibited from broadcasting advertisements under s. 31 of its Act. Interestingly, the original plan had been to allow the ABC to supplement its income through sponsorship. The Lyons Government had intended for the ABC to accept a limited amount of advertising, but was forced to abandon the plan owing to pressure from the commercial media (Inglis 1983, p. 19). In the 1980s, the issue was again revisited when the Dix review recommended that the ABC introduce sponsorship in order to alleviate some of its financial pressures. While the Hawke Government seriously entertained the prospect, the matter was dropped due to lack of support from both the **Senate** and the public. It would seem, in the short term at least, any attempt to remove the moratorium on paid advertising would be politically unpopular.

> **Senate** the (76-member) upper house of the Commonwealth Parliament; along with the House of Representatives (150-member lower house), the Senate is responsible for debating and scrutinising legislation

AUDIENCES

Both SBS and the ABC draw considerably smaller audiences than the commercial broadcasters. According to OZTAM, the official source of television ratings, the ABC averages 15 per cent national audience share during prime time, whereas the SBS reaches slightly over 4 per cent. This compares to 20–25 per cent audience share attained by each of the three commercial networks.

It is not without good reason that the ABC and SBS attract a smaller audience share than their commercial sector counterparts. It is important to bear in mind that both broadcasters, particularly at their inception, were not required to chase audiences but to provide services that the commercial stations were unwilling to deliver. One of the implications is that neither has prioritised the scheduling of populist-style programs that are likely to invite large audiences. Similarly, the broadcasters' comparatively weak television ratings reflect the relatively meagre financial resources on which they rely. Both public broadcasters operate on only a fraction of the budget of the commercial stations. Glenn Withers estimates that the ABC's television costs per hour of programming are around two-fifths of those of the commercial free-to-air stations. According to his calculations, using cost per station as the measure, the ABC costs $26.18 million, Channel 9 $88.59 million, Channel 7 $83.21 million and Channel 10 $46.39 million (Withers 2002, p. 109).

Debates and controversies

The ABC has been a fixture of the Australian broadcasting landscape for over 70 years. It is a popular institution, especially in regional Australia where it was the only broadcasting service that country people received for many years. The evidence shows that most Australians are highly supportive of both public broadcasters. A 2005 survey conducted by Newspoll revealed that nine in ten people believe the ABC provides a valuable service (Newspoll 2005, p. 15). The SBS also records high levels of public satisfaction. One survey showed that 89 per cent of respondents believed that 'it is important that SBS be available to provide an alternative to the commercial stations', and that 77 per cent find value in the services it provides (SBS 2004–05, p. 76). In fact, comparisons of consumer perception of the quality of programming of commercial and public broadcasting indicate that the public broadcasters return a higher satisfaction rating, particularly the ABC. Whereas 80 per cent of those surveyed believed that ABC television was 'good', only 38 per cent thought the same for commercial television (Newspoll 2005, p. 15).

Despite the high regard Australians hold for the ABC and SBS, both broadcasters have experienced their share of controversy. SBS has been criticised for promoting cultural separatism by enabling non-Australian born members of the community to retain their own (foreign) cultural identity— rather than embrace an Australian one—through the provision of foreign-language news services and movies. Some believe that SBS impedes, rather than encourages, new Australians from embracing the language, culture and traditions of their adopted country. More recently, SBS has been criticised for favouring certain ethnic groups over others, and, since accepting advertising, some commentators have noted 'it has been pandering to sponsors ... of currying favour with an affluent, Anglo-Celtic majority with advertising dollars to spend' at the expense of the demographic the broadcaster was established to serve (Simper 1996; Field 2001, p. 13; Jacka 2002, p. 3).

It is probably true to say that the ABC has been subject to the harshest censure. Crises within the ABC are not a new phenomenon (see Harding

1985; Inglis 1983; and Semmler 1981). The ABC enjoys the rather dubious honour of being one of Australia's most loved, yet controversial, public institutions. One commentator has even suggested that the 'perpetual crises' that plague the ABC are natural and inevitable, and 'constitute the institution as a natural broadcaster' (Craig 2000, p. 105).

While the ABC is far from perfect, it is also true that other factors have contributed to this state of affairs. The high costs associated with running the ABC compared with other public institutions results in fairly high expectations about the services it should provide. Whereas SBS is designed to fill a very particular niche in the market, the ABC shoulders the responsibility of having to be both a substitute and competitor to commercial broadcasting. Moreover, because the ABC is one of the most influential media organisations in the country, this increases sensitivity to its activities, particularly government sensitivity. The ABC's reputation for hard-hitting investigative journalism can have the effect of rendering it few friends among those who make important decisions about the public resources it receives (Inglis 2002, p. 11; Posetti 2001–02). In recent years, the ABC has been embroiled in three major controversies: political bias, funding and relevance. Each of these issues will be addressed in the next section of this chapter.

BIAS

The allegation that the ABC is biased in its coverage of political matters is time-honoured. Since its inception, the ABC has been accused of behaviour 'unbecoming' of a national broadcaster. Among its most vocal critics have been the ALP and the Coalition. Both the major parties, particularly when in office, have been openly hostile towards the ABC, complaining of bias in its presentation of news and information.

However, some believe that since the election of the Howard Government (Coalition) in 1996, relations between the ABC and the government have deteriorated. Coalition disaffection with the ABC is not a new phenomenon. According to Inglis, the Coalition's antipathy towards the ABC dates from the 1960s; crystallising in the 1970s owing to the ABC's perceived favouritism of the Whitlam Government (Inglis 1997, p. 8). The substance of the Coalition's concerns is that the ABC has a left-wing political bias, which causes the national broadcaster to be inherently hostile to the principles and values supported by conservatives. The Coalition believes this is the result of a lack of diverse views represented within the ABC, particularly among its journalists.

The Coalition is not alone in this view. A number of commentators have expressed similar concerns about a lack of balance at the ABC (Blair 2003; Blair & Morrow 2004; Bolt 2003; Kerr 2005; Luck 2003; Mackriell 2001). One critic, Michael Warby, has argued that the ABC is a 'staff-captured' institution. Warby believes that the organisation reflects the 'values, prejudices and perspectives of ABC staff' who, owing to the absence of a real owner, are unaccountable to the public (Warby 1999, p. 2). The problem is compounded because the organisation deliberately recruits those 'in their own likeness' (Warby 1999, p. 3). Warby maintains that the ABC's 'lack of objectivity' is beginning to have an 'invidious effect' on public debate, causing a narrowing of debate on issues such as the 'republic, indigenous affairs, the environment, migration, multiculturalism [and] labour market issues' (Warby 1999, p. 3).

In 2002, the ABC's coverage of the invasion of Iraq prompted a new wave of criticism from the Coalition. The then Minister of Communications, Senator Richard Alston, claimed that the ABC's coverage of events was biased against the US-led Coalition forces. He claimed to have found 68 occasions of anti-war bias in the ABC's reporting of events from 21 March 2003 to 14 April 2003. The Minister said he was motivated to act as a result of the 'groundswell' of complaints received by his office.

While the Minister was genuinely aggrieved at what he believed was a problem 'of one-sided and tendentious commentary by [ABC] program hosts and reporters' (Alston 2003), his claims were only partially vindicated. There was not quite the 'groundswell' of criticism of the ABC's coverage of the invasion as Senator Alston had alleged. Despite the Minister's claim that his office had been inundated with calls of complaints, his office could only substantiate 10 complaints (*Media Watch* 2003). While the ABC did record 291 letters of complaint from the public about its coverage of the invasion, this number represented only 0.65 per cent of the total. Even then, the complainants were fairly evenly split, with 147 complaining about pro-US coverage and 144 complaining about anti-US coverage (ABC 2003–04, p. 32). Moreover, subsequent reviews of Alston's complaint by an independent review body accepted 17 of his 68 complaints (26 per cent). While the review found that 12 of the complaints were serious, they nonetheless rejected the suggestion that the ABC was guilty of systematic (anti-war) bias (ABC 2003, p. 3).

There is little evidence that the public supports the Coalition's views in this matter. This is borne out in the ABC's summary of public contact in 2003–04. Of more than 50 000 letters or emails received by the ABC, only 0.7 complained of party-political bias, 0.7 per cent of bias, 0.9 per cent of factual inaccuracy and 0.3 per cent of a lack of balance. The ABC received fewer than 3 per cent of complaints that related, in some way or another, to the issue of bias (ABC 2004–05, p. 27). This finding is consistent with a recent Newspoll survey of audience perceptions of four of the ABC's news and current affairs programs, which revealed that 88–94 per cent of respondents believed that the ABC offers an even-handed and balanced presentation of news stories (Newspoll 2005, p. 47).

Moreover, there does not appear to be any factual evidence to back the claim of left-wing bias. If the ABC's coverage of the 2004 federal election is anything to go by, it has proven to be even-handed in its coverage of both the ALP and the Coalition. Table 9.1 shows that across radio, television and the internet, the Coalition enjoyed the largest voice time compared with other political parties. Table 9.2 reveals that not only did the Coalition gain the largest cumulative share of voice—which is, in part to be expected because the incumbent always attracts more media attention—but that it also drew more favourable coverage than the ALP. In combination, this evidence tends to suggest that the ABC is not any more or less biased against the Coalition than it is the ALP.

In response to the allegation of bias, the ABC has bolstered its complaints management mechanisms. A number of new review bodies have been created to consider complaints received by anxious members of the public about its conduct. Complaints are initially heard by the Audience and Consumer Affairs Unit (Unit). If the complainant is dissatisfied with the outcome of the Unit's investigation, the matter can then be referred to the Complaints Review Executive (CRE). Complainants also have recourse to one of two external review agencies. A complaint can be referred to either the ABC Board-appointed Independent Complaints Review Panel (ICRP), or alternatively, if it involves a matter pertaining to the ABC's code of practice, the Australian Communications and Media Authority (ACMA). It is interesting to note that the proliferation of the various review entities sits strangely at odds with the ABC's obligation to achieve greater fiscal stringency. It is safe to assume that the existence of such bodies imposes an enormous financial burden on an institution that is constantly under pressure to cut costs.

Table 9.1 Cumulative share of voice on ABC, 11 May–29 August 2004

Party	Television	Radio	Online
Coalition	56.8%	53.4%	54.4%
ALP	38.6%	39.8%	37.6%
Greens	2.0%	2.7%	3.5%
Democrats	0.5%	2.5%	3.0%
Other parties	2.0%	1.6%	1.5%
Total	*100%*	*100%*	*100%*

Source: ABC Election Coverage Review Committee (2004).

Table 9.2 Cumulative favourability within ABC coverage, 23 May–29 August 2004

Party	Television	Radio	Online
Coalition favourable	42%	43%	42%
Coalition unfavourable	23%	21%	25%
ALP favourable	21%	21%	17%
ALP unfavourable	13%	12%	13%
Total	*100%*	*100%*	*100%*

Source: ABC Election Coverage Review Committee (2004).

FUNDING ISSUES

The funding of the ABC has always been contentious. The Australian public broadcasting sector is one of the most under-funded among similar countries. In Germany, public broadcasting is funded at 80 cents per head, Japan,

45 cents per head and UK 59 cents per head, while in Australia it is around 23 cents per head (McKinsey & Company 2004). Moreover, international benchmarking reveals that the ABC is relatively efficient in its use of financial resources. Not only does the ABC operate on a much smaller budget than many of its international counterparts, but it is also among the most efficient in terms of it use of resources (ABC 2004–05).

Since the 1980s, governments of both political persuasions have reduced funding to the ABC. The ABC has been de-funded in real terms by 34 per cent in the last 15 years. There is no particular consensus about what has motivated the reduction in financial support. One argument is that the funding cuts are merely the consequence of radical public sector reforms initiated by the government in the 1980s. Across the public sector, the government has sought to ensure that its agencies model their work and organisational practices on the private sector. In the case of the ABC, it resulted in the shift to triennial budget proposals and the legal requirement to be more cost-effective (Craik & Davis 1995, p. 121). Because the government has made similar demands on all public institutions, the implication is that the funding cuts are 'not personal'. That is, they are not a reflection of deep animosity with the broadcaster per se, but merely the result of a new style of public sector management.

A second school of thought holds that the funding cuts are intended to debilitate the ABC for political reasons. Some contend that money has become the 'bludgeon' used by governments to control the ABC in light of its inability to directly control the broadcaster due to its status as a statutory body. Government, by its nature, naturally seeks to control the activities of the public institutions under its jurisdiction. If thwarted by legal barriers, governments typically respond by using its control over the purse strings to bring institutions into line. Over the years, governments have been quick to remind the ABC of its precarious financial position. In 2003, the Communications Minister issued this warning to the ABC: 'They are accountable to government in the same way any other organisation is, but if they choose to ignore it then it is a matter for the Parliament. If the Parliament thinks they have lost the plot they could be de-funded' (Alston quoted in Mac 2003).

The ABC's lack of direct control over its finances and budget places the government in a very powerful position. *Actual* funding cuts undermine the capacity of the ABC to provide not only comprehensive programming but also (more importantly) quality news services. The less money available to undertake this latter role, particularly, the less potent the ABC will be in performing its fourth-estate functions. ABC employees have expressed concerns they are being forced to make compromises in response to limited resources. Kerry O'Brien, presenter of the *7.30 Report*, explains that reductions in the news budget have meant that there is a growing tendency to 'shy away from a particular story because you know you simply won't be able to do it justice' (O'Brien quoted in Simons 2005, p. 124; Posetti 2001–02, pp. 6–7). Similarly, the mere *threat* of funding cut is often sufficient to curtail the activities of the broadcaster. It has been suggested that the ABC has become increasingly self-censoring in order to avoid attracting the government's wrath. This, some writers claim, is a long-standing practice known within the ABC as the 'pre-emptive buckle'. It refers to the practice of minimising potentially 'controversial' content and programming in response to the perception of likely political pressure from government (Dempster 2005, p. 108).

Box 9.3   **The pre-emptive buckle in practice: *Jonestown***

In 2006, the ABC Board was accused of having intervened to prevent the publication of a biography about Alan Jones, a well-known radio talkback broadcaster with close ties to the Howard Coalition Government. The book, titled *Jonestown*, was written by Chris Masters, an award-winning investigative journalist, and commissioned by ABC Enterprises. ABC Enterprises, the publishing arm of the ABC, claimed that it was forced to scuttle plans to go ahead with the book's release following legal representation from Jones's lawyers that he would commence defamation proceedings if the book was published. In a media release, ABC Enterprises claimed that it would be 'irresponsible' to proceed with publication on the grounds that 'it will almost certainly result in a commercial loss' (see Box 2006; Ricketson & Moore 2006).

However, the ABC *Media Watch* program disputed this explanation, claiming that the decision was prompted by the ABC's own board of directors—a view that was shared by the book's author. *Media Watch* claimed that ABC Enterprises, despite having made a strong case for publishing the book and having spent approximately $100000 in research fees and legal checks to limit the ABC's legal exposure, were forced to cancel plans to proceed with the book owing to pressure from the board. It was generally thought that while Jones would launch a defamation action, it would, in all probability, be unsuccessful. In their final assessment, *Media Watch* argued that 'direct involvement of the board in such decisions has to create the perception that the ABC is editorially timid or, worse, vulnerable to the influence of powerful men like Alan Jones' (*Media Watch* 2006).

Do you think the ABC should have proceeded with the publication of *Jonestown* despite the legal threats? Was it right for the board to intervene, or should the decision have been left in the hands of ABC Enterprises? Does this decision indicate that the ABC no longer has 'the money, freedom and the guts' to support its investigative reporters?

There are growing fears that the funding cuts are beginning to weaken the ABC's ability to deliver quality programming (Posetti 2001–02, p. 6). Since the 1980s, successive ABC boards and managing directors have spoken publicly of the need for the broadcaster to lift its audience ratings in order to guarantee its funding base. This, some claim, is beginning to have a damaging effect on ABC programming, prompting a shift to 'crowd pleasing', 'light weight programming' at the expense of 'quality' (Dempster 2005). As one commentator noted, ABC scheduling consists of 'cheap studio-based quiz shows and celebrity interviews' and 'contrived fly-on-wall reality shows', with 'arts criticism and genuine locally produced documentaries' a thing of the past (Dempster 2005. pp. 104–5). More worrisome is that, should the ABC's funding base continue to decline, it will lack the capacity to respond adequately to the changing technological media environment. If the ABC is unable to compete and maintain its position against the commercial broadcasters—particularly given the high costs associated with replacing, let alone updating technology infrastructure—this may give a non-sympathetic government all the ammunition it needs to **privatise** the broadcaster.

> ▶ **privatise** to sell government-owned enterprises or industries to private investors

Over the years, various solutions to the ABC's funding crisis have been proposed. In the 1980s, the Hawke Government suggested that SBS and

ABC be amalgamated. The Hawke Government claimed that this would allow both broadcasters to conserve scarce resources. However, the legislation was defeated in the Senate (Cockburn 1986). In June 2003, the matter was raised again, but this time from within the ABC. The new proposal sought to merge the 'back office' functions of the broadcasters. This entailed amalgamating their basic accounting and human-resource functions, with all other functions remaining separate. It was argued that $15 million dollars a year could be saved—money that could be better directed at producing additional local content. While a merger of basic administrative functions was in itself relatively innocuous, the concern was that it would provide the basis for a full merger between the two organisations later down the track. For now, at least, both major parties have expressed a desire to keep the institutions separate.

RELEVANCE

There are growing concerns about the relevance of the ABC to Australian public life. This argument is based on the belief that many of the reasons that prompted the establishment of the public broadcasting sector no longer exist. That is, some view public broadcasters as 'creatures of another time, when nation formation, citizenship development and quality programming were not so much contested and problematic notions' (Craig 2000, p. 107).

One of the arguments that has been put forward in support of this contention is that the ABC no longer provides a comprehensive service. The suggestion is that much of the ABC's programming is skewed in favour of the over 55s and the educated classes; in essence, the middle class. This has led some to argue that lower- and working-class Australians, through the allocation of their tax dollars, are being forced to subsidise the viewing preferences of the middle classes (Jacka 2003, p. 338).

Another line of argument is that a public broadcaster is no longer required to correct market failure. If you remember back to the beginning of this chapter, one of the justifications for public broadcasting is to ensure that all members of society, and not just the lucrative mass audience, have their viewing needs met. It is thought that certain minority groups with limited economic resources—such as Indigenous people, the disabled and children—would simply be overlooked. Today, however, this argument is thought to no longer be valid. New platforms facilitated by new technology, and digital and subscription services in particular, have resulted in a plethora of new channels capable of accommodating a broad cross-section of the community at relative little expense. Pay television particularly, with its capacity to generate hundreds of channels, can offer programs that appeal to very specific niche markets (Jacka 2003, p. 338; Long & Smith 1992). Also, new platforms, such as the internet, can transmit diverse public affairs information and educational material from a host of different providers. Essentially, new technology has increased the diversity and availability of new programming, thereby rendering public broadcasting redundant.

The traditional bases on which public broadcasting was cast are no longer thought to be persuasive. The great fear is that, given these developments, combined with government reluctance to sink funds into the public broad-casters, this will give a less-than-sympathetic government all the ammunition it needs to justify the privatisation of the broadcaster. For now, at least, neither of the major parties have openly challenged the validity of the ABC's existence. The election promises of the major parties still carry a commitment to the ABC, each continues to extol its virtues, and neither has yet to openly suggest that it be privatised. Despite this, there is a growing sense that the importance or the relevance of public broadcasting is beginning to diminish.

SUMMARY

This chapter has established that public broadcasting has been a feature of Australian society since the 1930s. Both the ABC and the SBS are intrinsically important cultural institutions—popular and respected by the Australian public. Despite this, Australia's broadcasters are frequently forced to defend their performance and, occasionally, even their very existence. The controversy that has engulfed both ABC and SBS, despite the decidedly local flavour of the criticisms, has occurred in the context of a much broader debate about the relevance of public broadcasting in Western liberal states. While the demise of public broadcasting is far from imminent, it is also true that the ideal of public broadcasting will be scrutinised, dissected and ultimately remodelled to suit the needs of the modern media age.

Questions

1 It has been said that the ABC suffers from a tendency to bias and, more particularly, the promotion of left-wing, politically correct views. Do you agree with this view? Why/why not?

2 Should a public broadcaster be permitted to accept advertising? What are the benefits and the costs associated with allowing a public broadcaster to raise funds from commercial advertising?

WEBSITES

ABC—The official website of the ABC, containing news, program information and corporate material (http://www.abc.net.au/corp/).

Friends of the ABC—A politically non-aligned interest group that represents the public's interest in the ABC (http://www.fabc.org.au/vic/index.html).

SBS—The official website of SBS, containing news, program information and corporate material (http://www20.sbs.com.au/sbscorporate/index.php?id).

FURTHER READING

Inglis, K. 2006, *Whose ABC? The Australian Broadcasting Commission 1983–2006*. Black Inc: Melbourne.

Jacka, E. 2006, 'The future of public broadcasting'. In S. Cunningham & G. Turner (eds), *The Media and Communications in Australia*. Allen & Unwin: Sydney.

NEW MEDIA AND THE PROSPECTS FOR DEMOCRACY

10

This chapter will:

- critically analyse the potential for new media to change the way news about politics is created and distributed
- discuss the ways in which new media are altering the structures of politics and communication in our society
- analyse the impact of new technologies on some of the essential parts of the media as we know it, such as news gathering and copyright protection.

New media: 'no centre, no gatekeeper, no margins'

(Jenkins & Thorburn 2003, p. 11)

In his novel *Nineteen Eighty-Four*, the great British writer George Orwell put forward a terrifying vision of governments using technology to enslave the populace. Orwell's was the original Big Brother—mass propaganda and thought police bringing about conformity and obedience in industrialised societies. Fifty years after the publication of that book, a quite different vision of technology and power has emerged. We may be moving away from an era when, between them, parliaments and media companies were the gatekeepers of what we can see, hear and read. The liberal vision of diverse and competing centres of power may be fully realised in the years to come.

Mass media and representative democracy have much in common. The profession of politics and the profession of journalism are both criticised for being the preserve of an elite. They both operate in a top-down fashion, making decisions every day that the majority of people feel they are unable to influence. The fact that both commercial media outlets and political parties must by their very nature take popular trends into account has not prevented a growing sense of public disillusionment with these crucial institutions. Australian society has changed a great deal in recent decades, yet the two-party system persists. Just as it is difficult for new parties to break into our political system, it has been difficult for new players to enter the mass media. Society has become ever more complex, with a host of new social movements and areas of employment. Yet, the structures of party politics and the mass media struggled to keep up with these changes. New media promises to undermine this top-down control of politics and the media by allowing much more **horizontal communication**, as with the world wide web, email and instant messaging (Rosen 2005, p. 28).

> **horizontal communication** communication between creators of content and their audience; the ability of new media to accommodate many more creators of content has made this much more common

Mass media are said to be responsible for the 'sensationalism, trivialisation, personality fixation, horse-race mentality' (Dahlgren 2003, p. 151) that we discussed earlier in this book. Unlike the printing press, which undermined government and religious monopolies on written communication, broadcasting brought us closer to the oppressive, Orwellian vision of mass communication as propaganda. Now, technology is once again promising a more diffuse set of messages. Indeed, Jay Rosen likens the current era to Revolutionary America, when **pamphleteers** like Tom Paine agitated for the American colonies to break ties with Great Britain (Rosen 2005, p. 23). We need not romanticise the way democracy worked before the onset of mass media. Voting then was restricted to property-owning white men. The parallels lie instead in the vitality of the political culture and the dynamic effects of new forms of communication. Now, every personal computer is a printing press. Further, the interactivity of new media makes possible a return to what the Americans call 'town hall democracy' (Mayer & Cornfield 2003, p. 299), where citizens gather in their local communities to debate issues and make decisions.

▶ **pamphleteers** those who spread political ideas during the eighteenth century through short pamphlets instead of books or newspapers

Van Dijk points out that information technology has the potential to both centralise and diffuse political power, depending on which groups are better organised to take advantage of the technology (1999, p. 84). The PR state techniques that we saw in Chapter 5 are examples of governments using their resources to take advantage of electronic media. Governments, as regulators and through their coercive power, are also in a position to use new media to their advantage. While new media might lend itself to decentralised power structures, the old, hierarchical structures will remain influential for some time to come. Many of the early predictions of the internet as the forerunner of radical social and political reform may prove to be overly optimistic. Still, the extensive debates over these issues are an indication of widespread disillusionment with the status quo. While critics from left and right have vastly different visions of what a communications nirvana might look like, they each have problems with the tendency towards monopolistic power that characterises traditional media (Jenkins & Thorburn 1993, p. 10).

The internet is quite different from broadcasting in that it was created through a system of government licensing. Indeed, it was not designed as a system of public communication at all. The US Department of Defense required a communications network that was decentralised and therefore less vulnerable to enemy attack (Barr 2002, p. 246). Computer experts in universities created the world wide web on the back of that defence network, although it was the advent of free browsing software that allowed the network to really take off. Companies such as Microsoft have experimented with ways of bringing the internet under greater corporate control. However, the complex work involved in turning the internet into a user-friendly network is still largely in the hands of a decentralised group of experts. In large part, the ethos of those who have created and continue to maintain the internet has been to resist either corporate or government control. Its unusual origins make the internet a unique and potentially revolutionary medium. Instead of a handful of people making decisions and creating content for the rest of us, it provides a grassroots or 'many to many' structure of communication. The explosion of personal computer use in the 1980s and 1990s made the internet what it is today. Just 90 000 computers were connected to the internet in 1989. Hundreds of millions are connected today.

Yet, pessimism about the relationship between technology and social trends may be warranted. As we have shown throughout this book, 'big power and big money always found ways to control new communications media when they emerged in the past' (Rheingold cited in Jenkins & Thorburn 2003, p. 8). We may, however, eventually come to see the twentieth century, with its representative politics and mass media, as an unusually hierarchical period. New technologies have the potential to allow much wider participation in both politics and the media. This will change the relationship between media institutions and their consumers, as well as that between citizens and political leaders. In turn, this may reduce some of the cynicism associated with politics. A more egalitarian forum for debate and influence in the political realm is, after all, what democracy is supposed to be all about.

Box 10.1 A revolutionary medium?

The internet was expected to be a boon for pro-democracy groups in developing countries. These groups, it was thought, could bypass state-controlled media and use new technology to communicate and organise. That early assessment, however, may prove to be too optimistic. Some countries, such as China, have been able to build a **firewall** around the internet in their jurisdiction. Because of the scale and dynamism of its internal market, China has been able to censor the internet without frightening off foreign investors from its technology sector. For example, a Google search for Falun Gong (a seemingly harmless lifestyle movement that seems to upset the Chinese government), when conducted outside China turns up sites critical of the Chinese government's imprisonment of Falun Gong members. The same search from inside China leads to government sites critical of Falun Gong. An American company, then, is not simply engaging in self-censorship, but is assisting the Chinese government in its own campaign to limit freedom of speech. Dissidents breaching China's censorship laws face lengthy jail terms.

Reporters Without Borders publishes *A Handbook for Bloggers and Cyber-dissidents*, which includes advice on how to remain anonymous when publishing incendiary material.

Think about the potential for the internet to undermine authoritarian governments. Do you think it is really possible for countries to effectively censor the internet?

▶ **firewall**   used to cordon off part of a computer network to protect it from unwanted influences

Empowering the individual

As we saw in Chapter 3, media audiences are not quite the passive 'couch potatoes' that some critics of mass media have portrayed (Barr 2002, p. 244). They have, however, had little control until now over the content broadcast to them or served up in newspapers and magazines. At the very minimum, the internet provides a different structure of communication from broadcasting. We engage with it actively, choosing content instead of letting editors make those choices on our behalf. Unlike reading a newspaper, mouse clicks give instant feedback to content providers about what is popular and what is not. Judgments about the proximity and depth of news stories are less important online. Readers can access stories in as much, or as little, depth as they prefer. The media consumer can become 'seeker, consultant, browser, respondent, interlocutor or conversationalist' (McQuail 1997, p. 129).

Advertisers are finding new ways to reach such audiences. Fully aware of the number of viewers who skip commercial breaks, television networks are experimenting with ways to embed advertising in programming. Email spam may irritate us and overload our in-box, but only a tiny proportion of recipients need to respond to these ads for them to be considered successful. Also popular, but less likely than spam to be outlawed, are innovative video clips circulated by email that depend on recipients enjoying the presentation and passing them on to friends. Some of the more successful 'viral marketing' campaigns promote products aimed at young people, such as Microsoft's X-

Box. All of this is happening because we as individuals have greater control of what we see, hear and read.

Another new and fast-growing source of online content is the **weblog**. There are already tens of millions of 'blogs' around the world, a remarkable phenomenon. Some American blogs average over a million hits per day. Even so, the resources of these blogs are very limited. It is through traditional media that blogs have had their biggest effects to date, correcting erroneous stories in the mainstream media (MSM, as they call it), and exposing stories that bloggers think have been underreported. Blogs have made an occasional splash in the mainstream media by breaking stories during election campaigns. In the 2004 US presidential election, bloggers showed that documents regarding George W. Bush's military service were forged. This incident led to the resignation of a CBS television producer, and the early retirement of its news anchor. The internet also makes fact-checking very simple. Media outlets simply cannot get away with sloppy journalism and editing anymore. Similarly, the comments facility on blogs allows instant response, debate and debunking.

> **weblog** an online diary (often shortened to 'blog') usually featuring comments from readers and links to other web sites

Many bloggers have a sense of mission, which often comes from their perception that their voices are underrepresented in traditional media. One of the most successful bloggers, Glenn Reynolds of *Instapundit*, puts the case succinctly in the title of his book: *An Army of Davids: How Markets and Technology Empower Ordinary People to Beat Big Media, Big Government and Other Goliaths* (2006). Blogs, and the internet more generally, are attractive to **libertarians** of the left and the right, due to the lack of government regulation of the internet. While Reynolds is sceptical of the notion that the power structures of media and government will change quickly, he believes that the internet will at least help keep them honest, and allow a good deal of social autonomy for those who have interests outside the mainstream. Indeed, for some libertarians, the technology is an end in itself. Their aim is not to influence government, but to have government leave them alone. The internet frees them from government and corporate control of what they read, watch and say.

▶ **libertarians** those who prefer minimal government intervention in both the economic and social spheres

Progressives, on the other hand, see the internet as an opportunity to bypass media companies that they see as perennial voices for conservatism. During the Iraq war, blogs played a unique role in questioning government spin and prodding the mainstream media into a more skeptical frame of mind. Bloggers like 'Salam Pax' gave an inside view of the American invasion of Iraq that reporters based at Allied Headquarters in Qatar, and even Baghdad, could not. Myths quickly spread about Salam Pax. How could he prove he was in Baghdad? Was he a creation of American intelligence services? He turned out to be an ordinary Iraqi. Salam Pax's creator soon formed an alliance with a British newspaper. His is an example of both the strengths and weaknesses of blogs. Their independence from government and corporate influence is invaluable. But we all have to make a living, and even the most successful bloggers have day jobs. Indeed, the fact that some of the most prominent bloggers are established journalists has given the movement a level of credibility in the mainstream media that they would arguably not have had if all bloggers were genuine media outsiders.

Traditional media has not enjoyed the onslaught against it from bloggers, launching some stinging attacks on the credibility of online commentary. *Forbes* magazine referred to bloggers as 'an online lynch mob spouting liberty but spewing lies, libel and invective' (Lyons 2005). Yet, it did not take long for the commercial world to see the potential of blogs. Popular blogs are often quickly incorporated into the mainstream media, either through the Google advertising (which can be automatically placed in blogs related to the subject matter of that blog), using blogs to promote new products, or simply by siphoning a blogger's output to a larger site. Glenn Reynolds, for example, has a second blog inside the Microsoft empire. He notes that the corporate bureaucracy dilutes the interactivity of that site, making it difficult to respond quickly to changing events.

Technorati.com tracks blogs to allow subject searches and to keep track of trends in the world of blogs. The number of blogs increased exponentially once software and a critical mass of potential readers became available. Yet, many bloggers seem completely unfazed by the fact that they have a minuscule audience. They write not for profit but because they enjoy it. They are satisfied if they reach a handful of interested souls. This is arguably a bigger problem for traditional media than commercial competition from blogs and other sites. The fact that there are an infinite number of people providing free content will change irrevocably the economics of the media. At the very least, the internet provides big media with competition for audience and agenda-setting, as well as an army of instant fact-checkers. More radical changes in our media environment may await the ability of new media sources to develop levels of brand recognition and accessibility that will give them access (collectively, at least) to mass audiences.

A global village

The internet does more than undermine the top-down structure of the media and politics in democracies. As well as a 'many to many' structure of communication, the internet allows 'any to any' exchanges—that is, we can communicate with anyone, anywhere in the world who has access to the technology. This provides challenges not only to the ways in which national governments can conceivably regulate media ownership and content, but will also affect our sense of social identity and cohesion. No matter how unusual your interest, or how radical your opinion, you will find websites that validate your world view.

The idea of the internet changing the way we live assumes ubiquitous access to computers. This is far from the case, even within a prosperous society such as ours. The internet opens up a 'digital divide' between information haves and information have-nots. This divide can be a result of geography (with rural areas feeling left behind), of wealth or a generation gap. Getting **broadband** technology to the majority of citizens in a decentralised population such as Australia's may also prove difficult. While Australians have historically been fast adopters of new technology, we are already lagging behind much of the developed world in broadband penetration.

> **broadband**   technology that allows access to the internet at a much faster rate than traditional telephone lines

In Chapter 8, we considered the impact of technology on media diversity and the consequences for government regulation of media ownership. Technology and globalisation may render all such discussions irrelevant. If anyone who owns a computer can download all their information and entertainment from a server located overseas, all of our debates about regulation of Australian content, censorship and ownership will not amount to much. The decline of mass media may see the decline of policy designed to enhance the public interest. Audiences will instead find themselves part of a segmented market, without a united public voice with which to influence politics and corporate behaviour (McQuail 1997, p. 134).

The internet supports virtual communities, bringing together groups of people with common interests regardless of where they happen to live. People who, for one reason or another, find social interaction difficult in their local community can find solidarity online. Paradoxically, given globalisation's dependence on improved transport and communications technology, the anti-globalisation movement has made extensive use of new media to pursue its agenda. Pressure groups make extensive use of new media, particularly those who feel the established media ignores their causes. Since the World Trade Organization meeting in Seattle in 1999, large protests against the organisations that are entrenching liberal economic policies have become commonplace (Juris 2004, p. 342). Such protests are in large part generated by sophisticated yet decentralised communications strategies using email, mobile phones and the internet. Images and stories from the protests are then circulated on sites such as the Independent Media Center (www.indymedia.org) to bypass mainstream media, which the protesters perceive as hostile to their cause.

In the USA, moveon.org uses new media to raise awareness of progressive issues and raise funds for its favoured candidates. Such activism is not simply a means to an end. This type of political participation, particularly for those alienated from mainstream politics, is often 'a highly valued cultural goal in itself' (Juris 2004, p. 353). Participants in these groups are not simply agitating for social change, they are also living it.

In some respects, those groups using new media to bypass existing political and media structures form the 'democratic laboratories' (Juris 2004, p. 357) of our age. Their experiences, however, are not uniformly positive. Freedom gives us the ability to be destructive as well as creative (McNair 2006, p. 14). The rules of conduct for new media are still evolving. For example, bloggers and cyber-activists must deal with anti-social components within their organisations and audiences. The internet helps all groups communicate, not just those who want to make the world a better place, and the web has been a boon for hate groups marginalised from traditional media. White supremacist groups quickly latched onto the freedom provided by the internet. The 2005 Cronulla protests-turned-riots were the result of an SMS campaign. Whether or not cyber-activists can be true to the ideals of democratic communication and at the same time limit access for those with destructive intent will be one of the defining questions of new media. In turn, the success or failure of these types of social and political movements in utilising new media may indicate the extent to which the economic and social changes described in this chapter can truly affect our democratic political institutions.

Debates and controversies

CAN QUALITY JOURNALISM SURVIVE IN THE DIGITAL AGE?

In Chapter 8, we noted how political journalism has historically been subsidised by classified advertising, which is migrating to the internet. Journalists, editors and media owners are already confronting the consequences of these changes for their profession. Eric Beecher describes the present period, where the possibilities of new media are still largely unknown, as waiting for a volcano to erupt (2005b, p. 65). Will the fast-moving information age have room for 'long investigations, thorough news coverage, extended arts and book reviews and opinion and editorial pages that debate about what is best for society?' (p. 70) Although he is now a proprietor of independent online journal *Crikey*, Beecher is pessimistic about the 'maintenance of serious debate in a society that seems more interested in instant gratification than in thoughtful reflection' (p. 75).

In a speech to the American Society of Newspaper Editors in 2005, Rupert Murdoch described the way young people approached the media:

> They don't want to rely on a god-like figure from above to tell them what's important … They want control over the media instead of being controlled by it. They want to question, to probe, to offer a different angle … Where

four out of five Americans in 1964 read a paper every day, today only half do. Among just younger readers, the numbers are even worse ... The data may show that young people aren't reading newspapers as much as their predecessors, but it doesn't show they don't want news. In fact, they want a lot of news, just faster news of a different kind and delivered in a different way.

Naturally, Murdoch hopes the existing print and video resources of his empire will translate profitably to the internet, and in turn bring readers and viewers to his established businesses. But can any media company, or any journalist, operate in a truly interactive manner? News Corporation is certainly trying, purchasing in 2005 MySpace.com, a youth-oriented networking site. Exchanging gossip and music files is a long way from journalism, though.

Optimists speak of a new era of journalism as a conversation instead of a lecture (see Rosen 2005). Newspaper editor Dan Gilmour put it this way: 'We tell you what we have learned, you tell us if you think we are correct, then we discuss it' (cited in Mayer & Cornfield 2003, p. 302). An online platform gives news outlets the opportunity to cover stories in much greater depth, to regularly update and correct those stories, and to link to other sites of interest. This can be particularly important for ongoing stories, such as public policy or constitutional debates (Hume 2003, p. 337). While much online content is 'easy to consume and easily available' (Packer 2004), there will always be a market for the sorts of facts and judgments that news organisations traditionally provide.

Journalists cannot hope to compete with the instantaneous nature of many parts of the internet, but do they need to? The instantaneous and interactive nature of new media has its advantages and disadvantages. Television news solicits story ideas and video of breaking news from the public. This method became famous when images of the 2005 London Underground bombings were taken from commuters' mobile phones and emailed to television stations. BBC journalist Nik Gowing said that his organisation received 20 000 emails, 3000 text messages, 1000 phone pictures and 20 video packages related to that story within hours of the blast. With such material, reporters could be confident about what just what had occurred well before official sources were ready to go on the record (*Australian* 2006).

Some sites seek to provide a better news service by allowing their readers to recommend stories from established media, submit their own stories and comment on the news. Newsvine.com claims to 'bring together big and little media in a way which respects established journalism and empowers the individual at the same time' (newsvine.com 2006). In 2006, internet entrepreneur Craig Newmark, whose online classifieds site *Craigslist* (www.craigslist.org) has contributed towards the drift of classified advertising revenue away from newspapers, provided seed funding for a new type of investigative journalism. *Newassignment.net* (http://newassignment.net/) aims to fund high-quality reporting, which will be assisted by the public providing ideas and checking facts—a technique called networked journalism. A number of similar experiments are also under way.

Box 10.2   **Crikey! Where's the independent media?**

One Australian example of internet-based media is *Crikey* (www.crikey.com.au). *Crikey* started out in 1999 as a website commenting on the Victorian election. It grew very quickly into a subscription-based email and web magazine. *Crikey* has been criticised (and sued) for simply trafficking in gossip. This shortcoming reflected *Crikey*'s modest resources and need to rely on anonymous sources. It has grown, however, into something resembling an online newspaper, with reporters and regular correspondents in a range of areas. *Crikey* was taken over in March 2005 by Text Media, a small publishing firm. Critics argue that since the takeover, *Crikey* has become more conservative in its approach; frightened of offending powerful interests.

Such criticism is, perhaps, an inevitable outcome of a small outfit like *Crikey* attempting to become a reliable source of independent information. Many independent (or indy media) sites are long on opinion and short on objective fact. Often, their rationale for existing is a perception that mainstream media does not cater to their point of view. However exciting it may be for new media to present us with a proliferation of opinion, many of us inevitably rely on trusted brand names to give us our daily fix of news.

Consider your own consumption of new media. Do you think that new media cover issues and people that are ignored by traditional media or is it simply a more convenient platform for communication?

Ultimately, the public will make judgments about which new media sources are credible and which are not. Technology provides us with an avalanche of information. Most of us will continue to rely on others to sort and prioritise that information, and present it to us in a manageable way. Just who these new gatekeepers will be is another question altogether. Some bloggers promote what they call citizen journalism. Bloggers can carry their laptops to an event and report live, alongside the broadcast journalists. Again reminding us of the way things were before the emergence of mass media, cyber-optimists see journalism as an activity that any concerned citizen can engage in, rather than an exclusive profession. No doubt, many trained and experienced journalists disagree. The way in which they wrestle with the challenges and opportunities of new media will be a major turning point for the profession.

HOW WILL NEW MEDIA CHANGE REPRESENTATIVE DEMOCRACY?

Politicians have always used whatever technologies are available at the time to spread their message. After the Second World War, Robert Menzies used radio to reach what he called 'the forgotten people': the middle class. The contemporary era has been dominated by television images. Will interactive technologies make politics more interactive, giving more citizens the opportunity to have input into the democratic process in addition to their occasional vote? Government bodies already make extensive use of new technology to carry out their day-to-day business. But they do so within the existing top-down framework of bureaucracy and representative democracy (although, on the other hand, confidential information stored electronically is easier to leak to the media). So, citizens can use the internet to fill in forms, make complaints, access information such as weather warnings or traffic snarls, and submit their tax returns. In the USA, some jurisdictions allow **online voting** in an attempt to improve voter turnout. All of this makes the business of government quicker and more efficient, but does nothing to change its basic structure. Of course, not everybody wants to be politically active. Representative democracy allows us to delegate responsibility for many complex and difficult decisions that most of us do not have the time or the inclination to wrestle with. For the structures of our democracy to change, significant legislative and constitutional change would be required. In spite of the disillusionment described above, Australians have been reluctant to embrace even incremental changes to the way we are governed.

If electronic democracy has to this point been about making things quicker and easier, some proponents of democratic reform would prefer our political process to be slower and more complicated. The idea of **deliberative democracy** predates the internet. It came out of the body of political theory, exemplified by Habermas, critical of the existing power structures of representative democracy and mass media. Deliberative democracy requires consensus over procedures and priorities. It may be as simple as deliberative polling, where groups of people gather together over a period of time to listen to all sides of a given issue, with their opinion on that issue monitored before and after the exercise. It could also involve deliberation over questions to be put to a referendum. Yet, while deliberative democracy encourages the horizontal—or many to many—communication exemplified by the internet, it also encourages time for reflection and compromise. The instantaneous nature of new media, where opinion and analysis quickly follows news events, may actually take us further away from the deliberative ideal.

> **deliberative democracy** the encouragement of extensive and rational public debate on political issues before decisions are made

Just because technology allows us to communicate with governments or new social movements, it does not automatically follow that most of us will bother. As well as giving us a window on the world, technology can also allow us to become more withdrawn from society. We can use television, computer games and the internet to escape from the problems of everyday life. Personal Video Recorders (PVRs) and **podcasts** allow us to watch and listen to only the programs that suit us, which may or may not have anything to do with politics or the wider world. Governments historically regulated radio and television broadcasting in order to expose citizens to a range of viewpoints, while at the same time providing shared cultural experiences. For a previous generation, the first moon landing was one such cultural marker. Is something missing from our social interaction if many of us miss out on such shared experiences because we have our own narrow set of interests?

▶ **podcast** a computer file containing news or entertainment, which has been either broadcast by media outlets or created expressly for the internet or replay on handheld devices

Many people find the social cohesion provided by mass media to be comforting, and have no wish to indulge in the multitude of choices that new technologies provide. They will be perfectly happy for existing broadcast networks to provide them with the types of news and entertainment they are used to. For those who wish to exercise a high degree of control over the sorts of images and messages that children, in particular, are exposed to, the internet is a threat. Given the flood of pornography, gambling and violence that the internet makes available to us, there have inevitably been attempts, unsuccessful to this point, to regulate the new medium. It is not yet clear whether the internet will be used more for information gathering and social networking or for 'cocooning' (Mayer & Cornfield 2003). Working from home, watching streaming video instead of going to the movies, and using the internet to satisfy our individual pursuits may make us more withdrawn from society rather than more engaged. At this point in its development, we are using new media, like television before it, for entertainment and commerce much more than for political engagement (Dahlgren 2003, p. 163).

DO NEW MEDIA UNDERMINE INTELLECTUAL PROPERTY?

While Western governments have been reluctant to regulate the internet, it is still subject to laws such as defamation and copyright, just like any other platform for communication. Enforcement of such statutes where online activities are concerned, however, is difficult. Making internet service providers responsible for every word and image that their customers choose to access, for example, is hardly fair on them.

Intellectual property is a unique subset of property rights. The state enforces property rights in order to resolve disputes over the ownership of scarce resources. The public benefit in such a system is clear; our market-based economy depends upon it. The case for intellectual property is more complex. Ideas are much cheaper and easier to copy than, say, motor cars. It's far from clear how copyright affects 'the public's right to a rich intellectual realm' (Raven 2005, p. 1). Patents are a type of intellectual property that protect design and innovation rather than content. The creators of intellectual property argue that ownership of their work provides an incentive for them to create more ideas and art. 'Thin' copyright protection provides such an incentive, but only for a limited period of time. Advocates of thin copyright protection point out that extending copyright for decades beyond the death of the author, as our current laws do, is not much of an incentive for creativity (Raven 2005).

Globalisation and new technology are pushing our thinking about intellectual property in different directions. On one side, computers make the flouting of intellectual property laws so easy and widespread that enforcement becomes difficult. You will be familiar with the debates over illegal copying of music and video on personal computers. How can such a simple and quick activity be illegal? Should the state be arresting people for a victimless crime? Copyright laws have provisions for 'fair dealing', but in the past these provisions have not even allowed you to make a copy of a CD for your own use. This is a sub-section of a wider debate about the nature of creativity, and whether society is well served by the ability of a few people to profit from something as abstract as words and ideas. We limit the length of time that intellectual property can be protected, but it is difficult to judge just what that length of time should be. We need to balance the financial incentives for the creators of songs and books with the public benefits of having their creative output distributed as widely as possible.

At the other end of this debate, big media companies, whose profitability depends on rigorous enforcement of copyright, have succeeded in extending the reach of intellectual property laws. Copyright in the USA now extends for 70 years after the death of the creator of the work (known as the 'Mickey Mouse clause' since Disney's copyright of Mickey Mouse was soon to run out when the law was amended). The USA is pressuring its trading partners to harmonise copyright laws. Australia has adopted the American law in accordance with the Australia–USA Free Trade Agreement. It's difficult to see how extending the length of copyright in this way encourages creation of content. Indeed, the increased market competition from the free availability of back catalogues as their copyright runs out increases the incentive for corporations to find new works to promote. Yet again, a small number of companies with strong incentives to change the law have convinced governments to act in a way contrary to the public interest.

Existing owners of copyrighted material feel threatened by the potential for internet piracy to undermine their industries. They lobby governments to enforce copyright laws, and take companies that benefit from piracy (such as or Napster or Kazaa) to court in order to close them down. Yet, while the short-term profits of companies that rely on copyrighted material might be under pressure from piracy, it is unlikely that entire industries will fall foul of this trend. We purchase creative content for a range of reasons. Just because something is available at no cost does not mean that there is not a large parallel market for identical products. We buy books even though they are available for nothing from the local library. We pay for cable and satellite television even though we have access to free-to-air networks. Record companies feared the onset of readily downloadable music. They delayed the introduction of pay-for-download sites to discourage piracy. Yet, as soon as commercial download sites such as Apple's iTunes became available, many consumers deserted the peer-to-peer networks and flocked to the legal sites. The professionalism of such sites makes them more user-friendly. Unknown musicians find the internet a better way to promote their work than relying on record companies who extensively promote only a tiny minority of artists.

The interests of copyright holders will ensure that our intellectual property laws will persist, and perhaps be strengthened, in spite of the ease with which intellectual property can be copied. However, not all creators of content want to be financially rewarded for their efforts. *Wikipedia* is one of the best examples of **open source** production of content. It is an online encyclopaedia written and edited by an army of volunteers. A wiki is a website that allows anyone to contribute and edit content. The open nature of *Wikipedia* is certainly a weakness. For example, politically contentious issues can be difficult to cover objectively. Staff members of American Members of Congress have contributed implausibly positive assessments of their employers to *Wikipedia*. However, a study of the accuracy of the scientific articles in *Wikipedia* by the journal *Nature* found that they were as accurate as those found in the more staid *Encyclopaedia Britannica*.

▶ **open source** computer code for a program that is made available to anyone who wishes to alter or improve it

The open source movement also provides competition to software companies such as Microsoft. Software tends towards monopolistic markets because users like to be able to easily exchange files, hence the dominance of Windows and Office. Proponents of open source software argue that this tendency delivers Microsoft inordinate profits and takes away its incentive to innovate and improve its products. By making software's computer source code freely available, anyone can improve upon it, making us all better off as more and better programs become available. The open source movement sees this method of production and distribution as a model for the rest of society, incorporating 'the twin goals of individual liberty and social democracy' (Bradley 2004). In the short term, however, Microsoft's profitability means it has been able to fight off most legal challenges to its market dominance, and extensively market its products. While the internet has been a boon to the open source movement, the resulting programs (such as the Linux operating system or the internet browser Firefox) have thus far achieved limited market penetration. While proponents of open source argue that their operating systems and web browsers are better than those sold by Microsoft, most people are reluctant to make the change to something new. We perceive that the costs of changing from something familiar outweigh the benefits that a new system may provide. The profits continue to flow to the incumbent centres of power, and society accepts second best. It's a problem familiar to anyone who studies politics and the media.

SUMMARY

In this chapter, we have shown some the possibilities that new media provide to those of us uncomfortable with the political and economic status quo. New media also presents challenges, however, to important established practices, such as quality journalism. Big changes in the way society is governed may be some way off, but the potential erosion of the top-down power structures of representative democracy and mass media posed by the application of technology are real. New media allows a less hierarchical structure of communication. Many people will continue to receive most of their information from the mass media. Yet, information technology is changing traditional platforms such as newspapers and television. One important source of revenue for media companies, classified advertising, is migrating to the internet. This may affect the resources available for investigative journalism. New media also makes it much easier for us to obtain information without paying for it. This raises questions about the role of copyright in the creative process. The open source movement provides a new model for creating and distributing all manner of information-based products. The future of the biggest media corporations and the smallest websites depends largely on the decisions that we make as consumers of media.

Questions

1   Given all the hype surrounding new media, will it actually change the way we engage with the wider world? Are new media sources more or less reliable than traditional sources? What problems does the proliferation of new media sources present?
2   Should copyright laws be rigorously enforced in an online world? How does society benefit from the enforcement of copyright?

WEBSITES

Berkman Centre for Internet and Society—Conducts research into, and surveys, the way the internet is affecting political activity (http://cyber.law.harvard.edu/home/).

Comment is Free—One newspaper to take the internet seriously has been the London Guardian (http://commentisfree.guardian.co.uk/index.html).

Creative Commons—A non-profit body offering a new approach to copyright (http://creativecommons.org/).

Medialens—Provides a critical view of new media and journalism (http://www.medialens.org/).

Pew Research Centre for the People and the Press—Has many projects on new media (http://people-press.org/).

The following sites are e-journals and blogs that deal with the impact of new media on society and government:

Hitwise (http://weblogs.hitwise.com/)

M/C Journal (http://journal.media-culture.org.au/).

Pressthink (http://www.pressthink.org)

Wired News (http://www.wired.com/)

The following sites feature community groups that use new media as a part of their political activism:

Greenpeace (http://www.greenpeace.org.au)

Independent Media Centre (http://www.indymedia.org)

MoveOn.org (http://www.moveon.org)

FURTHER READING

Jenkins, H. & Thorburn, D. (eds). 2003, *Democracy and New Media*. The MIT Press: Cambridge.

McNair, B. 2006, *Cultural Chaos: Journalism, News and Power in a Globalised World*. Routledge: London.

Mills, J. 2005, *Barons to Bloggers: Confronting Media Power*. The Miegunyah Press: Melbourne.

GLOBAL POLITICS, GLOBAL MEDIA

11

This chapter will:

- assess the role of the media in the determination of a state's foreign policy priorities
- weigh the priorities of national security and the public's right to know
- discuss the notions of truth, objectivity and the national interest in the reporting of Australia's involvement in various conflicts around the world.

The CNN effect

Many of the liberal concepts about the interaction of politics and the media described in this book have historically come under challenge during times of conflict. The media are in the business of revealing information, whereas governments have many things they wish to keep secret. In the past few years, we have seen debates about the balance between national security and civil liberties in the wake of September 11. In Australia, the federal Parliament has placed new restrictions on freedom of speech as part of an overall response to the threat of terrorism. There is an extra dimension to this debate, however.

The media plays an important part in the way we perceive the world and the threats to our way of life. Our priorities in foreign affairs are very much shaped by the episodic way in which we take in information about events that happen thousands of miles away. Some of the most important decisions we make as a society are based on a scant knowledge of the world we live in.

In October 1993, American military forces entered the Somali capital Mogadishu in order to capture militia leaders loyal to local warlord Mohamed Farrah Aidid, thought to be meeting in a safe house in the crowded city. Somalia had been in chaos since the overthrow of its president in 1991. The civil war triggered a famine that killed more than half a million Somalis. The American forces were part of a United Nations authorised multinational effort (including Australia) to feed starving Somalis, whose plight had been beamed around the world by news organisations. The UN Security Council authorised the use of force to ensure sufficient stability for effective famine relief and democratic elections.

The attempt to arrest the Somali militia leaders turned into a disaster for the USA, and arguably for the world. Eighteen Americans were killed in the battle—by historical standards a minor battle. However, in the context of domestic political support for overseas military intervention, the Battle of Mogadishu made an enormous difference. Re-created in the movie *Black Hawk Down*, the events in Mogadishu proved a turning point in American popular attitudes towards humanitarian intervention. In 1991, the United Nations had authorised member states to remove Saddam Hussein's Iraqi forces from Kuwait. US President George Bush declared that this successful imposition of international law marked the beginning of a 'new world order'. His successor, Bill Clinton, an opponent of the Vietnam War, was an idealist, prepared to use American power for the greater good. However, with the disastrous events in Mogadishu covered live on 24-hour news channel CNN, and quickly picked up by other news outlets, Clinton had to make an instant decision on the future of the US presence in Somalia. Images of the body of an American marine being dragged through the streets by angry Somalis caused Americans to question the entire concept of humanitarian intervention. Somalia was left to its fate. As one newspaper columnist wrote: 'We went into Somalia because of horrible television images; we will leave Somalia because of horrible television images.' However, a recent study found that media coverage of the Somali famine only reached blanket coverage after the US deployment was announced (Robinson 2002).

Clinton's experience with American military involvement in Somalia caused him to act with great caution as humanitarian crises unfolded throughout the 1990s. Television images brought to the world another African tragedy in Rwanda in 1994. A small United Nations force could do little as one ethnic group slaughtered another. Clinton later wrote that his failure to intervene in the Rwandan genocide was his greatest regret. Television cameras also rolled as ethnic cleansing took place in Bosnia. Western intervention was cautious and a long time coming. The West's failure to protect Bosnian Muslims provided easy propaganda for radical Islamists.

Whatever the idealistic impulses of their leaders, the American people had no wish to create a new world order; certainly not at the cost of the lives of their soldiers. In arguing to again go to war in Iraq, Bush's son George W. pitched his arguments in favour of deposing Saddam squarely in the American national interest. Australia's John Howard similarly calculated the interests of his country in his decision to support the Americans. The moment of post-Cold War idealism was brief. Its demise was thought to have much to do with something called the CNN effect. As we will see later in this chapter, political and military leaders go to great lengths to influence media coverage of war. The power of the media can be a 'strategic enabler' for those decision-makers if the right images and messages are harnessed (Belknap 2001). The instant and continuous coverage typical of our era, however, creates new challenges for those involved in war. It forces upon them decisions that they would rather delay. Anything broadcast on television can be accessed by both sides of a conflict. Livingston (1997, p. 2) identifies three elements of the CNN effect:

- Images of humanitarian disasters frame the foreign policy agenda away from hard-headed notions of the national interest towards emotional concerns.
- Instant coverage of events forces accelerated decision-making response time.
- Graphic images of war undermine public morale and support for a conflict.

Livingston notes that the type, level and influence of media coverage is different in any given situation. Different political leaders may be less swayed by fleeting changes in public opinion than Clinton was in 1993. Government officials, aid agencies and other **non-government organisations**

(NGOs) lobby news organisations to take their cameras to crisis-ridden areas. The CNN effect refers not just to television but also more generally to our globalised media (Louw 2005, p. 253). Agenda-setting is a complex process of interaction between a range of decision-makers, as we saw in the case of domestic politics.

Television, having been accused of closing the **public sphere** through its triviality, has arguably created a global public sphere. During the First World War, Australians would wait weeks for reports from the front. Photographs of battle were rare and heavily censored to maintain morale. Today, we have live images of war beamed into our lounge rooms. The CNN effect certainly causes greater urgency in debates over foreign policy, but also affects the priority that foreign affairs have in our wider political debate. Australia's geographic isolation has not prevented us from sending troops to far-flung parts of the world in support of our allies for more than a century. The media have a greater chance to affect policy debates when it comes to foreign affairs because few of us have direct experience of this area. Our experiences in our workplaces influence our attitudes to industrial relations law. Mortgagees do not need the newspaper to tell them what rate of interest they are paying to their bank. Our knowledge of the world is much more limited, and therefore susceptible to influence by the choices made by journalists, editors and media owners about international news.

> **non-government organisations (NGOs)** centres of power and resources alternative to nation-states
>
> **public sphere** the set of actors and activities that enable an exchange of ideas throughout society

One form of influence is the way in which political stories are framed. Hirst and Patching (2005) describe the 'terror frame' within which politics around the world has been discussed since the attacks on New York and Washington on 11 September 2001 (p. 143). After the Bali bombing in October 2002, the *Australian* editorialised that 'Bali proves that all freedom-loving peoples are at risk from terrorism, at home and abroad' (p. 147). That might be true, but such a claim illustrates the lack of a critical approach on the part of the media to such events, and to the government's response to them (p. 147). What are the parameters of the war on terror? How do we judge progress and how long will it last? Tragedies like those in Bali are designed by their perpetrators to grab our attention. Just whose agenda is served for us to concentrate on the effects of terrorism to the exclusion of an ongoing (but unspectacular) humanitarian crisis in Africa? On the other hand, the bombing of the Australian embassy in Jakarta during the 2004 election campaign did little to disturb the centre of gravity of that campaign. The Prime Minister had long succeeded in putting economic management at the forefront of voters' minds.

Box 11.1 A media tsunami

On Boxing Day 2004, the biggest news story in decades developed in Southeast Asia, when hundreds of thousand of people were killed by a tsunami caused by an earthquake off the Indonesian island of Sumatra. New media was important in the coverage of this story. Images from the hand-held cameras of tourists quickly found their way to news organisations. Yet, there is still no substitute for images flashed around the world by television. The power of mass media is still very strong. Within days of the tsunami, groups around the world were raising funds and mobilising resources. Benefit concerts, neighbourhood food stalls and telethons were quickly organised. Governments were slow to follow, but eventually organised the world's biggest-ever relief efforts. The Australian government, in recognition of the importance of South-East Asia to our future, promised its largest-ever aid donation.

If news coverage of a single event can move millions of people around the world to take action in support of their fellow human beings, surely the power of the global media can help to make the world a better place. Yet, the ability of news organisations to follow, and make a difference to, ongoing stories of tragedy and injustice are not very strong. In 1982, television pictures of starving Ethiopian children were the catalyst for an enormous effort to provide relief, headed by the Live Aid concerts.

More than twenty years later, however, many of the same participants rallied again for debt relief in Africa. It seemed that little had changed in spite of the huge amount of attention paid to the problems on the African continent around the world.

Ultimately, the factors that cause poverty and malnutrition can only be solved by effective national governments. Yet the media, as we have shown throughout this book, are crucial to the development of democracy. Indian economist and author Amartya Sen argues that 'in the terrible history of famines in the world, no substantial famine has ever occurred in any independent and democratic country with a relatively free press. We cannot find exceptions to this rule, no matter where we look' (1999, pp. 6–7). In countries where the media are free to report on disasters such as famines, the government comes under pressure to do something about them. Whatever else a free media might do for us, it compels us to empathise with our fellow citizens.

Why does it take war or natural disasters for Australians to take an interest in global politics? Would we be more generous in our dealings with developing states if we knew more about them?

It is in this 'terror frame' that Australia has debated such measures as the *Anti-Terrorism Bill 2005*, which contained measures such as detention of terrorism suspects without charge. We will discuss the balancing act between national security and freedom of speech in greater detail below. American, British and Australian governments have been keen to blur the line between protecting their citizens from terrorism and their reasons for attacking Iraq. Journalists have been sceptical of these tactics, but are less prone to question the priority that issues of conflict and terrorism should be given at a time when Australia's territory is not under threat. That is, their scepticism still accommodates the 'terror frame'. How many times have we heard that the attacks on America on September 11 'have changed everything'? For example, the large increases in funding for the Australian Defence Forces throughout the 1990s are a questionable response to the terrorist threat. The ADF's poor financial management and some disastrous acquisition programs would suggest that greater scrutiny of such a large reallocation of resources is justified.

The first casualty

Prussian military strategist Carl von Clausewitz argued that war is 'a continuation of politics by other means'. War is politics at its most brutal, emotional and desperate. Politicians who send their nations into war are making their most important decisions. When a nation's very existence is under threat, extreme measures can be expected in its defence. **Abraham Lincoln** is celebrated for his commitment to democracy and his emancipation of slaves. Yet, during the US Civil War (1861–64), Lincoln repeatedly infringed civil liberties and ignored the decisions of the courts in his determination to maintain order and achieve victory. Well before that conflict, governments had learned the value of controlling information during wartime. However, the mass media were becoming an important institution in our Western societies—and not one that could be easily intimidated by governments.

▶ **Abraham Lincoln**   the sixteenth and one of the greatest presidents (1861–65) of the USA

Newspapers first made their presence felt during the Crimean War (1854–56), with reporting critical of the tactics of the British generals, and first-hand descriptions of the appalling conditions of the common soldiers. Debates about the effect of the embryonic mass media were brought into focus during the Spanish–American War (1898), when American newspaper baron William Randolph Hearst told an employee: 'You furnish the pictures, I'll furnish the war' (Gorman & McLean 2003, p. 16). Stories like this one help to shape our perceptions about the power of the media. It is difficult to judge, however, the extent to which the press was shaping public opinion about the prospects for war, or merely following it (Gorman & McLean 2003, p. 16).

The First World War marked a turning point in the history of human conflict—the first industrial-scale war. The total effort required to prevail in a war between industrialised states led to the mobilisation of all sectors of society, including the media, behind the war effort. Governments saw the importance of psychological warfare, not just in shaping the thinking of opponents but also in getting the citizenry behind the war. This involved maintaining morale at home, as well as attempting to influence opinion in neutral and combatant countries. In Great Britain and the USA, new laws allowed extensive censorship of newspapers (Gorman & McLean 2003, p. 18). The attitude of the military towards the role of public information was typified by a remark from a British officer: 'It simply tells the people what it thinks will conduce to winning the war. If truth is good for winning the war, it tells them the truth. If a lie is likely to win the war, it tells them a lie' (cited in Knightley 2000, p. 483).

During the Second World War, the scale of the information campaign, like the scale of the war, was the biggest ever. Democratic nations, including Australia, created dedicated departments of information, something hitherto thought to be the province of dictatorships like Nazi Germany and the Soviet Union (Gorman & McLean 2003, p. 93). These departments had access to a truly mass media, with the development of cinema and radio broadcasting, and, in the USA, television. Cinema newsreels played an important role in reaching that part of the population who did not read newspapers.

Box 11.2 ... and now for some good news

With so much conflict in the world, news organisations have under-reported one of the most important trends in global politics: that military conflict is on the wane. The latest Human Security Report, sponsored by the United Nations, 'documents a dramatic, but largely unknown, decline in the number of wars, genocides and human rights abuse over the past decade' (Human Security Centre 2005).

Such a promising trend is difficult to report. Peace provides fewer graphic images than war. At the same time, there is no shortage of conflict to report. Indeed, the period after the Cold War is often considered one of increased conflict, partly because some of the most egregious events took place in Europe, with the ethnic cleansing in the former Yugoslavia. The facts, however, tell us otherwise.

Why do you think the decline in conflict in recent decades is 'largely unknown'? What role does the media play in our perceptions of conflict and the prospects for a more peaceful world?

The British government had learned from its experience in the First World War that outright propaganda was treated with suspicion by the populace. They attempted to find a balance between the need to influence the media and allowing the media to be independent and credible.

Pressure on the media under these conditions of national emergency comes not just from the government but from the public. Indeed, during the early stages of the **Cold War** newspapers needed little government prodding to take a fiercely anti-communist editorial line. Patriotic support for government policies carried over from the Second World War to the Korean War (1950–53). Television had not yet penetrated the majority of American households and was yet to be introduced to Australia. Coverage of the Vietnam War (1959–75) was more vivid and timely due to the evolution of television technology.

> **Cold War** the period from the end of the Second World War (1945) to the fall of the Berlin Wall (1989) that was a period of tension, but not direct conflict, between capitalist and communist states

A simple cause and effect between the extensive nightly television news coverage of the war and the fact that America and its allies lost the war is tempting. Indeed, the coverage of the Vietnam War still colours conservative perceptions of the trustworthiness of journalists on issues of national security. That war could have been won, many believe, had the media played a more supportive role in maintaining public morale. President Johnson believed that continual coverage of the horrors of war eroded public support (Gorman & McLean 2003, p. 172). More likely, however, is a more complex interaction of factors. Support for the war was initially very high. Without a rapid victory, however, the ongoing images of sacrifice fed into public debates about why the war was necessary. In a part of the world that most Americans knew little about, even the communist bogey was insufficient to buttress support for a war of attrition. As debate about the war on the home front became more intense, the ebbing of morale could not help but extend to the battlefield. Protests against the Vietnam War were part of a wider trend towards a society more critical of authority than had been the case during the two world wars. Scepticism of government claims about the need to send troops overseas, and of foreign policy priorities more generally, is a healthy part of democracy. However, such notions do not make military planners any less concerned about the potential impact of the media on the conduct of war. Since Vietnam, a range of strategies have been tried to better manage the effect of television coverage on the course of military conflicts.

The First Gulf War against Iraq in 1990–91 was the first to receive round-the-clock coverage. With both sides watching CNN, television was used as a source of misinformation, a conduit for communication with the enemy, and a means of propaganda aimed at civilian populations (Louw 2005, p. 253). This war probably marked the peak of military management of war coverage. This was partly because the conflict was brief, and journalists and news outlets had little opportunity to escape the military PR machine. Shortly after the war, a veteran of public affairs during the Vietnam War remarked: 'The Gulf War is over and the press lost' (cited in Knightley 2000, p. 500). Many news outlets shared this analysis, and vowed never again to be as tightly controlled as they had been during that conflict.

Terrorism brings in quite a different perspective to this argument since the security of our state is not under any serious threat, but the lives of our citizens may still be endangered. As we noted in the previous chapter, the decentralised nature of new media allows anyone to get their message to the world. That includes terrorist groups. Inexpensive and difficult to trace, the internet has allowed terrorists to bypass mass media in promoting their cause. This makes the internet an important tool not only for publishing training manuals and distributing propaganda aimed at recruitment and fundraising, but also for spreading messages and images that the mainstream media refuses to touch. For example, video of the beheading of an American hostage in Iraq, of which television news showed only the initial stage, was available uncensored over the internet.

One aim of terrorist groups is to spread fear among citizens in the hope that they will force governments to change their policies on issues of concern to the group. Television has been the perfect medium for terrorist propaganda. Widespread dissemination of images of destruction is usually more important than the act of terrorism itself. The destruction of the twin towers of New York's World Trade Center provided the most stunning images of the television age. Terrorists knew those images would be endlessly broadcast around the world. Even after the hundredth replay, the pictures are unnerving.

Debates and controversies

NATIONAL SECURITY VERSUS THE RIGHT TO KNOW

In an early attempt to wrestle with the consequences of war in the television age, veteran BBC broadcaster Robin Day argued: 'One wonders if in future a democracy which has inhibited television coverage in every home will ever be able to fight a war, however just … The full brutality of the combat will be there in close up and in colour, and blood looks very red on the television screen' (cited in Knightley 2000, p. 411). There is a healthy streak of journalistic idealism in such remarks. If only people knew the truth, they would do the right thing. It is difficult to judge the true effects of the type of coverage that Day imagined, since the bloodiest scenes of conflict are often omitted from news coverage. This is usually done in the interests of good taste, and to avoid offending the families of those involved. Thus, in dealing with debates about the public's right to know, we need to consider self-censorship as well as any restrictions governments may place on media freedom.

It is a long time since any Western state fought a war for its very existence. Our willingness to suspend civil liberties and sacrifice soldiers depends on perceptions about what is at stake. America and its allies faced this in Iraq from 2003. When the first phase of the war was over, with Saddam Hussein deposed as president of Iraq, public support soared, only to fall away again as the insurgency took hold. The Howard Government paid little political cost, however, and was fortunate that Australian casualties were, at least in the early years of the war, minimal. Public perceptions about war also depend on just who is expected to do the fighting. Australia has not experienced military **conscription** since the Vietnam War (1959–75). Debates about conscription were hugely divisive in Australia during the First World War and the Vietnam War (more so than the Second World War when Australian territory was under threat.) More recent wars in Iraq and Afghanistan have been extensively debated, but the smaller scale of Australian involvement has reduced their political saliency.

> **conscription** the compulsory recruitment of labour by the government, for war or any other purpose

Even under the most extreme circumstances, however, one might argue that open debate about military strategy, for example, should be allowed. Why should a nation's strategy during wartime be any less open to constructive criticism than any other area of policy? Limited conflicts—those where a state's territorial integrity is not under threat—make the suspension of civil liberties more difficult to justify. In addition, Australian involvement in conflicts well beyond our shores tends to be much more politically controversial. Under these circumstances, there is greater public support for critical media scrutiny of the conflict. Prior to the September 11 attacks on the USA, most Western countries already had strong anti-terrorism laws. One of the first government responses after that attack was legislation that undermined long-standing and fundamental rights, such as the right to a lawyer. This type of legislation may simply have been a tactic to sway public attention away from intelligence and operational failures. There were certainly many of these in the lead-up to September 11. In moving quickly to introduce or amend counter-terrorism laws, governments showed that they were acting to counter the threat of terrorism.

The first challenge to free speech in the enactment of such laws was the haste with which they were legislated. The *USA Patriot Act* was passed just six weeks after the September 11 attacks. The Howard Government allowed little parliamentary scrutiny of its second round of anti-terror laws in 2005. Public debate is curtailed by the security imperative. Yet, given the important departures from human rights values that counter-terrorism laws often contained, they should have received an above-average amount of scrutiny.

There is some justification for treating terrorism differently from other types of crimes. Terrorist acts are usually a means to an end, aimed at spreading fear. Communication is at the centre of terrorism, and also at the centre of efforts to prevent it. Australian law allows authorities a great deal of latitude in preventing the communication of information within suspected terrorist organisations, including the detention of non-suspects and restriction on media reporting on police counter-terrorism action. Suspects can be denied a lawyer for this reason. Further, terrorists who employ suicide bombing as a means of spreading fear are unlikely to be put off by the prospect of punishment, making prevention a more urgent method of dealing with this type of act than deterrence. Counter-terrorism laws are rightly very controversial. Even the definition of terrorism is not straightforward. Acts of terrorism are easy enough to recognise. Criminalising acts in support of terrorist groups tends to be much more contentious. Such acts might include selling books that incite violence or hatred. Differentiating between nascent terrorist groups and those hostile to the war in Iraq (even to the extent that they express sympathy for the insurgency there) can also been a problem. One would imagine, then, that the introduction of counter-terrorism laws would be cause for a high level of public debate.

One method used by governments to justify laws that depart from long-standing legal principles has been to stress the ways in which counter-terrorism laws add to human security. Attorney-General Phillip Ruddock argued that:

> Unfortunately the debate on counter-terrorism issues has been dominated by traditional analysis of protecting either national security, or civil liberties, as if the protection of one undermines the protection of the other. This course is unhelpful as it implies that counter-terrorism legislation is inevitably at odds with the protection of fundamental human rights (cited in Golder & Williams 2006, p. 50).

Human rights advocates have long accounted for the fact that some rights can come into conflict with each other. They accept that there must be a hierarchy that values some rights over others, but also maintain that some rights remain inalienable (Golder & Williams 2006, p. 50). Advocates of human security, on the other hand, point out that security is a precondition for the protection of rights.

This brings us back to the fundamental role of the media in democratic societies. How can we freely debate the appropriate balance between security and civil liberties when the media are not free to report the activities of our security agencies? Laws that restrict the flow of information about the activities of law enforcement agencies also make very difficult any assessment of the effectiveness of those laws in preventing terrorism. Australia's 2005 counter-terrorism laws also altered the law of **sedition**. Laws that prevent the advocacy of overthrowing the government have been long-standing exceptions to the principle of freedom of speech. A more controversial provision in the new law outlaws speech that may provoke violence between groups within society, where 'peace, order and good government' are threatened. While this provision allows for public debate in good faith, critics argue that this is a narrow exception that may not include academic and artistic endeavour.

▶ **sedition** subversion of the state

Box 11.3   Another view: al-Jazeera

Qatar-based satellite news station al-Jazeera came under heavy criticism from American officials for its purportedly biased coverage of events since 11 September 2001 and their willingness to air terrorist propaganda. The Arab broadcaster alleges that the American attack on its Kabul headquarters during the bombing of the Taliban in 2001 was deliberate. One important difference between al-Jazeera and its Western counterparts is the former's willingness to air explicit pictures of the casualties of war. American officials interpreted this as an attempt to inflame Arab opinion against the USA. More likely, al-Jazeera's audience, with long experience of the Arab–Israeli conflict, is simply more used to seeing the results of bloodshed.

The fact that, like its audience, al-Jazeera was editorially opposed to the war against Iraq did not stop them from trying to understand the American point of view. They aired extensive interviews with supporters of the war and attempted to give a balanced account of events. Balance never wins news outlets many friends, however. Both sides of the conflict within the Palestinian Authority, Hamas and Fatah, have accused the network of bias. Many al-Jazeera journalists were recruited from the Arabic service of the British Broadcasting Corporation, renowned for its pursuit of objectivity.

Western perceptions of al-Jazeera often compare it (favourably or unfavourably) to Western news outlets such as CNN or BBC World. Yet, a more apposite comparison would be with the official state media outlets that dominate newspapers and broadcasting in the Middle East. For example, we may see a translation of a debate on al-Jazeera where neither of the protagonists is painting a favourable view of the war in Iraq. While the parameters of such a debate may seem strange to us, the fact that debates take place at all is a vast improvement in freedom of expression in that part of the world. Television viewers are used to one view only—that of the state. The fact that citizens might openly discuss the big issues facing their societies is a quantum leap for journalism, and one of the reasons satellite broadcasters have proved to be so popular.

Al-Jazeera now has an English-language service. Do you think this a welcome competitor to the established international news channels that have had so much influence on the way we see the world?

JOURNALISTS AND THE NATIONAL INTEREST

Speaking against America's involvement in the First World War, Senator Hiram Johnson noted that 'when war comes, the first casualty is truth'. While truth and objectivity are sometimes seen as outdated notions, if they are of any value, it is surely in making the public fully aware of what is at stake in the decision to go to war. Why should we expect journalists to remain objective when issues of life and death are at stake? It would be foolish to think that journalists did not have a considered opinion on whether or not their country should go to war. Having an opinion is not the same as taking one side or the other in a debate. However, some journalists unashamedly do the latter. One of the most famous is Australian-born John Pilger. His passionate reports on conflicts around the globe have moved many, but angered others. For example, Pilger's advocacy of plight the East Timorese people under Indonesian occupation proved unpopular with Australian governments seeking closer relations with the Indonesian government (see Pilger 1992).

As prime minister, John Howard has frequently used the term 'national interest' to describe his actions, regarding both domestic and foreign policy. The government's 2003 foreign policy **White Paper** was entitled *In the National Interest*. The government, naturally, presents its own interpretation of what constitutes the national interest. This is important because the government is in a position to represent Australia's official position to other countries, and makes many foreign policy decisions without reference to Parliament. Yet, government policy and the national interest are not one and the same. Similarly, the national interest is not the same as public opinion. Governments often argue that they must make difficult and far-sighted decisions that conflict with majority public opinion. That was the case when the Howard Government deployed troops to Iraq in 2003. Media criticism of governments during times of conflict is sometimes portrayed as unpatriotic, putting journalists and news organisations in an invidious position.

▶ **White Paper**   a public statement of government policy in a given area

It is difficult for journalists to swim against the tide when a nation is at war. While some Australian media outlets, such as the *Australian*, supported war in Iraq, they have refrained from the unabashed patriotism of the American

Fox News Channel (even though both of these outlets are owned by News Corporation). Coverage of the Vietnam War is romanticised by journalists as an example of critical media coverage. Yet it was some years before American and Australian involvement in that war came under intense scrutiny. It took a breakdown in the consensus at government level for the media to outwardly question the position of the US government (Hirst & Patching 2005, p. 148). Similarly, in Iraq we look to experts such as retired generals to provide a signal that things are going badly. No single journalist can get a complete picture of both the front line of battle and the machinations of Washington or Canberra politics. It can thus take some time for the media to have the confidence to challenge political leaders about their decisions.

One dimension of the CNN effect is the surreal business of bringing warfare into our lounge rooms. The 1991 war against Iraq was the first to be covered around the clock. Government claims about the efficiency of their weapons systems were buttressed by repeated television images of a missile finding an impossibly small target. These 'smart bombs', however, still cause considerable damage, relied on human intelligence to select the right target and had a lower rate of accuracy in battle than under test conditions. Well after the Allies had claimed victory, the reality of the massive death toll during the Iraqi retreat from Kuwait began to emerge. By then, however, it was no longer headline news. Reflecting on the coverage of that war, journalists were angry that their ability to properly cover the Iraq war had been limited. Many media organisations were determined not to allow the military establishment to control what they could broadcast. Determined to continue to influence, if not control, media coverage, America and its allies in Iraq in 2003 allowed **embedded journalists** to travel with military units.

> **embedded journalists** journalists who become part of a military unit in order to gain first-hand access to their manoeuvres

Box 11.3   Dying for a story

More journalists have been killed since 2003 covering the war in Iraq than in any conflict since the Second World War. This is partly because of the record number of journalists covering that conflict. It also stems from a renewed determination on the part of many journalists to report the war from outside the protected areas of Baghdad. Once outside the 'green zone', there is no set battle front. Journalists have also become the targets of kidnappers in Iraq and the Philippines. Cameraman Jon Steel captured the feeling of many of those who enter battle zones in his book *War Junkie: One Man's Addiction to the Worst Places on Earth*. Steel captured images of the worst of human nature from Rwanda to Russia.

Journalists are not the only ones who risk their lives to get important stories to the world. In recent years, we have seen dissidents across the world risking the wrath of their governments by getting video of important events in areas where journalists are banned. We have seen images of violent confrontations over land in Zimbabwe and riots in rural China.

What do you think motivates journalists and their support crews to risk their lives in pursuit of a story? Is that level of close contact necessary for us to understand what is at stake in a conflict?

While being embedded in a military unit involved in a war gives a journalist direct access to the front line of battle, there are a number of problems with the arrangement in terms of maintaining objectivity. The first is the tendency to empathise with the aims of the soldiers. Reliant on the unit for protection, it would be surprising if any journalist could remain emotionally distant from the activities of that unit. Further, an embedded journalist has limited sources of information about the context of any battle that they witness. To be effective in furthering our understanding of the war, coverage from embedded journalists needs to be combined with that of other sources of information. Some embedded journalists managed to balance these competing demands in Iraq, giving close-quarters reports of important events. Satellite technology allowed instantaneous transmission of reports, limiting the opportunities for military censorship. Other embedded journalists were taken by the moment, only adding to the jingoistic coverage of certain media outlets, or content to let spectacular pictures of tank advances substitute for good reporting. Even this ultimate front-line reporting failed to lift the fog of war from that conflict. The fall of Basra in southern Iraq to British forces was reported numerous times over two weeks before events became clear (Hirst & Patching 2005, p. 152).

One decision that placed editors in the position of influencing political events was the publication of photographs showing abuses committed by American soldiers at Abu Ghraib prison in Baghdad. The photographs had been circulating among media outlets for some time before they were published, while generals tried to convince editors that the images would inflame Islamic opinion and put the lives of Americans at risk. It was a forlorn hope that the digital images would be secret for very long. The large amount of coverage that the prison torture story received, however, showed that the moral authority of the allied action in Iraq was coming under attack. This was the first of many occasions when Western media became openly hostile to the White House. The failure to find weapons of mass destruction caused the *New York Times* to revisit its coverage of the period running up to the war, and it published a public apology for being insufficiently sceptical of the case for attacking Iraq. Since the initial phase of the war, the media has been very sceptical of government pronouncements. With hindsight, it is easy to suggest that this scepticism would have been better placed before the war. We should not assume, however, that the media could have prevented the war. The political atmosphere after 11 September was such that showing strong leadership and defying popular opinion was the order of the day. A hostile press can make only a limited difference to that type of political dynamic.

SUMMARY

The debate about the effects of the media could have no higher stakes than the course of war and peace. The bluster and self-importance of media barons and journalists should not be mistaken for influence. Yet the media surely plays a crucial role in framing political debates. The ways in which foreign policy debates are framed, and the priority they take in our wider political discourse, have much to do with the startling images that reach us from around the world. Whether it is images of children in distress, or the bloody results of conflicts in which Australia is involved, television has sharpened our sense of what is at stake in our relations with the rest of the world.

Governments struggle to justify restrictions on media freedom when our sovereign territory is not at risk. Yet terrorism has brought an entirely new dimension to conflict, where the lives of citizens can be threatened by relatively small groups.

Australia has made compromises in its traditional protection of civil liberties as a result. The priority that the media gives to terrorist threat, encouraged by the government, has played a role in framing such debates. Over time, the media will tire of the 'terror frame', and the political agenda will move on to the next crisis. It is difficult to escape the conclusion that although television and the internet give an immediacy and relevance to global events that affect our debates on foreign policy, their coverage of those events can be shallow. The CNN effect notwithstanding, we correctly rely on authoritative and reflective journalism to guide our understanding of our place in the world.

Questions

1 What is the CNN effect? Do you think it applies to Australian foreign policy?
2 To what lengths should the Australian media go in order to ensure that we know the truth about conflicts in which Australian forces are engaged?
3 Think about the way in which the media 'frames' debates over terrorism. Do we worry too much about terrorist attacks? Has media coverage of terrorism influenced public debates about civil liberties?

FURTHER READING

Golder, B. & Williams, G. 2006, 'Balancing National Security and Human Rights: Assessing the Legal Response of Common Law Nations to the Threat of Terrorism'. *Journal of Comparative Policy Analysis*, vol. 8, no. 1, pp. 43–62.

Hirst, M & Patching, R. 2005, 'The Media Goes to War'. *Journalism Ethics*. Oxford University Press: Melbourne.

Knightley, P. 2000, *The First Casualty: The War Correspondent as Hero, Propagandist, and Myth-maker from the Crimea to Kosovo*. Johns Hopkins University Press: Baltimore.

Glossary

Abraham Lincoln

the sixteenth and one of the greatest presidents (1861–65) of the USA

agenda priming

coined by Iyengar and Kinder, it draws on and expands upon the agenda-setting thesis; Iyengar and Kinder argued that media helps to 'prime' or influence how people think about particular issues—the media sets the context (on the basis of the stories it presents) in which audiences make political judgments, not only about the 'issue' but also perceptions about how well political candidates and organisations are doing their job in relation to that issue

agenda setting

associated with the work of Shaw and McComb, it posits that the media does not tell us what to think, but rather tells us what to think about

agenda-setting role

the power of senior journalists to make choices about which news items make the front page of a newspaper, or the lead story on broadcast news, to shape the agenda in politics

analogue

A form of transmitting information characterised by continuously variable quantities, as opposed to digital transmission, which is characterised by discrete bits of information in numerical steps

anti-siphoning legislation

a scheme that ensures that certain events are available on commercial free-to-air channels by preventing pay-TV licensees from acquiring exclusive rights to certain listed events

Australian Journalists Association (AJA)

formed in 1910 and registered federally in 1911, this union served its members until 1991 when it amalgamated with the Australian Commercial & Industrial Artists Association; in 1993, the AJA (along with the Australian Theatrical and Amusement Employees Association and the Actors Equity of Australia) amalgamated to form the Media, Entertainment and Arts Alliance (MEAA)

Australian Press Council

The self-regulatory body of the print media, established in 1976 with two main aims: to help preserve the traditional freedom of the press within Australia and ensure that the free press acts responsibly and ethically

backgrounding

involves journalists seeking information from political actors without naming them in the resulting story

bourgeoisie

a term often used in reference to the middle class; in Marxist terminology, it is specifically applied to the ruling capitalist class that owns the means of production

broadband

technology that allows access to the internet at a much faster rate than traditional telephone lines

budget

all of a government's taxation and spending plans for the year combined in a single statement

cabinet government

the system where all important decisions are made by a group of senior ministers, for which they take collective responsibility

cabinet

the supreme decision-making institution of government, consisting of the prime minister/premier and his/her most senior ministers

censorship

the prohibition, control and suppression of ideas, speech and other forms of human expression

code of ethics

a statement of principles that outlines the expected behaviour of members of a professional group, and that reflects the values that it members are required to observe

Cold War

the period from the end of the Second World War (1945) to the fall of the Berlin Wall (1989) that was a period of tension, but not direct conflict, between capitalist and communist states

Committee to Protect Journalists

An independent, non-profit organization dedicated to the global defence of press freedom.

conscription

the compulsory recruitment of labour by the government, for war or any other purpose

Constitution

enacted in 1900, the Australian Commonwealth Constitution is a legal compact that sets out the fundamental political principles of government, describing important political institutions, actors and processes

convergence

the use of the internet to replace separate media platforms such as television, radio and newspapers

cross-media ownership

laws that until 2007 limited media companies to one type of platform—television, radio or newspapers—in each market

deliberative democracy

the encouragement of extensive and rational public debate on political issues before decisions are made

deregulation

the removal (either in part or in whole) of government controls over an industry, which is done ostensibly in the interests of improving the economic and productive efficiency of the industry in question

digital

information-processing techniques that convert the actual data into binary (or machine language) code for more efficient transmission and storage; it is regarded as being more secure than its sibling, analogue, and also relatively impervious to static or fading signals

digitisation

the use of digital technology to replace analogue technology; digital signals can be compacted and therefore carry more channels than the single, continuous analogue signals

Dix Review

a major review of the ABC in 1981, named after Alexander Dix, who chaired the review

embedded journalists

journalists who become part of a military unit in order to gain first-hand access to their manoeuvres

encoding/decoding

derives largely from the critical tradition; however, it does use tools of quantitative analysis; media messages are believed to be open and have multiple meanings, and are interpreted according to the context and culture of the receiver—it assumes that audiences can in fact resist ideological influence by applying oppositional readings according to their own experiences and outlook

false consciousness

the failure of the oppressed to recognise that their situation results from their acceptance of the views of their oppressors

federation

the unification of the six colonies that formed the Commonwealth of Australia in 1901; the process resulted in a new political arrangement whereby powers and functions were divided between the federal (or central) government and each of the states

firewall

used to cordon off part of a computer network to protect it from unwanted influences

first release

programs that have not been televised and that are no more than two years old

focus group

a small group of people, usually swinging voters, on whom political parties test policy ideas and slogans

fourth estate

thought to date from the first half of the nineteenth century, this term in its modern form refers to the role of the media (press) as a check and counterbalance on the power of the executive, Parliament and courts—the three arms of government

government department

a department established by the government in order to advise and assist in the formulation and delivery of policy in a specific area, such as health or defence; individual departments are directly answerable to the relevant minister

Governor-General

the Queen's representative in Australia; the formal head of the Australian state

governors

officials of the UK government who were appointed to manage the affairs of the various Australian colonies

Great Depression

a period during the 1930s in which Australia, along with a host of economies throughout the world, experienced high unemployment and stagnant economic growth

High Court

the highest legal body in Australia, which, among other things, is charged with the responsibility of interpreting the Australian Constitution

horizontal communication

communication between creators of content and their audience; the ability of new media to accommodate many more creators of content has made this much more common

ideology

a comprehensive set of beliefs, ideas or values that inform how people order and make sense of the world around them

industry code of practice

a document that outlines how to achieve the standard required by the relevant government act and regulation; codes of practice are generally developed through consultation with representatives from industry and the relevant government agency or agencies

Internet Content Host (ICH)

persons, groups or organisations that host internet content

Internet Service Provider (ISP)

a company that provides access to the internet to individuals or companies; they provide local dial-up or broadband access from your personal computer to their computer network and their network connects you to the internet

Karl Marx

a key nineteenth-century thinker and co-author (with Frederick Engels) of *The Communist Manifesto*

libel

a false and malicious publication that injures someone's reputation or defames them

liberal/pluralist perspective

a view that holds that power in society is diffused and rented among a number of competing groups

libertarians

those who prefer minimal government intervention in both the economic and social spheres

licence

a contractual arrangement between the government and an individual/organisation, which affords to the latter the right to operate broadcasting services; since 1992, the process of assigning broadcasting licences is based on a price-based system whereby they are auctioned to the highest bidder

limited effects

sometimes referred to as minimal effects theory, this school of thought has its genesis in the work of Paul Lazarsfeld and his colleagues, and champions the view that media effects are largely of an indirect nature and minimal

market failure

the inability of the market to achieve an efficient allocation of resources due to incomplete or asymmetric information

media adviser

an employee of a politician, often with experience in journalism, whose job it is to manage the politician's relationship with the media

media effects

attempts to account for how the media affects audiences; it is associated with an empirical, qualitative research approach that attempts to scientifically measure the relationship between the media and audience behaviour

Media, Entertainment and Arts Alliance (MEAA)

The Alliance is the union and professional organisation that covers everyone in the media, entertainment, sports and arts industries; it was created in 1992 and consists of 36,000 members, including people working in TV, radio, theatre and film, entertainment venues and recreation grounds; journalists, actors, dancers, sportspeople, cartoonists, photographers and orchestral and opera performers, as well as people working in public relations, advertising, book publishing and website production

media monitoring

transcripts of radio and television programs that are made available to politicians and government departments so that they can keep track of what is making news and check on the results of their media management techniques

Media Watch

an ABC television programme dedicated to exposing deceitful and duplicitous behaviour in the Australian media

minister

a person appointed to head an executive or administrative department of government; in the Australian context, a minister is in charge of one or more portfolio areas and is answerable to Parliament for both his/her actions and those of the department under his/her jurisdiction

negative campaigning

a campaigning style that highlights the bad things about the opposing party and its leader

non-government organisations (NGOs)
centres of power and resources alternative to nation-states

oligopolistic
refers to a situation in which there are only a few competitive firms operating in a market; while competition between the different sellers can sometimes lead to lower prices, in some contexts the firms may collude to raise prices and restrict production, thereby leading to higher prices for consumers

open source
computer code for a program that is made available to anyone who wishes to alter or improve it

pamphleteers
those who spread political ideas during the eighteenth century through short pamphlets instead of books or newspapers

Parliament
an assembly of those men and women who have been democratically elected to make laws for the country

party organisation
a complex set of official structures common to all parties, ranging from local branches to national secretariats, that support their Members of Parliament

permanent campaign
the use of the resources of government to promote a political party over the entirety of the parliamentary cycle

plausible deniability
when no official records exist of what a minister was or was not told of a given matter, the politician is said to have plausible deniability of any knowledge of that matter

podcast
a computer file containing news or entertainment, which has been either broadcast by media outlets or created expressly for the internet or replay on handheld devices

privatise
to sell government-owned enterprises or industries to private investors

prescribe
in this context, to issue an order or command that something must be done or shown

proscribe

to prevent or exclude something from use or mention

public sphere

the set of actors and activities that enable an exchange of ideas throughout society

qualitative research

attempts to 'study the lived experience' by 'observing how individuals act' and by 'describ[ing] their actions in society' (Traudt 2005, p. 30); Turow describes this approach as one that endeavours to 'make sense of an aspect of reality by showing how different parts of it fit together in particular ways' (2003, p. 131)

quantitative research

attempts to measure quantitatively the impact that exposure to media has on our actions and attitudes by 'converting observed behaviours into numbers that can be systematically analysed using mathematical tools generally known as statistics' (Traudt 2005, p. 16)

radio frequency spectrum

alternating current having characteristics such that if the current is input to an antenna, an electromagnetic field is generated suitable for wireless broadcasting and/ or communications.

reinforcement thesis

linked to the limited effects school, it suggests that the media tends to reinforce existing attitudes rather than change or create new attitudes

Reporters Without Borders

an international organisation that fights for the freedom of the press and freedom of expression, and ensures protection of journalists by denouncing human rights breaches

representative

a form of democracy wherein voters choose representatives to act on their behalf

responsible government

a form of government wherein the party or parties that win the most seats in the lower house of Parliament, or have the support of a majority of members in that house, form the government of the day

sedition

subversion of the state

Senate

the (76-member) upper house of the Commonwealth Parliament; along with the House of Representatives (150-member lower house), the Senate is responsible for debating and scrutinising legislation

separation of powers

the separation of government responsibilities into executive, legislative and judicial realms

shield laws

laws that protect the right of journalists to keep their sources private

socialisation

the process whereby individuals learn to behave in a manner consistent with societal expectations as regards the norms, values and culture of their society

spin

an effort to persuade individuals or the public of a given proposition; the term is usually used pejoratively to suggest that the proposition in question is an unlikely one

statutes

laws that have been devised and sanctioned by Parliament

statutory body

a form of government department that has a largely corporate function and is, for the most part, autonomous in its operations as compared with government departments

structural power

a consequence of the inherent importance of a particular section of society, such as the role of the media in reporting on politics

swinging voters

voters who are prepared to change the party for whom they vote between elections

uses and gratifications

a theory that focuses on how audiences use media and why; it assumes an active audience that selects different media based on fulfilling their particular needs

weblog

an online diary (often shortened to 'blog') usually featuring comments from readers and links to other web sites

White Paper

a public statement of government policy in a given area

References

ABC Election Coverage Review Committee. 2004, *Monitoring ABC Pre-Election Coverage*, 3 October. http://www.abc.net.au/corp/pubs/monitoring_elections.htm (accessed 24 November 2005).

ABC, see Australian Broadcasting Corporation.

Abetz, E. 2004, 'Abetz Accuses Latham of Avoiding Scrutiny'. *The World Today*, 5 July.

ABS, see Australian Bureau of Statistics.

ACMA, see Australian Communications and Media Authority.

Albon, R. & Papandrea, F. 1998, *Media Regulation in the Public Interest*. Institute of Public Affairs.

Alger, D. 1989, *The Media and Politics*. Prentice Hall: New Jersey.

Alliance Online (MEAA). http://www.alliance.org.au/ (accessed 1 December 2006).

Alston, R. 2003, 'The ABC of Politics'. Transcript of a speech delivered at *The Brisbane Institute*, 18 November. http://www.brisinst.org.au/papers/alston_richard_abc/ (accessed 25 May 2004).

ANAO, see Australian National Audit Office.

Australian Broadcasting Corporation. 2003, *Independent Complaints Review Panel Review of the Minister's Complaint*, 10 October. http://www.abc.net.au/corp/pubs/ICRP.pdf (accessed 24 November 2005).

Australian Broadcasting Corporation. 2003–04, *ABC Annual Report 2003–04*. http://www.abc.net.au/corp/annual_reports/ar04/pdf/ABC_AR_03-04_Complete.pdf (accessed 5 February 2007).

Australian Broadcasting Corporation. 2004–05, *ABC Annual Report 2004–05*. http://www.abc.net.au/corp/annual_reports/ar05/pdf/ABC_AR05_Complete.pdf (accessed 5 February 2007).

Australian Broadcasting Corporation Act. 1983, http://scaleplus.law.gov.au/html/histact/10/5029/top.htm.

Australian Bureau of Statistics. 2004, *Arts and Culture in Australia: A Statistical Overview*. Catalogue number: 4172.0.

Australian Bureau of Statistics. 2004–05, *Household Use of Information Technology*. Catalogue number: 8146.0.

Australian Communications and Media Authority. 2005, *Financial Trends in commercial radio 1978-79 to 2003-04*. December. http://www.acma.gov.au/acmainterwr/aba/newspubs/radio_tv/licensing/documents/financial_trends_05.pdf (accessed 1 February 2007).

Australian Film Commission. 2006, *Get the Picture: Fast Facts*. http://www.afc.gov.au/gtp/fastoverview.html#Raj67744 (accessed 6 February 2007).

Australian National Audit Office 1998, *Community Education and Information Program*. Commonwealth of Australia.

Australian Press Council. 2002, *General Press Release*, no. 253, November. http://www.presscouncil.org.au/pcsite/activities/guides/gpr253.html (accessed 1 February 2006).

Australian. 2004a, 13 July.

Australian. 2004b, 21 October.

Australian. 2006, 18 May.

Ball, T. & Dagger, R. 2004, *Political Ideologies and the Democratic Ideal*, 5th edn. Pearson Longman: USA.

Bandura, A, 1977, *Social Learning Theory*. Prentice Hall: Engelwood Cliffs.

Bandura, A. 1965, 'Influence of models' reinforcement contingencies on the acquisition of imitative responses'. *Journal of Personality and Social Psychology*, vol. 1, pp. 589–95.

Barnes, G. 2006, 'New laws on suicide attacks freedom'. *Online Opinion*, 9 January. http://www.onlineopinion.com.au/view.asp?article=4022 (accessed 11 November 2006).

Barns, G. 2005, *Selling the Australian Government: Politics and Propaganda from Whitlam to Howard*. UNSW Press: Sydney.

Barr, T. 2002, 'The Internet and online Communication'. In S. Cunningham & G. Turner (eds), *The Media and Communications in Australia*. Allen & Unwin: NSW.

Beecher, E. 2005a, 'The Decline of the Quality Press'. In R. Manne (ed.), *Do Not Disturb. Is the Media Failing Australia*? Black Inc. Agenda: Melbourne.

Beecher, E., 2005b, 'The End of Serious Journalism?'. In J. Mills (ed.), *Barons to Bloggers: Confronting Media Power*. The Miegunyah Press: Melbourne.

Belknap, M. 2001, *The CNN Effect: Strategic Enabler or Operational Risk?* U.S. Army War College. Strategy Research Project. http://www.iwar.org.uk/psyops/resources/cnn-effect/Belknap_M_H_01.pdf (accessed 27 April 2006).

Berg, C. 2006a, 'Only the market can properly re-shape the media'. *Australian Financial Review*, 15 September.

Berg, C. 2006b, *IPA Submission to Meeting the Digital Challenge: Discussion Paper on Media Reform Options*. April, pp. 1–8. http://www.ipa.org.au/files/IPA_Digital %20Challenge%20Submission%202006.pdf (accessed 6 February 2006).

Berkowitz, L. 1984, 'Some effects of thought on anti- and pro-social influences of media events: A cognitive-neoassociation analysis'. *Psychological Bulletin,* Issue 95, pp. 410–27.

Blair, T. & Morrow, J. 2004, 'Anti-American Biased Collective: Your ABC and the Iraq War'. *IPA Backgrounder*, Institute of Public Affairs, vol. 16, no. 1, pp. 1–20.

Blair, T. 2003, 'ABC Journalism…One Huge Humanitarian Crisis'. *IPA Review*, September, pp. 8–10.

Bolt, A. 2003, 'High price of bias'. *Sydney Morning Herald*, 24 July.

Box, D. 2006, 'ABC betrayed me on Jones book: Masters'. *Australian*, July 10.

Boyd-Barrett, O. 2002, 'Theory in Media Research'. In C. Newbold, O. Boyd-Barrett & H. Van den Bulck (eds), *The Media Book*. Arnold Publishers: London.

Bradley, D. 2004, 'Open Source, Anarchy and the Utopian Impulse'. *Media/Culture Journal*, vol. 7, no. 3, July.

Brown, A. 1986, *Commercial Media in Australia*. University of Queensland Press: St Lucia.

Brown, A. 2000, 'Media Ownership in the Digital Age: An Economic Perspective'. *Media International Australia*, no. 95, May.

Butler, D. & Roderick, S. 2004, *Australian Media Law*, 2nd edn. Law Book Co.: NSW.

Cameron, A.J., Welborn, T.A., Zimmet, P.Z. et al. 2003, 'Overweight and Obesity in Australia: The 1999–2000 Australian Diabetes, Obesity and Lifestyle Study. *Medical Journal Australia,* no. 178, pp. 427–32.

Catalano, C. 2006, 'Advertisers start to tap online potential'. *The Age*, 22 February.

Centre for Health Promotion. 2006, http://www.chdf.org.au/ (accessed 1 February 2006).

Chadwick, P. 1994, 'Creating Codes: Journalism Self-regulation'. In J. Schultz (ed.) *Not Just Another Business*. Pluto Press: NSW.

Chaples, E. 1997, 'The Australian Voters'. In R. Smith (ed.), *Politics in Australia*, 3rd edn. Allen & Unwin: Sydney.

Cockburn, M. 1986, 'ABC-SBS Merger Bill Rejected'. *Sydney Morning Herald*, 8 December.

Coleman, P. 2000, *Obscenity, Blasphemy, Sedition: The Rise and Fall of Literary Censorship in Australia*. Duffy and Snellgrove: Sydney.

Commercial Radio Australia. 2000, *Radio Facts*. http://www.commercialradio.com.au/ (accessed 4 February 2007).

Committee of Review of the Australian Broadcasting Commission. 1981, *The ABC in Review: National Broadcasting in the 1980s* [Dix Review], vol. 2. Australian Government Publishing Service: Canberra.

Committee to Protect Journalists. 2006, http://www.cpj.org (accessed 7 September 2006).

Communications Law Centre. 2003, *Communications Update*. Issue 165. Communications Law Centre: Sydney.

Coonan, H. 2006, 'Meeting the Digital Challenge: Reforming Australia's media in the digital age'. Address to CEDA (Sydney), 14 March.

Craig, G. 2000, 'Perpetual Crisis: The Politics of Saving the ABC'. *Media International Australia*, no. 94, pp. 105–16.

Craik, J. & Davis, G. 1995, 'The ABC goes to Market: Transformations of the Australian Broadcasting Corporation'. In J. Craik & A. Moran (eds), *Public Voices, Private Interests: Australia's Media Policy*. Allen & Unwin: Sydney.

Curran, J. 2000, 'Mass Media and Society'. In J. Curran & M. Gurevitch (eds). *Mass Media and Society*. (3rd edn) Oxford University Press: New York.

Curran, J. 2002, *Media and Power*. Routledge: London.

Dahlgren, P. 2003, 'Reconfiguring Civic Culture in the New Media Milieu'. In J. Corner & D. Pels (eds), *Media and the Restyling of Politics*. Sage Publications: London.

Davies, A. 2006, 'Truth Loses When Only Half the Story Will Do', *Sydney Morning Herald*, 3 July.

DCITA, see Department of Communications, Information Technology and the Arts.

Dempster, Q. 2005, 'The Slow Destruction of the ABC'. In R. Manne (ed.), *Do Not Disturb: Is the Media Failing Australia?* Black Inc. Agenda: Victoria.

Denemark, D. 2002, 'Television Effects and Voter Decision Making in Australia: A Re-examination of the Converse Model'. *British Journal of Political Science*, vol. 32, pp. 663–90.

Denemark, D. 2005, 'Mass Media and Media Power in Australia'. In S. Wilson, G. Meagher, R. Gibson, D. Denemark & M. Western (eds), *Australian Social Attitudes: The First Report*. Sydney: UNSW Press.

Dent, C. & Kenyon, A. 2004, 'Defamation law's chilling effect: a comparative content analysis of Australian and US newspapers'. *Media and Arts Law Review*, vol. 9, no. 2, pp. 89–113.

Department of Communications, Information Technology and the Arts. 2006, *Statistical Highlights*. Prepared by the Research, Statistics & Technology Branch, Department of Communications, Information Technology and the Arts. http://www.dcita.gov.au/_data/assets/pdf_file/14310/Statistical_Highlights_Feb_2006.pdf (accessed 1 March 2006).

Department of Health and Ageing. 2005, *Obesity: Trimming the Fat*. http://www.health.gov.au/internet/wcms/publishing.nsf/Content/factsheet-obesity.htm (accessed 12 September 2006).

Doyle, J. 2005, *The Andrew Olle Media Lecture*. ABC: Sydney.

Durkin, K. 1995a, 'Changing the Effects of Media Violence'. *ABA Update*, 29 March.

Durkin, K. 1995b, *Computer Games and their Effects on Young People: A Review*. Office of Film and Literature Classification: Sydney.

Errington, W. & P. van Onselen. 2005, 'Public servants or partisan dirt diggers? Inside the Government Members Secretariat'. *Australian Journal of Communication*, vol. 32, no. 2, pp. 25–39.

Fairfax Holdings. 2005, *Fairfax Annual Report 2005*. http://www.fxj.com.au/announcements/sep05/Fairfax%20AR%20web.pdf (accessed 9 January 2006).

Feinberg, J. 1985, *Offense to Others: The Moral Limits of the Criminal Law*. Oxford University Press: New York.

Field, J. 2001, 'Public Broadcasting and the Profit Motive: The Effect of Advertising on the SBS'. *Policy*, vol. 17, no. 1, Autumn, pp. 13–18.

Flint, D. 1995, 'A Dangerous Dinosaur'. *Australian Press Council News*, vol. 7, no. 3, August.

Gardiner-Garden, J. & Chowns, J. 2006, 'Media Ownership Regulation in Australia'. *E-Brief*, Australian Parliamentary Library, Canberra.

Gaze, B. & Jones, M. 1990, *Law, Liberty and Australian Democracy*. The Law Book Company: NSW.

Given, J. 2003, *Turning off the Television: Broadcasting's Uncertain Future*. UNSW Press: NSW.

Golder, B. & Williams, G. 2006, 'Balancing National Security and Human Rights: Assessing the Legal Response of Common Law Nations to the Threat of Terrorism'. *Journal of Comparative Policy Analysis*, vol. 8, no. 1, pp. 43–62.

Gordon-Smith, M. 2002, 'Media ethics after "Cash for Comment"'. In S. Cunningham & G. Turner (eds), *The Media and Communications in Australia*. Allen & Unwin: Sydney.

Gorman, L. & D. McLean, 2003, *Media and Society in the Twentieth Century*. Blackwell Publishing: Oxford.

Graber, D. 1989, 'Media Impact on Attitudes and Behavior'. In *Mass Media and American Politics*, 3rd edn. CQ Press: Washington.

Grant, R. 2004, 'Federal government advertising'. *Research Note no. 62*, June. Parliamentary Library: ACT.

Grattan, M. 1998, 'The Politics of Spin'. *Australian Studies in Journalism*, vol. 7, pp. 32–45.

Griffen-Foley, B. 2003, *Party Games: Australian Politicians and the Media from War to Dismissal*. Text Publishing: Melbourne.

Griffith. G. 2002, 'Censorship in Australia: Regulating the Internet and other recent developments'. *Briefing Paper*. NSW Parliamentary Library.

Habermas, J. 1989, *The Structural Transformation of the Public Sphere*. Trans. T. Burger in association with F. Lawrence. MIT Press: Cambridge.

Hague, R. & Harrop, M. 2004, *Comparative Government and Politics: An Introduction*. Palgrave: Basingstoke.

Hamilton, P. 1999, 'Journalists, Gender and Workplace Culture 1900–1940'. In A. Curthoys & J. Schultz (eds), *Journalism: Print, Politics and Popular Culture*. UQP: St Lucia.

Hansard [Parliament of Australia]. 2005, *Criminal Code Amendment (Suicide Related Material Offences) Bill 2005*. Second Reading Speech. House of Representatives, 10 March, pp. 1–179.

Harding, R. 1985, 'Australia: Broadcasting in the Political Battle'. In R. Kuhn (ed.), *The Politics of Broadcasting*. Croom Helm: London.

Herman, E. & Chomsky, N. 1988, *Manufacturing Consent: The Political Economy of the Mass Media*. Pantheon Books: New York.

Herman, E. & R. McChesney. 1997, *The Global Media: The New Missionaries of Corporate Capitalism*. Continuum: London.

Herman, J. 2005, 'The urgent need for reform of Freedom of Information in Australia'. *Australian Journalism Review*, vol. 27, no. 1, pp. 95–104.

Hirst, M. 1997, 'MEAA Code of Ethics for Journalists'. *Media International Australia*, no. 83, February, pp. 63–76.

Hirst, M. & Patching, R. 2005, 'Infotainment and Digital Dilemmas'. *Journalism Ethics: Arguments and Cases*. Oxford University Press: South Melbourne.

Holland, I. 2002, 'Accountability of Ministerial Staff?'. *Information and Research Services*, Research Paper no. 19, 2001–02. Department of the Parliamentary Library: ACT.

Huesmann, L.R. 1998, 'The social role of information processing and cognitive schemas in the acquisition and maintenance of habitual aggressive behavior'. In

R.G. Green & E. Donnerstein (eds), *Human Aggression: Theories, research and implications for social policy.* Academic Press: San Diego.

Human Security Centre. 2005, *Human Security Report—2005.* http://www.humansecurityreport.info/ (accessed 1 January 2007).

Hume, E. 2003, 'Resource Journalism'. In H. Jenkins and D. Thorburn (eds), *Democracy and New Media.* The MIT Press: Cambridge.

Inglis, K. 1983, *This is the ABC: The Australian Broadcasting Commission 1932–1983.* Melbourne University Press: Melbourne.

Inglis, K. 1997, 'ABC Shock Treatment'. *Media International Australia*, no. 83, pp. 5–10.

Inglis, K. 2002, 'Changing notions of public sector broadcasting'. *Southern Review*, vol. 35, no. 1, pp. 9–20.

Jacka, E. 2002, 'Digital Spaces, Public Places'. *Southern Review*, vol. 35, no. 1, pp. 1–8.

Jacka, E. 2003, 'The Future of Public Broadcasting'. In S. Cunningham & G. Turner (eds), *The Media and Communications in Australia.* Allen & Unwin: Melbourne.

Jakubowicz, A. & Newell, K. 1995, 'Which World? Whose/Who's Home?: Special Broadcasting in the Australian Communication Alphabet'. In J. Craik & A. Moran (eds), *Public Voices, Private Interests: Australia's Media Policy.* Allen & Unwin: Sydney.

Jenkins, H. & Thorburn, D. 2003, 'Introduction: The Digital Revolution, the Informed Citizen, and the Culture of Democracy'. In H. Jenkins and D. Thorburn (eds), *Democracy and New Media.* The MIT Press: Cambridge.

Juris, J. 2004, 'Networked Social Movements: Global Movements for Global Justice'. In M. Castells (ed.), *The Network Society: A Cross-cultural Perspective.* Edward Elgar: Cheltenham.

Kaiser Family Foundation. 2003, *Key Facts: TV Violence.* The Henry J Kaiser Family Foundation: California. http:kff.org/entmedia/upload/Key-Facts-TV-Violence.pdf (accessed 11 June 2006).

Keane, J. 1991, *The Media and Democracy.* Polity Press: Cambridge.

Kerr, C. 2005, 'The ABC's paralysis on Bias'. *IPA Review*, March, pp. 37–8.

Kingston, M. 2004, *Not Happy, John! Defending Our Democracy.* Penguin Books: Melbourne.

Kirkpatrick, R. 2000, 'Chronic circulation decline: regional dailies succumb to metropolitan virus'. *Australian Studies in Journalism*, vol. 9, pp. 75–105.

Knightley, P. 2000, *The First Casualty: The War Correspondent as Hero, Propagandist, and Myth-maker from the Crimea to Kosovo.* Johns Hopkins University Press: Baltimore.

Koutsoukis, J. 2004, 'Treasurer Defends $20m Advertising Blitz'. *The Age*, 11 May.

Libertus.net. 2001, *Australian Censorship History.* http://libertus.net/censor/hist20on.
html (accessed 14 November 2006).

Livingston, S. 1997, *Clarifying the CNN Effect: An Examination of Media Effects
According to Type of Military Intervention.* Joan Shorenstein Center for Press and
Politics. http://www.ksg.harvard.edu/presspol/Research_Publications/Papers/
Research_Papers/R18.pdf (accessed 27 April 2006).

Lloyd, C. 1999a, 'Journalism: Print, politics and popular culture'. In A. Curthoys &
J. Schultz (eds), *Journalism: Print, Politics and Popular Culture.* UQP: St Lucia.

Lloyd, C. 1999b, 'British Press Traditions, Colonial Governors, and the struggle for
a 'Free' Press'. In A. Curthoys & J. Schultz (eds), *Journalism: Print, Politics and
Popular Culture.* UQP: St Lucia.

Long, M. & Smith, J. (1992) 'ABC: Towards 2000'. *Media International Australia*,
no. 61, November, pp. 28–35.

Louw, E. 2005, *The Media and Political Process.* Sage Publications: London.

Luck, G. 2003, 'Bias in the ABC'. *The Sydney Institute Quarterly*, vol. 7, no. 21 (3 &
4), pp. 19–24.

Lumby, C. 2002, 'The Future of Journalism'. In S. Cunningham & G. Turner (eds),
The Media and Communications in Australia. Allen & Unwin: Sydney.

Lyons, D. 2005, 'Attack of the Blogs'. *Forbes Magazine*, 14 November.

Mac, P. 2003, 'Media ownership changes behind "bias" attack on ABC'. *The
Guardian*, June 4.

Mackriell, K. 2001, 'Promise Deferred'. *IPA Review*, June, pp. 10–13.

Macnamara, J. 2003, 'Mass Media Effects: A Review of 50 years of Media Effects
Research'. *CARMA White Paper.* http://www.masscom.com.au/book/papers/
mass_media.html (accessed 1 February 2007).

Magnusson, R. 1999, 'Media rites (and the public right to know)'. *AQ*, March–April,
pp. 34–41.

Majoribanks, T. & Kenyon, A. 2003, 'Negotiating news: Journalistic practice and
defamation law in Australia and the US'. *Australian Journalism Review*, vol. 25,
no. 3, pp. 31–49.

Marr, D. 2004, 'The Shape of the Argument', *Overland*, 176.

Martin, P. 2005, 'Bracks Attacked Over $9m Ad Campaign'. *The Age*, 22 November.

Mayer, H. 1964, *The Press in Australia.* Lansdowne Press: Melbourne.

Mayer, J. & Cornfield, M. 2003, 'The New Media'. In M. Rozell (ed.), *Media Power,
Media Politics.* Rowman and Littlefield: Lanham.

McCullagh, C. 2002, *Media Power: A Sociological Introduction.* Palgrave: Hampshire.

McKinsey & Company. 2004, *Review of Public Service Broadcasting around the World*. September, McKinsey & Company: London.

McKnight, D. 1999, 'The Investigative Tradition in Australian Journalism 1945–1965'. In A. Curthoys & J. Schultz (eds), *Journalism: Print, Politics and Popular Culture*. UQP: St Lucia.

McLuhan, M. 1964, *Understanding Media: The Extensions of Man*. Routledge: London.

McNair, B. 2006, *Cultural Chaos: Journalism, News and Power in a Globalised World*. Routledge: New York.

McQuail, D. 1994, *Mass Communication Theory*, 3rd edn. Sage Publications: London.

McQuail, D. 1997, *Audience Analysis*. Sage Publications: London.

Media Watch. 2003, 'The Minister's Complaint'. 3 November. http://www.abc.net.au/mediawatch/transcripts/s981335.htm (accessed 5 January 2006).

Media Watch. 2004, 'Aren't there any rules?'. 28 June. http://www.abc.net.au/mediawatch/transcripts/s1142382.htm (accessed 20 August 2006).

Media Watch. 2005, 'The Tele's Sordid Shame'. 5 September. http://www.abc.net.au/mediawatch/transcripts/s1453097.htm (accessed 11 September 2006).

Media Watch. 2006, 'The ABC Board and Jonestown'. 3 July. http://www.abc.net.au/mediawatch/transcripts/s1677828.htm (accessed 15 February 2007).

Miller, T. & Turner, G. 2002, 'Radio'. In S. Cunningham & G. Turner (eds), *The Media and Communications in Australia*, Allen and Unwin, Sydney.

Mills, S. 1986, *The New Machine Men*. Penguin Books: Melbourne.

Miskin, S. 2005, 'Campaigning in the 2004 Federal Election: Innovations and Traditions', *Research Note no. 30*. Department of Parliamentary Services: ACT.

Moore, N. 2005, *Secrets of the censors: obscenity in the Archives*. National Archives of Australia. http://www.naa.gov.au/About_Us/nicolemoore.html#secret (accessed 15 December 2006).

Murdock, G. 1982, 'Large Corporations and the Control of the Communications Industries'. In M. Gurevitch, T. Bennett, J. Curran & J. Woollacott (eds), *Culture, Society and the Media*. Methuen: London.

Murray, L. 2006a, 'SBS caves in over ads'. *Sydney Morning Herald*, June 2.

Murray, L. 2006b, 'Murdoch U-turn: More TV licences or no media deal'. *The Sydney Morning Herald*, 17 June.

Napoli, P. 1999a, 'Deconstructing the Diversity Principle'. *Journal of Communication*, Autumn.

Napoli, P. 1999b, 'The Marketplace of Ideas Metaphor in Communications Regulation'. *Journal of Communication*, Autumn, pp. 151–69.

Nash, C. 2004, *Freedom of the Press in Australia*. Democratic Audit of Australia.

News Corporation. 2007, http://www.newscorp.com/index2.html (accessed 9 January 2007).

Newspoll 2005, *ABC Appreciation Survey—Summary Report*. http://www.abc.net.au/corp/pubs/documents/ABC_Summary_Report_05.pdf (accessed 5 February 2006).

Newsvine.com. 2006, www.newsvine.com (accessed 17 August 2006).

Nikkhah, R. 2006, 'Square Eyes means Round Tums'. *New Zealand Herald*, 15 April.

Norris, P. 1996, 'Does Television Erode Social Capital? A Reply to Putnam'. *PS: Political Science and Politics*, vol. 29, no. 3, September, pp. 474–80.

Office of Film and Literature Classification. 2006, *Annual Report 2005–2006*. Commonwealth of Australia.

OFLC, see Office of Film and Literature Classification.

Ornstein, N. & Mann, T. (eds). 2000, *The Permanent Campaign and its Future*. American Enterprise Institute: Washington.

Oxford English Dictionary Online. 2007, http://www.oed.com/ (accessed 1 February 2007).

Packer, G. 2004, 'The Revolution Will Not Be Blogged'. *Mother Jones*, May/June. http://www.motherjones.com/commentary/columns/2004/05/04_200.html (accessed 5 April 2006).

Papandrea, F. 2001, 'Digital Television Policy: A Squandered Opportunity', *Agenda*, vol. 8, no. 9, pp. 65–78.

Papandrea, F. 2002, 'Reform of Media Ownership Regulation'. *Agenda*, vol. 9, no. 3, pp. 253–66.

Pearson, M. 2004, *The Journalist's Guide to Media Law*, 2nd edn. Allen & Unwin: Sydney.

Pilger, J. 1992, *Distant Voices*. Vintage: London.

Posetti, J. 2001–02, 'The Politics of Bias at the ABC'. *Australian Studies in Journalism*, no. 10–11, pp. 3–32.

Productivity Commission. 2000, *Broadcasting*. Report no. 11. AusInfo: Canberra.

Publishing and Broadcasting Limited. 2006, http://www.pbl.com.au/ (accessed 7 November 2006).

Putnam, D. 1995, 'Tuning In, Tuning Out: The Strange Disappearance of Social Capital in America'. *PS: Political Science and Politics*, vol. 28, no. 4, December, pp. 664–83.

Radio National. 2005a, 'Media Futures'. *The Media Report*, 12 May. http://www.abc.
net.au/cgi-bin/common/printfriendly.pl?http://www.abc.net.au/rn/talks/8.30/
mediarpt/stories/s1354234.htm (accessed 17 May 2006).

Radio National. 2005b, 'A Conversation With the Minister'. *The Media Report*, 16
June. http://www.abc.net.au/rn/talks/8.30/mediarpt/stories/s1391952.htm
(accessed 11 December 2005).

Raven, F. 2005, 'Copyright and Public Goods'. In *M/C Journal*, vol. 8, no. 3, July.
http://journal.media-culture.org.au/0507/06-raven.php (accessed 6 April 2006).

Reporters Without Borders. 2006, *Worldwide Press Freedom Index*. http://www.rsf.
org/rubrique.php3?id_rubrique=639 (accessed 15 January 2007).

Reynolds, G. 2006, *An Army of Davids: How Markets and Technology Empower
Ordinary People to Beat Big Media, Big Government and Other Goliaths*. Nelson
Current: Nashville.

Ricketson, M. & Moore, M. 2006, 'ABC directors accused of intervening to scrap
Jones book'. *The Age*, 4 July.

Robinson, P. 2002, *The CNN Effect: The Myth of News, Foreign Policy and
Intervention*. Routledge: London.

Rosen, J. 2005, 'Each Nation its Own Press'. In J. Mills (ed.), *Barons to Bloggers:
Confronting Media Power*. The Miegunyah Press: Melbourne.

Roy Morgan Research. 2003, *Reading: Looking into ...Logging onto*. October 26–29.
http://www.roymorgan.com/resources/pdf/papers/20031002.pdf. (accessed 7
February 2007).

Roy Morgan Research. 2005, *Image of Business Executives and Politicians Down,
While Nurses Once Again Most Ethical and Honest Profession*. Finding no. 3938,
November 24. http://www.roymorgan.com.au/news/polls/2005/3938/ (accessed
30 January 2006).

Ruthven, P. 2005, 'Mediocre media'. *Business Review Weekly*, 21 April.

SBS, see Special Broadcasting Service.

Schultz, J. (ed.). 1994a, *Not Just Another Business*. Pluto Press: Leichhardt.

Schultz, J. 1994b, 'Reinventing Journalism Education—for Journalists and Citizens'.
In A. Curthoys & J. Schultz (eds), *Journalism: Print, Politics and Popular
Culture*. UQP: St Lucia.

Schultz, J. 1998, *Reviving the Fourth Estate*. Cambridge University Press: Melbourne.

Schultz, J. 1999, 'The many paradoxes of independence'. In A. Curthoys & J.
Schultz (eds), *Journalism: Print, Politics and Popular Culture*. UQP: St Lucia.

Schultz, J. 2002, 'The Press'. In S. Cunningham & G. Turner (eds), *The Media and
Communications in Australia*. Allen & Unwin: Sydney.

Semmler, C. 1981, *The ABC—Aunt Sally and Sacred Cow*. Melbourne University Press: Melbourne.

Sen, A. 1999, 'Democracy as a Universal Value'. *Journal of Democracy*, vol. 10, no. 3. pp. 3–17.

Senate Standing Committee on Legal and Constitutional Matters. 1994, *Off the Record: Shield Laws for Journalists' Confidential Sources*. Parliament of the Commonwealth of Australia: Canberra.

Simons, M. 2005, 'Inside the ABC'. In R. Manne, (ed.), *Do Not Disturb: Is the Media Failing Australia?* Black Inc. Agenda: Victoria.

Simper, E. 1996, 'Identity Crisis at SBS'. *Australian*, 16 November.

Sinclair, J. 1992, 'Television and Australian Content: Culture and Protections'. *Media Information Australia*, no. 63, February, pp. 23–8.

Sinclair, L. 2005, 'Murdoch calls summit on net strategy'. *Australian*, 8 September.

Special Broadcasting Service. 2000–01, *Annual Report 2000-01*. http://www.sbs. com.au/annualreports/sbsannualreport2001.pdf (accessed 5 February 2007).

Special Broadcasting Service. 2002, *SBS Corporation Overview*. http://www20.sbs. com.au/sbscorporate/index.php?id=. (accessed 5 February 2007)

Special Broadcasting Service. 2002–03, *Annual Report 2002–03*. http://www20.sbs. com.au/sbscorporate/index.php?id=392 (accessed 19 November 2006).

Special Broadcasting Service. 2004–05, *Annual Report 2004–05*. http://www20.sbs. com.au/sbscorporate/index.php?id=392 (accessed 18 August 2006).

Special Broadcasting Services Act 1991. http://www.comlaw.gov.au/ComLaw/ Legislation/ActCompilation1.nsf/0/A3FB3BA07ADD47D3CA2571FD001FC 54B?OpenDocument (accessed 1 February 2007).

Spry, M. 1997, 'What is political speech? Levy v. Victoria'. *Research Note no. 2*. Australian Parliamentary Library, Canberra.

Steketee, M. 1996, 'The Press Gallery at Work'. In J. Disney and J.R. Nethercote (eds), *The House on Capital Hill*. The Federation Press: Sydney.

Strasburger, V. & Wilson, B. 2002, *Children, Adolescents, and the Media*. Sage Publications: USA.

Street, J. 2001, *Mass Media, Politics and Democracy*. Palgrave: Hampshire.

Sydney Morning Herald. 2004, 'Howard campaign based on fear: Latham'. 6 October.

Sydney Morning Herald. 2005, 22 November, p. 7.

Taylor, L. & Willis, A. 1999, *Media Studies: Text, Institutions, and Audiences*. Blackwell Publishing: UK.

Thompson, B. 1995, *Media and Modernity: A Social Theory of the Media*. Polity Press: Cambridge.

Tiffen, R. 1989, *News and Power*. Allen and Unwin: Sydney.

Tiffen, R. 2002, 'Political Economy and News'. In S. Cunningham and G. Turner (eds), *The Media and Communications in Australia*. Allen and Unwin: Sydney.

Tiffen, R. 2004, 'The news media and Australian politics'. In P. Boreham, G. Stokes and R. Hall (eds), *The Politics of Australian Society*, 2nd edn. Pearson Longman: NSW.

Tiffen, R. 2006, 'The Press'. In S. Cunningham & G. Turner (eds), *The Media and Communications in Australia*, 6th edn. Allen & Unwin: NSW.

Tracey, M. 1992, 'Our Better Angels: The Condition of Public Service Broadcasting', *Media International Australia*, no. 66, pp. 16–27.

Traudt, P. 2005, *Media, Audiences, Effects*. Allyn & Bacon: Boston.

Turnbull, S. 2001, 'Once more with feeling: talking about the media violence debate in Australia'. In M. Barker & J. Petley (eds), *Ill Effects: The Media/Violence Debate*, 2nd edn. Routledge: NY.

Turner, G. 1994, 'Journalist ethics in Australia: Raising the standards'. *Australian Journalism Review*, vol. 16, no. 1, pp. 1–14.

Turner, G. 2002, 'Public Relations'. In S. Cunningham & G. Turner (eds), *The Media and Communications in Australia*,. Allen and Unwin: Sydney.

Turow, J. 2003, *Media Today: An Introduction to Mass Communication*. Houghton Mifflin Company: Boston.

Uhr, J. 2005, *Terms of Trust: Arguments Over Ethics in Australian Government*. UNSW Press: Sydney.

van Dijk, J. 1999, *The Network Society*. Sage Publications: London.

Van Evra, J. 1990, *Television and Child Development*. Lawrence Erlbaum Associations: New Jersey.

van Mill, D. 2002, 'Freedom of Speech'. *Stanford Encyclopedia of Philosophy*. http://plato.stanford.edu/entries/freedom-speech/ (accessed 8 April 2006).

Vivian, J. 1999, *The Media of Mass Communication*, 5th edn. Allyn and Bacon: USA.

Von Dohnanyi, J. 2003, *The Impact of Media Concentration on Professional Journalism*. Organisation for Security and Cooperation in Europe (OSCR): Vienna.

Warby, M. 1999, 'Whose ABC? The ABC, Staff Capture and the Obstacles to Accountability'. *IPA Backgrounder*. Institute of Public Affairs, vol. 11, no. 2.

Ward, I. & Stewart, R.G. 2006, *Politics One*, 3rd edn. Palgrave: Melbourne.

Ward, I. 1995, *Politics of the Media*. MacMillan: South Yarra.

Ward, I. 2002, 'Talkback Radio, Political Communication and Australian Politics'. *Australian Journal of Communication*, vol. 29, no. 1, pp. 21–38.

Ward, I. 2003, 'An Australian PR State?' Proceedings of the *Australian & New Zealand Communications Association Conference*. Brisbane, July.

Ward, I., 2006, 'Cartel Parties and Election Campaigning in Australia'. In I. Marsh (ed.), *Political Parties in Transition*. The Federation Press: Sydney.

Waterford, J. 2005, 'The Press Gallery: A Balance Sheet'. In R. Manne (ed.), *Do Not Disturb: Is the Media Failing Australia?* Black Inc. Agenda: Melbourne.

Weller, P. 2002, *Don't Tell the Prime Minister*. Scribe Publication: Melbourne.

Westerman, H. 2006, 'Investors Bet on Media Shakeup'. *The Age*, March 15.

Wheeler, M. 1997, *Politics and the Mass Media*. Blackwell Publishers: Oxford.

Williams, D. 1997a, *From censorship to classification*. An address to Murdoch University, 31 October.

Williams, P. 1997b, *The Victory*. Allen & Unwin: Sydney.

Windschuttle, K. 1988, *The Media*, 2nd edn. Penguin: Melbourne.

Withers, G. 2002, 'Funding Public Service Broadcasters'. *Southern Review*, vol. 35, no. 1, pp. 107–19.

Wood, L. 2005, 'Newspapers dog days'. *Sydney Morning Herald*. 11 November.

Woolfe, K. 2006, 'Legislation victory in fight for life'. *The Courier Mail*. 11 January.

World Bank. *Global Distance Educationet*. http://www1.worldbank.org/disted/glossary.html (accessed 4 February 2007).

Young, S. 2004, *The Persuaders: Inside the Hidden Machine of Political Advertising*. Pluto Press: Sydney.

Index